ESCAPING THE
ENDLESS
ADOLESCENCE

ESCAPING THE ENDLESS ADOLESCENCE

How We Can Help Our Teenagers Grow Up Before They Grow Old

Joseph Allen, Ph.D.
Claudia Worrell Allen, Ph.D.

BALLANTINE BOOKS NEW YORK

Published in the United States by Ballantine Books, an imprint of The Random House
Publishing Group, a division of Random House, Inc., New York.

BALLANTINE and colophon are registered trademarks of Random House, Inc.

ISBN 978-0-345-50789-1

Printed in the United States of America on acid-free paper

www.ballantinebooks.com

2   4   6   8   9   7   5   3   1

First Edition

Book design by Karin Batten

To Luke, Liv, and Eve

CONTENTS

INTRODUCTION

In this book we want to challenge you to think differently about the adolescents in your lives, whether they be your children, your students, your relatives, or your neighbors. It has become a truism not only that adolescence is a troubled and troubling part of the life span, but also that these troubles are inevitable—driven by hormones and immature brains in ways that we are relatively helpless to change. It's this truism that we intend to challenge.

We're going to ask you to reconsider notions about adolescence that you've likely held for a long time. We want to explain why the disturbing behaviors and attitudes that we've grown to believe are "just part of being a teenager" actually have more to do with an adolescence that has come to seem endless than with anything intrinsic to teens' bodies or psyches. There's been a gradual, insidious change occurring in the very nature of adolescence over the past several generations—a change that has been stripping this period of meaningful work and of exposure to adult challenges and rewards, and undermining our teens' development in the process. The good news is that in our years of work with thousands of teens in our clinical practices, our research, and even our own family, we've learned that teenage entitlement, apathy, surliness, and cynicism are far from inevitable. Most important, we've learned that we can change teens' behaviors and attitudes dramatically for the better with relatively modest, well-targeted efforts to change their environments. That's what this book is about.

Of course, the teenage years have always involved some waiting, but lately something has changed. For most of human history adolescence was a fleeting phase—a microsecond, or at most a few months, from the time when a teen first gained adultlike capacities to when some adult noticed and insisted on putting those capacities to use. Even well into the twentieth century, adolescence was brief. For the grandparents of today's teens, adolescence was pretty clearly considered to end at seventeen or eighteen. A generation later it became twenty-one or twenty-two for many. And now young people in their midtwenties are often still living at home and just starting to chart their course in the world. (We'll refer to all these young people as adolescents, because the term so clearly applies to those who haven't yet established adult-level maturity, whatever their chronological age.) While we may have noticed that this extension of the adolescent phase has been unfolding for several generations, we've failed to notice what pushing adulthood further and further back into the future is doing to our teens.

Think of it this way: Waiting at a doctor's office for thirty minutes is annoying; three hours becomes a problem; and three days would be a qualitatively different and surreal experience. Similarly, the extension of adolescence from months to years to more than a decade has led to a qualitatively different and often surreal experience for most teens. The period of preparation has expanded so boundlessly that many teens no longer have any realistic sense of what they're ultimately preparing for, or even that they *are* preparing for something. Their motivation, morale, and character all ultimately take hits.

Even for highly successful teens, school has become less about learning and more about getting good grades to get into good schools to prepare for the next hurdle. Work is no longer about future careers or saving, but about pocketing quick spending money. Adults are no longer guides to future maturity, but annoying rule-setters to be avoided. Worse yet, just as waiting drains adults' energy, waiting *for years* is sapping teens' energy for the hard work needed to grow up. And many teens simply don't believe that any energy they do have is worth expending for this increasingly distant future. It's simply not clear to them that adolescence will ever end. And that makes preparing for an eventual adulthood a rather low priority. They can hardly be blamed.

It wasn't always this way. Through much of human history teenagers' energy and efforts were routinely and immediately put to full use in their communities (and they still are, in societies that differ from our own). Teens were put in charge of younger children, relied upon to carry out important household tasks, and enlisted as crucial assistants in the family restaurant, business, or farm. Over summers, teens were often sent to help extended family with a new baby, sick elders, or home projects. Adolescence, to the extent it existed as a separate phase at all, was productive and short. Not coincidentally, societies (including our own, not all that long ago) in which teens' skills were heavily used frequently even lacked the words for phenomena such as juvenile delinquency that plague our current culture. The idea that the teenage years must inevitably be filled with surliness, entitlement, passivity, and anxiety was simply alien to such societies.

In the first half of this book we'll outline the ways adolescence has been extended. We'll consider why it's happened, how it fits (and doesn't fit) with what we know about teens' biological maturation, and most important, we'll take a look at just what this Endless Adolescence is doing to our teens. We'll revisit and debunk long-held beliefs that most problematic teenage behavior is just the result of raging hormones and immature brains. One of the things we know for certain about teens' development, for example, is that our species did not evolve over millions of years to prepare its young to spend a decade nearing peak physical and mental capacity by passively waiting to someday take a useful role in the world. We'll examine the effects of our placing our teens in a bubble, removed from much of the responsibility, challenge, and gratification of the adult world, and we'll shine a spotlight on the ways our efforts to parent our teens through this period often exacerbate their difficulties.

But ultimately we know that any argument that suggests that problems with our youth are a result of social and cultural factors must overcome years of assumptions that adolescence is inevitably a period of great struggle. We are not only clinicians, but social scientists, well-versed in the caveat that "correlation does not equal causation." Maybe society has changed, maybe teens do struggle. But are these two really connected?

In the end, the most persuasive evidence for what we're proposing will come from the results of successful efforts to *change* adolescents' experiences of themselves and their world in ways that undo—or at least compensate for—some of the larger societal changes we describe.

Fortunately, such evidence exists in abundance. In terms of hard research, we'll show that teen pregnancy rates can be decreased by fifty percent in programs that take just a few hours per week and don't even need to broach the hot-button issue of sex education. We'll show how otherwise stultifying high school classrooms can come alive, with both students and teachers finding meaning and motivation in their work. Closer to home, in our own clinical practices (and our own family), we'll show how modest, but carefully directed, changes in young people's lives can yield huge benefits.

All of these approaches work on the same overarching principle, which we refer to as "Putting the Adulthood Back into Adolescence." We'll spend the second half of the book outlining these approaches and their practical implications for the ways we can improve our teens' lives. Ultimately, we'll ask the reader to judge the ideas we present by the extent to which they can aid in understanding and helping adolescents close to home.

Let us be clear: We do *not* see ourselves as misty-eyed sentimentalists longing for a return to raising our youth in the days of yore. The technological changes and lengthening of the human life span that have supported an extended adolescence—both by delaying entry into the adult labor force and by removing restrictions on our natural tendencies to nurture and *over*nurture our young—have brought much that's positive in their wake. No one who cares deeply about teenagers would want to return our youth to the days of dangerous factory work, poor education, or physical hardship (and we know that some teens today in extreme conditions are still forced to grow up far too quickly). But just as the automobile moved society forward while leaving us needing to exercise our bodies in other ways to stay healthy, so too do the changes that have extended adolescence leave us needing to find other ways to exercise our teens' developing cognitive and emotional capacities, lest they atrophy. We'll outline the kinds of "exercise" that developing adolescent spirits need to thrive in a changed world.

Nor are we parent-blamers. Quite the opposite. We've increasingly come to recognize that the problems we face with many of our teens are not about the lectures we give, the rules we set, the misbehaviors we catch, or the lies they tell. Rather, the problems reflect the fundamental structure of adolescence in our culture. Yes, parents can sometimes make things worse, but by and large they have their hands full trying to cope with the fallout of the massive environmental changes that leave our teens burdened by multiple demands, yet with very little sense that they are doing anything that matters to anyone in the larger world. Although there are shelf-loads of books out there on helping troubled teens, there's very little that goes beyond telling parents how to talk to their teens or how to set rules for them. In this book, we aim to go a step further and reflect on—and ultimately work to change—the very environments in which our teens are growing up.

To make our case, we'll draw heavily upon our own experiences working as therapists and researchers with thousands of adolescents, along with our experiences as parents, with teens of our own. Just as we try to do as parents, we'll speak with a single, first-person voice, in order to focus most clearly on the overarching points that we have drawn from both sets of our experiences (for the curious, we'll make clear which of us is speaking in the notes section at the end). We'll also rely heavily on the stories of the families and teens with whom we've worked (which we've reshaped into composites to protect their privacy), to outline key principles.

Our ultimate goal in this book is to chart routes *out* of the Endless Adolescence . . . to use our clinical, research, and parenting experience to provide signposts, not simply to allow us to survive the adolescent years, but to help our teens move confidently beyond them to grow into *adults* of good character. If there's one thing that continually strikes us in our work with teens, it's their tremendous potential. It's remarkably untapped for most, even for the apparently successful, but it's waiting. Freeing that potential is not only the key to unlocking a productive future adulthood, but also to bringing our teens to life *now*. But we're getting ahead of ourselves.

The first thing we need to do is understand just what's been happening to adolescence in the years since most of us have lived through it. As we see the effects of this changed world through adolescents' eyes, much of their problematic behavior comes into focus in a different way.

So-called "crazy" teenage actions begin to look more and more like the desperate attempts of all-too-sane young people to manage in a world that makes increasingly irrational demands upon them. And this shift in perspective is the first step toward recognizing what's been going wrong in their worlds, and ultimately toward changing those worlds for the better.

PART ONE

THE ENDLESS
ADOLESCENCE

1

Is Twenty-five the New Fifteen?

As fifteen-year-old Perry shuffled into my office, with his parents trailing tentatively behind, he glanced at me with a strained neutral expression that I'd found usually masked either great anger or great distress; in Perry's case it was both. Although anorexia is a disorder most often associated with girls, Perry was the third in a line of anorexic boys I had recently seen. When he came to see me, Perry's weight had dropped to within ten pounds of the threshold requiring forced hospitalization, yet he denied there was any problem.

"He just won't eat," his mother began. Then, turning to Perry as if to show me the routine they'd been enacting, she asked with tears in her eyes, "Perry, why can't you at least have a simple dinner with us?" Perry refused to eat with his family, always claiming he wasn't hungry at the time and that he preferred to eat later in his room. Except that that rarely happened. New menus, gentle encouragement, veiled threats, nagging, and outright bribes had all been tried, to no avail. Why would an otherwise healthy fifteen-year-old boy be starving himself? The question hung urgently in the air as we all talked.

Let's be clear from the outset: Perry was a smart, good kid: shy, unassuming, and generally unlikely to cause trouble. He was getting straight A's in a challenging and competitive public school honors curriculum that spring. And he later told me that he hadn't gotten a B on his report card since fourth grade. In some ways he was every parent's dream child.

But beneath his academic success, Perry faced a world of troubles, and while he took awhile to get to know, eventually the problems came pouring out. The problems weren't what I'd expected, though. Perry wasn't abused, he didn't do drugs, and his family wasn't riven by conflict. Rather, at first glance, his problems would seem more like typical adolescent complaints. And they were, in a way. But it was only as I got to understand him that I realized the adolescent problems Perry experienced weren't just occasional irritations, as they'd been for me and my cohort as teens, but rather, had grown to the point where they cast a large shadow over much of his day-to-day world. I'd later come to realize that Perry wasn't alone in that regard.

One big problem was that while Perry was a strong achiever, he was not at all a happy one. "I hate waking up in the morning because there's all this stuff I have to do," he said. "I just keep making lists of things to do and checking them off each day. Not just schoolwork, but extracurricular activities, so I can get into a good college."

Once he got started, Perry's discontent spilled out in a frustrated monologue.

"There's so much to do, and I have to really work to get myself motivated because I feel like none of it really matters ... but it's really important I do it anyway. At the end of it all, I stay up late, I get all my homework done, and I study really hard for all my tests, and what do I get to show for it all? *A single sheet of paper with five or six letters on it.* It's just stupid!"

Perry was gifted enough to jump through the academic hoops that had been set for him, but it felt like little more than hoop-jumping, and this ate at him. But that wasn't his only problem.

Perry was well-loved by his parents, as are most of the young people we see. But in their efforts to nurture and support him, his parents inadvertently increased his mental strain. Over time, they had taken on all his household chores, in order to leave him more time for schoolwork and activities. "That's his top priority," they said almost in unison when I asked about this. Although removing the chores from Perry's plate gave him a bit more time, it ultimately left him feeling even more useless and tense. He never really did anything for anyone except suck up their time and money, and he knew it. And if he thought about backing off on his schoolwork . . . well, look how much his parents were pouring into making it go well. Sandwiched between fury and guilt, Perry had literally begun to wither.

The upcoming summer break initially seemed to offer some potential relief for this anxious and distraught young man. I saw the first brightening of Perry's countenance as I suggested that this might be a time when he could explore something other than school. But it was not so simple. Financial constraints, and more important, his parents' fears, quickly brought the dark clouds back to his face. Perry had been mind-numbingly bored alone at home in previous summers, especially during those times when other kids were off on vacation or at camps. I asked him about activities he might do on his own.

Tennis, it turned out, was a sport he was trying to learn, and he even liked just practicing by hitting a ball against a wall. Okay, I thought, that's something we could build on. Yet when I suggested he could ride his bike to nearby tennis courts to practice, his parents cut me off.

"That road's too busy to bike on," his mom interjected.

"And the courts by the high school are awfully isolated. It just doesn't seem safe," Dad added, even though the high school was in a tame residential neighborhood, and six-foot-tall Perry did not look like an easy mark.

"They won't even let me have my best friend over to hang out unless they're home," Perry complained. In the name of safety, his parents had indeed ruled out such activities. "Trouble" could be the result, although Perry, save for his weight loss, was not a troublemaker.

Perry's parents were just trying to do what all parents do: keep their child safe. But they were keeping him "safe" at home, while exacerbating a condition that eventually kills one in ten young people. As other options for the summer fizzled one after another, Perry just stared silently out at me, looking away only to discreetly wipe the tears that kept welling up in his eyes. He'd spent a good part of the prior summer reading books on a sofa in his dad's office and didn't want to do that again.

With an illness as life-threatening and dramatic as anorexia, I was expecting, and even wanting, to find some equally dramatic set of causes. But the more I learned about Perry, the more surprised I was to discover that what was pushing him to the breaking point could best be described as an extreme form of modern adolescent life. Though he had his own unique vulnerabilities, most of what burdened him was just a more intense version of what many teens face: endless hoops to jump through, high pressure, lack of the chance to do anything meaningful for anyone, and numerous constraints designed to keep floundering teens "safe." We might wonder if we'd missed something with Perry, except that addressing these problems, as we'll describe later, was indeed enough to turn his life around—these "typical" adolescent experiences had in fact been precisely his problem.

In one sense Perry was not unusual in that adolescent problem behaviors are often bizarre and exasperating. But what was ultimately most disconcerting about his story was just how mundane and prosaic his motives were. We've often found that identifying the underlying intent behind teens' behaviors—finding out what they are really trying to get at, however ineptly—is a critical first step toward identifying ways to help them. And so it was with Perry.

"BUFF"

As I got to know Perry, it became clear that the only thing "real" that he could easily feel any mastery over was his weight. He had stumbled into his eating disorder almost by accident. It started with a growing adolescent awareness of his body and his wish to be fit and in shape. He began working out and reading fitness magazines, and soon took to watching what he was eating. He liked the initial results as some visible muscle replaced what had been baby fat. He found the idea of having a body that was "buff" quite appealing, and even more than that, he liked being able to make a difference in something real and immediate in his life that *he* actually cared about.

No one else needed to help him, and this wasn't part of someone's agenda about maximizing his potential. In some ways Perry was doing what adolescents have no doubt been primed by thousands of years of evolution to do: see a challenge and take steps, however dramatic, to master it. And the results, unlike in school, weren't years in the future. If he worked hard at school, Perry got abstract feedback that he wasn't sure he cared about weeks or months down the road on his report card. In contrast, if he watched what he ate and worked out, he could see the results on the scale and in the mirror within a few days. The irony, of course, is that the best way Perry could find to nurture his cravings for control and autonomy was to starve himself.

If he had been "working his tail off" to buy himself a car or to master a first job—as his dad had once done—his sense of accomplishment might have served as a counterweight to the intense pressure, grinding drudgery, and boredom he felt. He could have been throwing his efforts into these tasks (or even overdoing it, as adolescents have often been wont to do) in productive ways that might have provided immediate satisfaction. But like most of his peers, Perry was on a high-achieving track where the real payoff for his work wouldn't come until after his graduate or professional training was complete. That was so far in the future that he couldn't even accurately estimate the years involved. Perry didn't feel he was so much on a path as on a treadmill. And though he could scarcely allow himself to verbalize it, he wanted desperately to get off.

PERRYS OF THE PAST

On the one hand, the pressures Perry faced were remarkably mundane and typical. But one of the more intriguing aspects of his situation was

that just a few generations ago—for example, in his grandfather's generation, or perhaps his great-grandfather's—most of Perry's problems *simply
wouldn't have existed.* Yes, school has always mattered a great deal for
some, but it was only the rarest of teens who could expect to spend a
decade or more in school after ninth grade. And even for those teens, parents wouldn't have had the time to remove all other meaningful work
from their lives. On the contrary, if we go back a little further, say a hundred years or so, typical teenagers in a family were not only essential to
making a household run each day, but contributed almost a third of the
family's total household income.

In many ways, teenagers were already functioning as adults then.
Yes, working extremely hard, but also experiencing the gratification of
seeing the tangible results of their efforts in a way that mattered not just
to them, but to their entire family. Today's parents can wistfully imagine
how this might have been good for the family. What they might not
realize was just how good, indeed critical, it was for the teens as well.
And while parents have always sought to keep their offspring safe, earlier generations simply lacked the resources to hypermonitor their teens'
activities. No one had the luxury to be a "helicopter parent," and teens
had plenty of room to exert control over their lives in ways other than by
starving themselves.

Perry's problems, unfortunately, represent just the visible and dramatic tip of a very large iceberg. Even as our teens have become better
nourished, and the stresses of untreated illness and material deprivation
have become rare, rates of eating disorders and adolescent depression
and anxiety have skyrocketed. Some of the changes have been building
for a while, but some have occurred across just a single generation. For
example, the average college student now reports as much anxiety as did
the average *psychiatric patient* forty years ago. While some of this is
undoubtedly due to a greater willingness to acknowledge mental problems, much appears to be a truly new phenomenon. At the other end of
the socioeconomic spectrum, we find that more than one in every four
teenagers in America is still failing to complete high school after twelve
years.

We start with Perry's story because much of what he experienced—
from his anxiety and misguided efforts to gain a sense of control to the

seemingly supportive but ultimately suffocating environment in which he lived—is reflective of what many of our teens are going through. Perry's weight loss made the problems all too visible, but the strains can appear in many guises. Often the problems grow quietly over years, with only the occasional disturbing behavior to indicate that something may be seriously wrong just beneath the surface. Such was the case with Ellen.

WHAT WAS THERE TO LOSE?

Ellen was a gifted eighth-grade lacrosse player, with visions of college scholarships dancing in her parents' heads. She was also a fine student in school, though not hitting her full potential, but then how many students do? And while there were the usual adolescent ups and downs at home, life generally proceeded smoothly. So Ellen's mom was shaken to her core one cold Tuesday night a few Februarys back when a friend and fellow "lacrosse mom" informed her of the rumors that Ellen had been having oral sex, not only with her boyfriend, but with several boys in her class. A long night of harsh questions and tears all around revealed the truth to these rumors, but no hint of their root cause.

Ellen's parents were devastated. "How could this be happening with our little girl?" her dad asked. Ellen herself was sheepish and a bit frightened. She hadn't expected things to turn out this way. In some ways, her behavior was a mystery to her as well. Was she "seriously disturbed," as her dad angrily suggested? If only that were the case, we could at least write off Ellen's behavior as something that needn't concern most parents.

But as Ellen thought later that night about what had happened, and talked with friends the next day about it, she felt less sheepish and more frustrated. What else was there really to do? She did okay in school, but it was boring, and seemed fairly pointless as well. This was an area of consensus among Ellen's friends, even those who got good grades. Yes, lacrosse was great. The competitions and practices were crazy and tense, but overall it was fun. If only it lasted more than an hour or two a few times a week. And beyond that . . . well, as far as she could see, nothing else was all that interesting. There was plenty of idle chatter about a friend's new jeans, the idiocy of her algebra teacher, and who had the coolest addition to their Facebook page. But when Jake started making out with her in the back of the bus coming home from a long school trip just after Thanksgiving break, a whole new world opened up.

It wasn't so much the sex—Ellen later admitted that it seemed a little "gross" at first, and ultimately was just "okay"—but everything that went with it. Intensity. Connection. Doing things that only adults did. Risk. Mattering to someone. It was almost as exciting as lacrosse, though the rules were less clear. The rest of life seemed dull and one-dimensional compared to those times with Jake, and later, with his friends. Ellen did have the occasional second thought, but then again, what was there to lose? And the person who had the most intense involvement in her day-to-day life—Jake—was quite clear about what she should do when she had doubts.

Ellen went further than she probably wanted to with Jake, and certainly with the boys who followed, until her mother learned of her activities. And when this new game came abruptly to an end on that cold Tuesday night, Ellen could at least quietly admit later that she was also a bit relieved. In the days after her mother's discovery, her life returned to normal and was far healthier. (Not until a few months went by would she learn that she'd contracted a sexually transmitted infection, as do one in every four American teens.) But deep down Ellen also knew that the life to which she was returning didn't seem as exciting as the life she'd left behind. Peer pressure and preoccupation with meaningless competitions could certainly occupy one's time. Nothing was necessarily all *that* unpleasant. But face it, life was basically flat in many ways. She knew it, as did many of her friends. It would take an entire stable of activities to get Ellen out of this state, but that's a story we'll get to in a bit.

TODAY YOU BECOME AN ADULT?

The question is: How did we arrive at a point where even our successful teens are so likely to be struggling? Neither Perry's nor Ellen's parents were doing anything so terribly wrong. In fact, they were doing many things quite right and they clearly cared deeply. So what's going on?

In our research, clinical practices, and conversations with friends and family, the answer—once we were caught sight of it amid all the distractions—was almost impossible to overlook.

The end point of adolescence has been creeping upward in many ways and for many years. But gradual changes often catch us by surprise in the end. The most obvious change—that schooling now routinely extends for many years beyond twelfth grade—has brought many other far-reaching changes with it. Financial dependence on parents lasts longer. Exposure to real employment is delayed. The result is that the teenage years have gradually evolved into something quite different than they used to be.

But it's only when we catch glimpses of the past and present side by side that the sheer magnitude of the change that has occurred starts to come into focus.

We recently attended the bar mitzvah of Max, the son of two close friends. The traditions of the ceremony were simple yet powerful, as Max took the reins of adulthood in speaking about the meaning of the Torah to the congregation in which he grew up. And yet there was something that felt vaguely incongruous about the ceremony. Max's father captured it succinctly when he offered a toast to his son at the reception that followed.

"Today, you become an adult . . . " he began proudly, in a tradition that goes back thousands of years. Then, in an effort to avoid meaning-less formalities and to keep things real, he added with friendly good humor, "yeah . . . right!"

Everyone laughed, including thirteen-year-old Max, sitting a bit uncomfortably at the head table. Max's dad's toast was gracious, elo-quent, and loving. If there was any awkwardness, it was not in the toast, but in the fundamental truth it had revealed: Max's dad's humor had been dead-on, and it pointed up just how out of synch modern times and modern adolescence had become with the wisdom of this centuries-old ceremony.

But of course the tradition Max was reenacting that day goes back thousands of years, when the physical and intellectual development of most youths were far *less advanced* than Max. But like some well-preserved archeological artifact, this particular tradition made clear just how different things used to be for thirteen-year-olds. And how different they've become. Becoming an adult at thirteen? Not these days.

We'll say more about how this change has come about in the next few chapters. For now, our point is that as it has unfolded over the past few generations, it's left teens like Perry, Ellen, and Max in an awkward and indeed precarious position. And these changes and problems aren't just confined to what we used to think of as the adolescent years. In fact, we can see some of the effects of these changes most clearly *after* we think adolescence should have ended. Even if our teens seem to fare okay as adolescents, we're often surprised and disappointed to later realize that they weren't being well-prepared to enter adulthood.

AFTER ADOLESCENCE . . . MORE ADOLESCENCE!

I was discussing this book with one of my former advisees at the University of Virginia, a talented and ambitious young woman who'd graduated with high honors nine months earlier, when she casually mentioned that *three-fourths* of her friends had gone back to living with their parents after graduating. Not just those in large cities—where expensive rents may force the issue—and not just for a few months. Rather, she had friends in large towns and small, male and female, all living with their parents.

"Why?" I asked, struck by what a setback this must have seemed to these accomplished young people.

"Mostly because they don't know what they want to do with their lives," she replied. They were waiting tables, working as receptionists, and a few were just hanging out.

"Doesn't this make them crazy?" I asked (while also wondering how crazy their parents must feel). Well, my student told me, maybe. She said one friend had described the feeling to her in a phone call the night before:

"It's not that I feel depressed, actually. I'm just very sad. I visit my friends living on their own and I feel good and all, but then I come back to my old room and it just feels sad."

And this, among the most talented and ambitious young students in America.

One might think the young people lost in this postcollege world will grow up and out of such behavior soon enough, but that's true only if we stretch the definition of "soon." Almost half of all men and women in the United States between the ages of eighteen and twenty-four live with one or both parents, and as many as sixty percent are still receiving financial support from them *after* the college years have passed. Recent analyses make clear that these behaviors cannot be written off as a result of changing economic circumstances in our society. Even after they turn twenty-five, more than a quarter of all young adults in this country still receive ongoing financial support from their parents.

This "boomerang" generation continues to bewilder its parents. Showered with material goods like no other generation in history, with more opportunities, more years of education, less trauma, and better health care, a remarkable number of the young people in this generation consistently fail to move out and take wing as adults. Indeed, the "failure to launch" has now become not just a popular movie, but a distressing phenomenon that is becoming one of the defining features of a generation.

Even young people who appear to be succeeding by conventional standards often find themselves waking up in their midtwenties clueless about how to get a job, manage money, cook, or live on their own. They may be highly educated. They may have gotten good grades. But many find themselves like Scott, who says this in *The Quarterlife Crisis* by Alexandra Robbins and Abby Wilner:

> "Now I find myself questioning how and when I will find my life's work. I am, after all, nearly 27 years old . . . And here I am stranded in a never-never land of my own making. I've committed myself to exploring other options that interest me, but I'm having a hard time actually thinking of a career that sounds appealing. There is one that I've been meaning to explore, but sometimes I'd rather just watch TV or play guitar or go out with my friends. So maybe I'm not really meant to do that either. When is something going to fall from the sky and hit me on the head, knock me out, and when I wake up I see clearly the road that lies ahead?"

EMERGING ADULTHOOD

I stumbled upon this problem in a different way as I grappled with an intellectual challenge in my field over the past fifteen years. I was struggling to come to terms with a new domain of developmental psychology that had sprung into being during this period. It's the study of what's been called "emerging adulthood." And it focuses on the ways in which individuals, typically in their twenties, are learning to act as adults and take on adult roles in society. Researchers in this field study entry into the labor force, moving out of one's family of origin, and entry into long-term romantic relationships.

As an adolescence researcher with interests in development across the life span, I knew I should welcome the development of this new field, but almost from the start there was something about it that made me uneasy. I could never quite put my finger on it, but sensed something that seemed redundant and old hat. But my personal misgivings aside, the field grew by leaps and bounds and has clearly established itself as a viable, indeed thriving intellectual enterprise. It has textbooks, and its own conferences of thoughtful scholars studying whether and how our youth in their twenties do or do not learn to become adults during this period.

Then one day it hit me. Wait a minute. *Adolescence* was supposed to be the period during which the traits of adulthood gradually emerged. Now the emergence of these same traits was being studied, but a decade later in the life span! And if the twenties are when adulthood is supposed to be just emerging, what does that mean our teens are supposed to be doing? Have we turned the teen years into a supersized extension of childhood? And if so, what does this do to these teens' efforts to grow up?

DRIVEN TO SCHOOL BUT NOT DRIVEN TO GROW UP

The problem, of course, with putting our teens in a world where they have nothing much to do that matters to anyone else (besides college admissions officers) is that they learn to do . . . nothing much. As a result, even when not displaying obvious psychological symptoms, we see a generation emerge that is increasingly slow to launch and appears help-less in the face of modest challenges. We see fifteen-year-olds who don't believe they can walk a mile to get somewhere in their own hometown. We see teens struggle to do even the most trivial adult tasks: "Sorry, Ma, I don't think the grocery store had any orange juice, or at least I couldn't find it." A degree of self-centeredness and surliness creeps into the speech and thought of these often-anxious and dependent teens as they wander through these years, uncertain about their future goals and obliv-iously ignorant of many basic adult responsibilities.

It's partly a matter of what the extension of adolescence has done to the desire to grow up. Even when teens engage in many of the same activities that we did when we were younger, they're doing so with a dif-ferent pace and sense of urgency. One of the surprises in our clinical practices in recent years has been our dawning awareness that many teens now almost seem to *welcome* the delay of adulthood. Growing up in the 1970s, for example, youth in our cohort couldn't wait to drive. Across diverse cultural groups, the sixteenth birthday was invariably marked by two universals—a birthday cake and a trip to the Depart-ment of Motor Vehicles to pick up a learner's permit. Increasingly, now we run into youths like Sarah, who was a few months past the age of eli-gibility to get her permit when I first asked her about it.

"Oh, yeah," she said. "I know I should get it soon, but it doesn't mat-ter all that much because my mom drives me to school and someone can usually bring me anywhere I need to go."

At first we just wrote off Sarah's behavior, until pretty much the exact same thing occurred with Jamal, Mark, and Emily, and then we realized something had changed. A recent report by the Federal High-way Administration confirmed our suspicion, revealing that the number of youths who get licenses at age sixteen has dropped by almost fifty percent in just the past ten years, though at sixteen, teens are still eligi-ble for some type of license in almost all states. No doubt the cost of auto insurance partly accounts for this change, but the change in teens' attitudes toward driving is clear.

We also see changes when teens head off to college. At parents' behest, college administrators have come to treat their students, who are legally adults, more as kids in need of guardianship than adults making their way in the world. But even more important, the students are behaving differently as well. As little as a generation ago college created a fairly sharp break in the emotional dependence of teens on their parents. Teens were on their own, they knew it, and most cherished it. Certainly our own generation was immature and dependent in many ways, but most of today's parents would have been *mortified* had their own parents called their professors or tried to check in multiple times each day to see how they were doing and remind them of upcoming deadlines.

In prior generations, some fared better than others in college, but most young people fared or failed largely on their own. Now it's far more typical for college students to consult with their parents via cell phones, e-mails, and instant messaging about even fairly mundane decisions, like, "Do you think I should write a paper or do a PowerPoint presentation for this assignment?" As one parent described it in a survey conducted by psychologist Barbara Hofer, "My parents and I talked once a week by phone, and a letter once a month. My daughter and I talk several times a day." And this isn't just because teens have such great, close relationships with their parents. Most adults have best friends with whom they're close, but they don't need to consult with them five times a day, as many college students do with their parents! Indeed, Hofer and her colleague Elena Kennedy have found that even by their senior year of college, the *average* student is in contact with his or her parents more than thirteen times each week.

I was recently chatting with a department chair at a large midwestern university who described how students continuously came into her office with cell phones glued to their ears, hanging up as they entered to say, "My mother says I should ask you about whether I can get out of this class I'm taking that's not going very well." In a few particularly exasperating instances, the chair's dialogue with students devolved to the point where the student ultimately said, "Maybe you should just talk to my mom, as she's the one who really understands this. I know she's home now. Should I just call her?"

Our generation *did* depend on parents, even in college, but we didn't depend on them as heavily, and we were actively striving not to lean on them. We *wanted* to grow up. And our generation was already at a midpoint in the current phenomenon of lengthening adolescence. When we speak to members of the generation that serve as grandparents to today's teens, they consistently make clear that as they were growing up, this level of dependence into one's twenties would have seemed farcical.

Generations ago, fourteen-year-olds used to drive, seventeen-year-olds led armies, and even average teens contributed labor and income that helped keep their families afloat. While facing other problems, those teens displayed adultlike maturity far more quickly than today's, who are remarkably well kept, but cut off from most of the responsibility, challenge, and growth-producing feedback of the adult world. Parents of twenty-somethings used to lament, "They grow up so fast." But that seems to have been replaced with, "Well . . . Mary's living at home for a bit while she sorts things out."

What used to occur during the teenage years is now happening far later. Twenty-five is becoming the new fifteen. And it's not just delaying our kids' maturity, it's changing who they become.

A MATTER OF CHARACTER

Ultimately, the problems created by the extension of adolescence aren't just a matter of moving (or not moving) expeditiously into adulthood, or even of the anxiety and assorted other problems that accompany teens along the way. Ultimately, the problem with these structural changes in the nature of adolescence lies in how they affect teens' very character. "Character" isn't a word that psychologists typically throw around easily, yet it seems quite apt here. Interestingly, problems that we call "matters of character" can appear in almost opposite guises at different times. For some adolescents, they show up as a deep-seated sense of incompetence and inadequacy that makes them hesitant to even face the larger world.

I once treated an accomplished carpenter in his midforties who'd become disabled working with some faulty equipment. He'd received a large financial settlement that enabled him to manage without ever working again, but he'd lost his means of contributing and his sense of place in the world. Financially, he was set; emotionally, he was miserable, as the experience ate away at his sense of himself. I'll never forget the vulnerable, uncertain glare this man would give me whenever I started to ask him a question—a look that captured a deep-rooted sense of worthlessness and the expectation of another psychic blow from the outside world: "You mean you just sit around at home all day and collect a check?"

What I've realized recently is how often I see this deer-in-the-headlights look when teens interact with new adults in their lives, as they sense the precariousness and awkwardness of their position: Is everything just given to them? Don't they know how to do anything? What responsibility do they handle? Unlike the carpenter, they've never even known that they *could* thrive in the adult world. We've worked with macho teenage boys—high school seniors who were more than able to take their licks on an athletic field or jousting with peers—who were reduced to near paralysis when told to go to a shopping center on their own and approach store managers about possible job opportunities. So far removed and so beyond them did the adult world seem that these teens felt unable to enter it alone, even in the most rudimentary ways. They were almost afraid to grow up.

WILL I HAVE TO BE BORED?

With other young people, the problems show up in an almost opposite fashion: as a sense of surly entitlement, of almost *deserving* to have things presented to them without having to struggle to earn them—an entitlement that seems a natural response to living in a world that's been far more geared to entertaining teens than to expecting anything from them.

Recently I was interviewing a bright college graduate for a challenging job working as a full-time coordinator of one of my research projects. The interview had gone well, but toward the end, when I asked if he had any questions, he replied, "As people have described the job to me, I get the sense that sometimes parts of the work can be a little boring, and I don't want to be bored." As gently as I could, I replied that this job, like all jobs, had its boring elements (although most people had found it more than challenging enough over the years). The applicant's question, told me that he hadn't yet learned the do's and don'ts of coming off well in a job interview. But more than that, I was concerned that he didn't seem to understand that *all* jobs have some boring elements. How did one make it to age twenty-three without knowing that?

THE TEACHER'S AXIOM

Is something wrong with these kids? Experienced teachers rely on a simple axiom that applies here: If one or two students fail a test, it's likely the students' own fault; if large numbers fail, look not to the students for an explanation, but to the learning environment. Applying that axiom: If just a few of our teens were failing to make it through adolescence successfully, whether failing to graduate from high school, succumbing to anxiety disorders, acquiring sexually transmitted infections, or depending on their parents financially in their late twenties, it might make sense to just look at what's wrong with those unfortunate individuals. But when the problematic cases reach into the millions and recur year after year—and when even otherwise successful teens often fail to fully complete the transition to adulthood—we need to begin to take a look at the environments in which our teens are growing up.

For many years we've treated teens like Perry and Ellen, and increasingly we've seen young people like my advisee's friends who are still living at home after college. But over time we've come to realize that while their problems appeared in different guises, there was an underlying thread that bound them all together. And it's a thread that's getting stronger. The thread is what we've come to call the Endless Adolescence.

If the problems created by the Endless Adolescence were limited to only a few extreme cases, we might not be so concerned. But the problems that Perry, Ellen, and their peers display are mirrored in large and small forms among most of our teens. We see the problems in males and in females and across all facets of society, from affluent teens—who turn out to be at particular risk for anxiety disorders and alcohol and substance abuse—to impoverished teens who drop out of school and watch as real adulthood appears less and less within reach. Some teens do much better than others, of course (although many of the struggles are quiet and easy to miss). But if you observe almost any teenager—and we have seen thousands over the years in our classrooms at the University of Virginia, in our research, and in our clinical practices—you can see the effects of an environment that is making it increasingly difficult for our adolescents to mature into adulthood.

In the rest of the first half of this book we will consider the ways that the radical extension of this formative life period has altered our teens' experience and development. We'll consider the ways our beliefs about teens and even our efforts to help them have at times led us badly astray. Perhaps counterintuitively to a generation of hyperattuned and watchful parents, solving the problems created by the Endless Adolescence requires a tack fundamentally different from adding more camps, lessons, tutors, and charter schools to our teens' lives, or tweaking our parenting styles with more consequences or tough love. Indeed, without first recognizing and addressing the fundamental problems created by the Endless Adolescence, even the best of parents often find their teens imprisoned in a world characterized by passivity, boredom, anxiety, and a lack of concern about the future.

But to maximize their chances of escape, we first need to understand our prisoners: how they got where they are, and then, through their own eyes, how being in this prison has changed them. Most important, we need to understand the ways we've unintentionally undermined their chances of escape by underestimating their capacities—and the ways we've been pushed by everyone from the media to eminent psychologists into doing so. For the most formidable prisons are not those made with thick walls, but with impenetrable ideas—ideas that seem deceptively simple and appealing at first glance, but that ultimately hold our teens back.

2

In Search of the Teenage Brain

Age is foolish and forgetful when it underestimates youth.

—IRISH PROVERB

One of the greatest challenges we've confronted in helping people understand the Endless Adolescence is not in showing them that it exists, but in getting them to consider the possibility that things could be any different than they are.

"Teenagers have always been this way."

"It's just wired into their brains."

"They're victims of their own raging hormones."

We've heard these laments from parents of our clients, from friends, from neighbors, and certainly from the media. In our experience, many parents instinctively react to the immaturity of their mid- to late-teens with dismay and concern—reactions that seem sensible to us. But then these parents are quickly told by "sophisticated" friends and neighbors, who cite a rash of popular books with titles like *Secrets of the Teenage Brain* and *Why Do They Act that Way?: A Survival Guide to the Adolescent Brain*, that such immaturity is simply to be expected. Adolescents, we're told, just come with immature brains and raging hormones; their behavior has always been pretty much like it is now, probably always will be, and we should all just settle in for the ride.

One doesn't need strong locks on a prison door if one can convince the prisoners there's no chance of escape, which is what we've done and continue to do by writing off all teen misbehavior as being caused by their brains. If we're going to help our teens escape the Endless Adolescence, we'll have to start by recognizing that escape is indeed possible. That's what this chapter is about.

Now we're quite aware of the growing body of research showing that teen brains and adult brains are different, and we'll talk about that research in this chapter. But knowing such differences exist still begs all the real questions of interest: Do these brain differences actually explain the adolescent behaviors we find most troubling? Alternatively, might some of these differences work in teens' favor and suggest areas of untapped potential? And have teens always behaved as they do now, or does history perhaps tell us that there is far more promise lurking within the adolescent brain than we've let ourselves realize?

To answer these questions and begin charting our escape routes from the Endless Adolescence, we'd like to take a brief tour of the teen brain, and how it has behaved throughout history, to try to get a sense of what is and is not inevitable about adolescent behavior. We think this tour can put a few chinks in the armor of the idea that teens' problematic attitudes and behaviors can merely be explained away by their hormones and brains. We'll take this process even further in the next chapter when we examine the Endless Adolescence from the inside out—from teens' own perspectives and in their own words—showing how their environment is producing much of what we find disturbing. This in turn leads to thinking about just what it is we're doing that creates this morass, and how to change it. But again, we're getting ahead of ourselves. First, the teen brain.

One of the very first things we notice as we begin our tour of efforts to understand the capacities of the teen brain is that we find ourselves bumping into some unsettling information that is well-established in research but has received almost no attention in the popular media. Ironically, one of the more intriguing pieces of such information comes not from those studying adolescents, but from our associates who study the aging process.

FAST THINKING

Our colleague Tim Salthouse studies how people think and how their thinking changes as they age; he is recognized as one of the world's leading experts on cognitive aging. As part of his research, Tim observes volunteers ranging from their teens to their eighties as they tackle myriad mental challenges, from keeping track of tidbits of information as he distracts them with arithmetic problems, to rapidly shifting their attention between multiple tasks, to mentally manipulating abstract figures. If you're an adult, you may want to sit down and slowly take in what Tim has learned.

Tim's research shows that many facets of cognitive ability, from the capacity to retain information in memory to sheer processing speed, decline with age *after the teen years end.* That's not just with old age, and not just a little. Rather, from age eighteen to age forty-five, individuals drop about a standard deviation in their cognitive capacities across a whole host of indices. Stated in everyday terms, this means that the typical forty-five-year-old is already far enough along in this cognitive aging process that he or she will process many kinds of new information more slowly than about eighty percent of typical eighteen-year-olds. Similar though slightly smaller declines are also found in abstract and spatial-reasoning skills and with certain types of memory. While teen brains are still immature in some ways (and we'll get to those in a bit), our adult cognitive advantages over our teens are not as clear-cut as we might imagine.

Tim's findings are a cold splash of water on the hot and trendy notion that immature adolescent brains are the driving force behind our teens' problems. To absorb the implications of his research, let's turn his findings around and view them in their more positive light. After all, most forty- and fifty-year-olds manage cognitively in the world just fine, thank you. The positive implications of Tim's research are that, in comparison to their elders, late adolescents have some remarkable and ephemeral cognitive talents. Yes, they lack the knowledge base and worldly wisdom that accrue across the life span. (Thankfully, there are some compensations that come with age!) Their brains even lack some other adult capacities that we'll describe in just a bit. But while we've always known that teenagers are at their peak in terms of physical strength, flexibility, and energy levels, research makes clear that in some important ways adolescents are approaching their *cognitive* peaks as well. These supposedly incompetent young people may have more going for them than we've realized.

I first saw what Tim was talking about on a baseball field. Actually, behind a baseball field. Another dad and I had volunteered to run the electronic scoreboard for our sons' Little League game. You wouldn't think it would be that hard, but we found it challenging to manage the slightly quirky control device while also keeping track of the game in order to change batter numbers, balls, strikes, outs, and runs scored, especially when the action on the field got chaotic, as it often tends to do in Little League games. Our task was made more challenging by two rambunctious fourteen-year-olds who insisted on joining us in the "control tower" to get a better view of the game. Instead of watching, however, they goofed around, threw things, and screamed (in our ears) as the action got intense.

By the fourth inning we'd had enough, and my friend finally blew up at them: "Look, guys, this is hard enough to keep track of without all your distractions. If you'd like to take it over, feel free, but otherwise you need to leave."

Their quick, eager reply: "Sure. We'll do it."

Skeptically, we explained how the system worked, then moved to the back of the booth to be ready to step in when things fell apart. But they didn't. In fact, these kids put us to shame! They'd never done this before, but after five minutes they were doing it like they'd done it all their lives, and it barely seemed to tax their capacities. They kept up an animated chatter with each other. They took cell phone calls. They talked to friends who came up. And they rarely missed a beat. They simply had raw cognitive-processing power that left us forty-something guys feeling ready to head out to pasture. Oh, and they seemed to be enjoying themselves. All of their arguing and mischief stopped. They'd found a way to use their energy and skill, and for once we'd let them.

So before we write off the Endless Adolescence as being due teens' brain development, we should remember these boys and Tim's research. Yes, adult brains are in some ways more mature than those of adolescents, but in other ways adults have less capacity—a set of ongoing trade-offs that continues to evolve right up through old age.

Tim's findings that cognitive decline starts so early come as a surprise to most people. But even more intriguing than his research findings is the question: Given all the attention paid to adolescent brain development these days, why are these well-replicated findings so poorly disseminated to the broader public? The answer to this mystery ultimately provides one of the keys to breaking out of the mind-set of the Endless Adolescence. But it's an answer that lies more in *adults'* motivation than in our teens' motivation, and it took one very sullen teenager in one very unsettling situation to ultimately help me discover it.

SILENT SAM

Sam, as Samantha preferred to be called, was seventeen when I first saw her, but she looked much younger. We'd had quite different life experiences to that point. I'd come from graduate school at Yale and a post-doctoral fellowship at Harvard. She'd come from twelve different residences in the previous twelve months, including foster homes, group homes, shelters, hospitals, and detention centers, *all* of which she'd run away from or been kicked out of. There was a real mismatch here, and it only took me a short time to realize that I was the one who was badly disadvantaged.

Coming to see me was emphatically not Sam's idea. On the contrary, Sam was in my office because individual counseling (at least one session weekly) was required for all residents of the treatment center I'll call SafeHaven, a home for troubled teenagers where Sam had lived for the past five months. Sam objected and had held out against this requirement for her entire stay up until the day she came to see me. During this time, she'd been pained to watch other residents progress through a level system, quickly earning more and more of the basic privileges of life, privileges that she craved. Finally, after five months of forgoing everything from using the phone to watching TV, Sam gave in and came to see me, but I was soon to discover that her "retreat" had been only tactical.

"Hi, Sam," I said to her. "Can you tell me a bit about what brings you here?"

"Because they made me come," she mumbled so quietly I could barely hear her, while never looking up.

"What did they do to make you come?"

"Only took away all my privileges," she replied, this time with more force and anger.

Not a terrible start for therapy with an adolescent who'd experienced such upheaval and undoubtedly had a lot on her mind. Unfortunately, though, this modest beginning would be the high point of my work with Sam for a number of weeks. Shortly after that, Sam, for all her troubles and all her distress, fell silent. And stayed silent for longer than any patient I'd seen before or since. Her stance was certainly challenging to me as a therapist, but ultimately it would place a spotlight on a far more general lesson about adolescents that I would never forget.

SOCRATIC MISCHIEF

As Sam's story eventually unfolded, she would show that in spite of all she'd been through, she was anything but "mental," to use her term. For a while, though, she would drive *me* just a bit crazy as I looked in vain for a way to help this troubled young woman, or even just get her to talk to me. At the time, her obstinate behavior left me seeking solace in the long-held truism that "adolescents have always been this way and always will be." But while I didn't realize it at the time, history's lessons about teens aren't what we might think.

"Teens have always been this way," we're told. But when we look closely at what we actually know from history, we see that we've gotten some of our history lessons wrong. Consider perhaps the most widely cited description of youth in antiquity—a passage attributed to Socrates that is often presented to show that those who are concerned about "teens today" are just overreacting out of an ignorance of history:

> Our youth now love luxury.
> They have bad manners, contempt for authority;
> They show disrespect for their elders and love chatter in place of exercise;
> They no longer rise when elders enter the room;
> They contradict their parents, chatter before company; gobble up their food and tyrannize their teachers.

It's a compelling passage that shows up everywhere from textbooks to parenting guides to Dear Abby, and suggests that problems like Sam's are so universal and endemic to the adolescent species that they've been with us for thousands of years. The only problem is that Socrates never wrote or uttered these words, nor did anyone of his era. Rather, this passage appears to have been fabricated (or perhaps misattributed) as a juicy addition to a psychology textbook first published in the 1950s. Nevertheless, the quote thrives, perhaps because we'd *like* to believe that teens have always been the way they are now.

But haven't teens always been a real pain to adults, quote or no quote? If we look at what another philosopher, Aristotle, actually said about youth in antiquity, the answer appears to be no. Aristotle provides a remarkably balanced picture. He does, on the one hand, acknowledge teen impulsivity: "Young men have strong passions, and tend to gratify them indiscriminately . . . They are changeable and fickle in their desires . . . They are hot-tempered, and quick-tempered . . . " So, yes, adolescents have never been perfect, and impulsivity does seem to come with the territory, and we'll say more about the possible brain bases for this impulsivity later on. But Aristotle also made observations that upend much of our thinking about the supposed inevitability of the problems of modern teenagers. About teens, he goes on:

They look at the good side rather than the bad . . .

They trust others readily . . .

They are sanguine . . .

They are shy, accepting the rules of society in which they have been trained . . .

They have exalted notions, because they have not yet been humbled by life.

What's striking about this picture is just how *positive* a view Aristotle takes of the young people around him. While acknowledging their impulsivity, he also ascribes to them many traits that are uniquely desirable—from trust to optimism to willingness to accept the rules of society—traits that are in all-too-short supply among teens in our society now. Even as we move 1,500 years forward from Aristotle, we find Shakespeare as likely to rejoice in the innocence and passion of youth as to complain about its impulsivity. Nowhere do we find descriptions of the cynicism, passivity, anxiety, or prolonged dependence that trouble adolescents today. History not only doesn't let us off the hook in this regard, it suggests that the teen problems that most bother us not only aren't inevitable, but may instead be a rather unique and unfortunate by-product of our modern age.

A FATHER'S BIAS

This tendency to view teens' behavior as something unchanging and universal appears to have gotten under way well before the 1950s textbook that misquoted Socrates. Some would trace it to 1904, when G. Stanley Hall, a brilliant, difficult man who would later be described as the "Father of Modern Adolescence," published perhaps *the* classic work on teenagers, titled *Adolescence*. Hall looked around him and saw a world with teens running amok. During the industrial revolution, teens flooded into small and large urban areas seeking employment, but often ended up roaming in unruly and often frightening gangs, literally taking over the streets of many cities, including, in all likelihood, Hall's own Worcester, Massachusetts. In his book, he offered one of the first modern, brain-based explanations for adolescent behavior, with graphic and vivid descriptions of adolescents as captives of their own "raging hormones" that drove them into conflict with authorities and into generally disagreeable behavior. Hall cast adolescents as victims of their own biology, living through a period of "storm and stress," and requiring careful monitoring. With its vivid prose, his book spoke to people's fears and dismay, shaping our views of adolescence right into the present.

Although Hall was a visionary in many ways, this aspect of his vision may have misled us almost as much as the fabricated Socrates quote. For at the time when Hall described the debilitating effects of "raging hormones" on teens' brains and behavior, there was scant actual evidence to support his novel thesis. In fact, the next hundred years of research largely failed to uncover substantial links between teen hormones and many of the most common and troubling traits of teens. Indeed, although some effects of hormones on behavior have been found (and we'll consider them in just a bit), we haven't detected any strong links to most of the behaviors we care about, particularly past age fifteen or so—when for many teens, adolescence is just getting fully under way and has many years to run.

For example, most adults have levels of sex hormones that match or exceed those found during the most volatile periods of early to mid-adolescence. But like the apocryphal quote from Socrates, the reality of this research never quite caught up to the seductive nature of Hall's vision. Something about the idea that teens' difficulties can be explained by their physiology appealed to the public. Many adults still write off teens' behaviors as "raging hormones." So even as the hormone research has failed to give us the answers we expected, we have subtly shifted our attention to emerging brain research to take its place.

I had little knowledge of any of this backstory when I was working with Sam. Frankly, given the challenges she offered, I think I would have been sorely tempted to cling to Hall's vision and Socrates's fabricated quote in any case.

THE ENDLESS THERAPY

Therapists are trained to deal with at least short periods of silence, and in Sam's case it was lucky I'd had that training. Thirty seconds of silence in a conversation is quite noticeable. A minute makes almost anyone uncomfortable, though therapists expect this at times. But after fifteen minutes of silence in that first session with Sam, I was already starting to lose my bearings.

"You're not sure you want to talk to me."

"You're just feeling like being quiet right now."

"You're probably mad that you're being made to come here."

I quickly went through all my usual approaches. And then went through them again, in all the creative iterations I could think of. And again. All met with the same reply.

Nothing.

The silence continued for weeks. Session after endless session. The group home where Sam was living reported that she remained equally unreachable there. Everyone agreed that she seemed deeply troubled and distressed. Numerous adults, including myself, had repeatedly reached out to Sam, but all of us were rejected. Why was she behaving so irrationally, we all wondered. As her therapist, the specific challenge for me was how I might help someone who was so determined to not even talk to me. With Sam, I wasn't so much discovering the Endless Adolescence as the endless therapy.

If most adults have a bias toward wanting to think about teens' behavior as being hardwired and largely uncontrollable, my experience with Sam and numerous other teens who've followed her helps me understand why. Adolescents' behavior can be exasperating, infuriating, inscrutable, and unmovable. Faced with onslaught after onslaught of challenges, it's not entirely unreasonable that most parents are willing to grasp at any available explanation for their teens' behavior—and the broader and more objective-sounding, the better.

And those conditions set a dangerous trap.

What began with fabricated quotes from Socrates and G. Stanley Hall's influential work has now been incarnated in popular interpretations of modern brain research. Parents, desperate for some explanation of why the teen years can be so trying, are all too eager to latch on. Teens *do* seem different from adults. They certainly act differently, so wouldn't it be reassuring if at last the brain scientists were starting to tell us why?

And yet as I recently sat listening to a panel of the world's leading experts on adolescent brain development present their work at a national conference, I was most struck by their great modesty in presenting their claims. "We don't yet know how most of the brain changes we've observed actually affect behavior," was a frequent refrain, typically followed by, "We need to constantly make clear that we are not saying our findings can explain all of teens' problematic behavior." They were enthusiastic about their research, and for good reason, but from the frequency of their disclaimers, it was obvious that these experts were concerned lest their research be misused to support the popular media message about brain immaturity as the cause of all teen problematic behavior. To their great credit, they were dogged in trying to resist it. But in some ways their message about the limits of what we know seem to be getting much the same treatment as the debunking of the raging-hormones theories and Socrates's supposed quote.

BEFORE THE ENDLESS ADOLESCENCE

The careful qualifications these brain researchers place upon their findings don't just reflect an excess of academic caution. The evidence that juvenile delinquency and other forms of misbehavior are not hardwired into the teenage years is actually rather compelling, but comes from a different source. Anthropologists Alice Schlegel and Herbert Barry, for example, have engaged in one of the farthest-reaching and most exhaustive studies ever conducted of adolescents across diverse cultures, reviewing interviews and descriptions of adolescents from 186 different preindustrial societies, ranging from Russian peasant villages in Khrushchev's era to the Kurds of northeastern Iraq. What would it do to brain and hormone explanations of widespread juvenile misbehavior if such behavior wasn't found in teens from other cultures and times? That's precisely the dilemma that Schlegel and Barry present with their findings.

They found that juvenile delinquency, for instance, was largely non-existent in more than half the societies examined. When individual young people in these societies did behave in troublesome ways, it was considered striking and unusual, rather than typical. In fact, many of these societies didn't even have *words* for delinquency in their language—"juvenile delinquency" was no more a part of their lexicon than "elder delinquency" would be a part of ours. Notably, teenagers in these societies tended to be incorporated quickly into the adult world. They worked side by side with adults. They socialized with adults. And they took part in adult rituals. When they were grouped with peers, it was to accomplish particular tasks for the community, and they learned to take pride in doing so. Adulthood came rapidly in these societies, and delinquency did not, just as was the case in our own society until a few generations ago.

In fact, we don't even have to look to foreign societies to see that the Endless Adolescence isn't hardwired into teens' biology. Just considering our own society not that many generations ago makes it quite clear how great the potential is for teens to function independently.

Historian Joe Kett, for example, describes the life of a young man of modest means, William Otter, who signed on to a merchant ship in 1803, worked for a while, was shipwrecked, and later drafted into the British Navy, deserted, smuggled himself to New York, and there became an apprentice—all by age sixteen. Susan Hull has written an entire book, *Boy Soldiers of the Confederacy*, describing the remarkable accomplishments of teenagers in the Civil War, many as young as thirteen. My own great-grandfather left his home and family at seventeen to sail to America and start a new life on a new continent speaking a new language, *completely on his own.* And he was not unusual, as the rosters at Ellis Island so eloquently attest. It's clear that these adolescents had the potential to survive and thrive independently; they were putting it to use!

Given what we know about the effects of nutrition and education, these teenagers of the past likely had brains that were, if anything, less mature than those of their contemporaries today. And we certainly have no reason to think that hormonal development didn't occur for them as well. No, if we want to say that teens' dependence, obstinacy, cynicism, and passivity are hardwired into their brains, we've got some pretty stark counterexamples, from all over the world and all over history, arguing against us.

THE FUNDAMENTAL ATTRIBUTION ERROR

If the theories about the hardwiring of teens' behavior and the way teens have been viewed throughout history are so weakly supported, why do we grasp onto them so readily and cling to them so tenaciously?

Judging from the enduring popularity of the Socrates "quote," the modern "teen brain" books, and G. Stanley Hall's original thesis, it's hard to escape the conclusion that in some ways we *want* to attribute adolescent behavior to something innate and physical about our teens—particularly behavior we don't like. My experience with Sam certainly made me want to do so, and one of the most important lessons she taught me was just how much one's exasperation with a teen's behavior could affect one's judgments about them. It's probably no surprise that unsettling behavior can distort the judgment of almost anyone, from textbook authors to time-honored theorists.

This search for physical deficiencies as causes of unsettling behavior doesn't begin or end with adolescents, of course. Across human history, various groups on the margins of mainstream society have often found themselves in the spotlight of this search. "Scholarly" works over the centuries have attributed the problems of a wide range of "troublesome" minority groups—from nineteenth-century immigrants to the United States, to Catholics in Northern Ireland, to slaves in America—to their innate physical deficiencies. Even very recently, a woman's capacity to handle the demands of the male workplace has been challenged by references to supposedly "innate" cognitive and emotional limitations of the female gender.

This pejorative tendency is so central to how we humans explain behavior that psychologists have coined a name for it: the "fundamental attribution error." It seems we humans have a strong, persistent bias to attribute behavior to innate qualities of individuals even when the objective evidence that their environment is shaping their actions is overwhelming. We do this in ways large (attributing evil to the motivations of rival nations) and small (not recognizing that a partner's short temper reflects a bad day or our failure to do the dishes, more than a latent mean streak). This bias is at its most persistent and most dangerous when applied to groups that lack the social status or verbal skill needed to articulate just how much they are affected by their environments. Groups like adolescents.

Most parents will tell you that this idea of the immature teen brain is one of the few notions that truly provides them comfort. "At least I don't have to feel like it's all my fault," is the way one parent put it to us. Yet, this idea also keeps teens and parents locked together in a prison of passivity and low expectations. For if poor behavior is all driven by the hormone-infused brain, what options do parents have to improve things? What else should teens even expect of themselves? This idea can become a prison so imposing that we give up on even looking for escape routes.

G. Stanley Hall was not immune to this quirky form of human blindness. In fact, had he looked more closely at the *environments* of the adolescents he was writing about, he would have noticed that adolescents' disturbing behavior had been increasing pretty much in direct proportion to the progress of the industrial revolution and the rise in compulsory education, which were changing the adolescent experience in a way never before seen. This simple point—that adolescence has changed radically over the years, and that teens used to behave more maturely than they do now—has the potential to act like a stick of dynamite in the prison of the Endless Adolescence. Once we recognize it, we must also realize that teens' poor behavior can't have been completely hardwired in their hormones and brains. Much as I might have resisted it, I'd ultimately need to find another explanation for Sam's behavior.

THE AUTONOMY CHALLENGE

I'd started to dread my weekly sessions with Sam, in which fifty minutes could seem oh so much longer. And then, just when I felt the situation had reached its low point, an ironic twist on the old saying "It's always darkest before pitch-black!" came to pass, and things got *worse*.

As Sam came in for her fourth session, she was wearing headphones. I explained to her that in order for me to be able to sign the form at the end of the session stating that she'd attended, she needed to not be listening to music. She sighed, said okay, made a motion toward turning off her Walkman, and sat down, pointedly leaving her headphones on! I could have challenged her on this, but somehow I trusted that this spirited young woman didn't feel any need to be dishonest with me and that the risk of antagonizing her further was simply too great to push it. But it left me deeply uncomfortable that perhaps she was enjoying a musical world while I sat in frustrated silence.

I had little to worry about, however, as Sam soon made clear to me that she wasn't just happily listening to music. How did she make this clear? She started to fall asleep! I insisted that she had to stay awake in order for the session to "count." Again she reluctantly agreed, and opened her eyes, but promptly began to flag. We spent most of the rest of the session with me calling her back to consciousness every few minutes and wondering if this was what I'd spent five years in graduate school to learn to do. What was wrong with this kid? What was wrong with *me* that I couldn't find a way to even communicate with this young woman who was so obviously in pain and in need of help? Was I a fool to be devoting my life to helping those who didn't even want to be helped?

I would eventually learn that in some ways I was right in thinking Sam's behavior was related to her brain development. But the brain development in question wasn't what I thought it was, and it wasn't a reflection of any sort of brain *under*development. Quite the opposite. What I finally saw in Sam was a part of adolescence that *does* appear to be hardwired—that is, universal across time and culture. Indeed, we even see it in the juvenile members of other primate species, including juvenile chimpanzees. It's the striving for independence, self-direction, and autonomy—the striving to move into adulthood, and it largely appears designed by evolution to propel development forward. And it's a force that we ignore at our own peril. I nearly misunderstood these strivings with Sam and was literally on the verge of giving up on her. But fortunately she didn't let me. Addressing this autonomy challenge was ultimately the key to helping her.

"It's not you."

The first three words she'd spoken to me in almost a month came at the very end of another silent session, and I had to reassure myself that I had heard Sam correctly as she was walking out the door.

I'd reached my breaking point with her by this time, and I'd said so in that session.

"Look, Sam, I'm not sure why you're not talking. I'd really like to try to be at least a little bit helpful, and I know you have to come here anyway. But if you don't want to talk, I clearly can't make you, or even convince you. So I just don't know what to do."

In retrospect, she had felt sorry for me. And indeed, as a young, novice therapist, I had degenerated into a state of blathering helplessness. But the irony is, my helplessness had given Sam a dose of *exactly* what she'd needed: a chance to show some autonomy *and* to step outside of the care-receiving role. She helped me out with that remark and we both knew it.

I came into the next session eager for more, and Sam quickly gave it to me.

"Are those my records?" she began, pointing to the large chart on my desk, filled with reports from her numerous placements.

"Yes," I answered hesitantly.

"Can I read them?"

This question—a challenge, really—was similar to many of the questions that followed. Each had a laserlike focus on one issue: Would I be willing to treat her as something other than an erratic kid and give her some control of our interaction?

Ultimately, I let Sam read her files (she'd have had the legal right to demand this in a matter of months anyway), but I insisted on reading them with her, a few pages at a time, and talking about what was in them.

When I asked her why she was so interested in her files, her answer made complete sense: "Everyone else gets to see what all these people have said about me. I'd just like to know what they're reading."

This was only one in a line of many challenges Sam made to the normal structure of therapy. She wanted—indeed needed—some sense of control over what was going on. At her request, we sometimes had sessions in the courtyard in front of the building. I once met her in the waiting room, only to see her chatting with two friends and have her then ask if it was okay if her friends joined us. On the spot, I said all right, at least for a few minutes. It turned out I had little to worry about. Sam's friends were far tougher on her—and armed with far more real-life data—than I could ever have been. It was a great session, though the friends never got invited back.

Sam's "pathology," it was to turn out as we talked, was sadly well earned. What she'd been through was more than sufficient to explain her long silence with me. The clues had been in her files, but it took Sam to help me put them together. She'd grown up in a just-getting-by family with poorly educated parents who'd tried in vain, but with brutal, sadistic physical force and repeated threats, to control her every move. They would fly off the handle if they didn't like how she styled her hair, who she dated, or even what books she read. As she described the horror of the repeated abuse she experienced—and the very physical ways in which her parents sought desperately to assert their control—I found her halting words far more disturbing than any violence I'd ever seen on a movie screen.

Once removed from her home, Sam went straight into a residential-care system that not only couldn't handle this angry young woman, but also ended up reenacting at least some of what she'd experienced at the hands of her parents. She experienced repeated physical confrontations with a poorly trained and overtaxed worker during one of her group-home stays. She was forcibly strip-searched by the police when picked up sleeping in a park one night. She was moved from residence to residence as a result of the financial needs of the larger social-service system of which she'd become a part.

As Sam came to talk about how these events affected her, her struggle for control and autonomy began to make a great deal more sense. She hadn't wanted to go to SafeHaven, and the staff there were less than receptive when she arrived, focusing more on "clamping down" on her from the get-go than on helping her. Sam connected the dots of all these experiences and concluded, not without justification, that she was in real danger of losing any vestiges of her own autonomy or capacity for self-direction. She might easily be kept in a passive, childlike, and dependent role forever, or so it seemed to her.

Fortunately, Sam was a fighter. The staff at SafeHaven (like her parents before them, and the social workers in between) could make her do many things, she realized, but the one thing they couldn't control was what was inside her head. She could still think for herself and decide for herself and that was what she was going to do. And she had decided that the staff couldn't make her talk about her painful experiences to some stranger. She realized that if she was going to make it as an adult, she'd have to stop letting herself be pushed around.

It wasn't until I'd seen many more adolescents over the years that I realized that what was so unusual about Sam was not the strength of her striving for autonomy, but just how stifled her strivings had been before she saw me. Her desire for autonomy was like a great river whose power isn't always visible on the surface—unless one tries to dam it up. Her struggles were wild and flailing at times, but had a single, focused purpose. Sam had been willing to blast her way out of placement after placement, lest she feel others were successfully pushing her around again. She was willing to give up even the most basic privileges to avoid coming to therapy, and once there, was willing to endure long and painful silences to make the point to me (but even more so to herself, I suspect) that she *was* in control, at least of her own thoughts and words. No one could make her talk, and that one small victory became a point of pride and perhaps even comfort.

All healthy adolescents want and need to develop their autonomy. The key point here is that Sam was *not* unusual in how much she wanted autonomy; what was striking in her case was that she felt so in danger of losing her chance to obtain it. Like the act of breathing, gaining autonomy for an adolescent can often proceed quietly and uneventfully, but let someone's oxygen be cut off even briefly, or a teen's autonomy appear seriously threatened, and panic and thrashing about is likely to result. What Sam displayed so clearly was what happens when this fundamental drive for autonomy is stifled, and how quickly the pressure builds when the relief valves are all closed.

Sam's push to gain adultlike autonomy is one facet of adolescent behavior that does appear to have a clear biological basis. The early stirrings of autonomy strivings, for example, are one of the few teen behaviors that researchers have clearly linked to hormonal changes. But in general these are natural and healthy strivings, not a source of great irrationality . . . unless, of course, they get dammed up. Yes, strivings for autonomy appear driven in part by hormonal changes and *can* look counterproductive if given no good outlets. But these strivings can also help adolescents move forward to achieve remarkable independence and self-sufficiency, just as they did with my great-grandfather as he made his way to Ellis Island.

It would have been easy to write off Sam's behavior as the nonsensical and irrational result of her hormonal state. Easy, but dead wrong, and a huge disservice to this feisty and determined abuse survivor. It took me awhile before I learned that the Socrates quote on which I'd relied was a fiction, and that there was much that raging hormones could not explain. But after seeing Sam, I was never again nearly as tempted to write off an adolescent's behavior as being fundamentally irrational and hormone-driven before making an effort to understand its source.

RISK-TAKING

Once we're aware of the danger of falling into the trap of using biology to explain away problems that have other causes, we're in a much better position to look at what we can actually learn from recent research on adolescent hormones and brain development. We'll be able to do so while recognizing that seeing adolescent brains as *different* should not automatically mean seeing them as *less capable*. With that perspective in mind, let's look at one of the areas that has received the most attention with regard to brain development: the adolescent propensity for risk-taking.

Deep within the brain, in an area called the *nucleus acumbens*, development is occurring during adolescence that increases sensitivity to rewards. When observed in laboratory paradigms, teens literally seem to get more out of rewards in a variety of experimental situations, and to seek out such rewards more so than adults do. Conversely, buried deep in the *amygdala* and other more-primitive parts of the brain where sensitivity to punishment is located, development isn't complete until about age thirty. Apparently as a result, adolescents do indeed seem less sensitive to punishments (that is, the negative consequences of their actions) than do adults. Or again, as Aristotle captured it several thousand years ago, "They look at the good side rather than the bad." We've also recently learned that several major areas of the brain across the prefrontal cortex that are responsible for judgment and risk-assessment don't fully come online until somewhere in the twenties.

Put these findings together and we get a picture that can be seen from several vantage points. On the one hand, we can begin to explain some of adolescents' propensity toward risky behavior—the impulsivity that even Aristotle noticed. The thrill of fast driving can sometimes outweigh the potential negative effects of a crash or a speeding ticket. In particular, the immaturity in the prefrontal cortex probably does suggest the need for guidance around teens' judgments in areas where the dangers are great. Teens don't fare well when treated as large children, but neither are they full-fledged adults.

But let's be careful not to go too far with this logic. We can also see these findings from a different angle. The focus on rewards over punishments not only leads to risk-taking, it also leads to a strong bias for action at a point in the life span when teens have a huge amount to learn about the world and yet are likely to stumble and fall on their faces frequently while doing so. Whether it's trying a new sport, learning to speak in front of a class, or heading off to college not even knowing who will be sleeping in a bed across the room each night, the risks of painful stumbles are huge. Perhaps teens' brains are wired to help them take on the risks they need to take on in order to grow up. The openness to new experience, even risky experience, that seems to be at least partly hardwired into their brains doesn't just cause problems, it propels teens to stretch themselves to learn and develop. It probably got my great-grandfather to America. So, the impulsivity and adventurousness of youth may indeed be biologically driven, but it may also have a larger purpose. Perhaps we can even learn to take advantage of it.

PUPPY LESSONS

The bias toward new experiences in teens is complemented by a related adolescent characteristic that appears equally likely to be hardwired. Observations of other mammalian species clearly show that juvenile primates of all sorts (including those in the human species) have an almost insatiable appetite to be active in the world. The same brain wiring that may account for some risky behavior is also likely to underlie teens' insatiable appetite for activity and action and agency—demands that modern adolescence seems uniquely set up to frustrate. In this regard, teens and puppies appear as close cousins in some ways.

We know a bit about puppies firsthand, as our family of two parents, two teens, and a preteen recently gained a sixth member—an energetic Labrador retriever named Butter. In preparing for her arrival, we did what many good, eager, and anxious "parents" do when preparing as adults to adopt their first puppy—we read books. But as we skimmed through the surprisingly voluminous literature on training puppies, we were struck by a theme that emerged with remarkable consistency: "Your puppy needs something to do. Keep your puppy active. Puppies like a challenge. They want to perform. An engaged puppy is a happy puppy." The warnings were equally consistent. If a family fails to provide such challenges and leaves a puppy with too little to do, the result will be a puppy that is bored, anxious, destructive, and poorly behaved.

Bored, anxious, destructive, and poorly behaved. Sound familiar? Might it be that our teens are in some ways like their puppy brethren in the family of juvenile mammals? That they are impulsive and have remarkably high levels of energy; that they aren't fully trained, but have capacities that, if not challenged and developed, may turn into significant liabilities and lead to significant problems?

And maybe the puppy people know something that those of us who work with adolescents have been missing. We've found, for example, that Butter does indeed behave far better on days when she's expended lots of energy, and like a bored adolescent when she hasn't. By the end of an inactive day, she's raiding the wastebaskets (getting into other people's stuff), chewing the edge of the rug (destroying property just for fun!), and jumping all over us (rude behavior!). To most dog owners, this sequence of events is utterly predictable. Yet we take teenagers at the height of their energy levels, individuals who crave stimulation and excitement, individuals with the capacity for tremendous amounts of physical activity (try keeping up with one on a basketball court), and ask them to do . . . almost nothing. Yes, we place demands on them, but the demands mostly involve enforced passivity and relatively meaningless tasks. To sit for hours at a time in a classroom and take notes or fill in bubble sheets for exams. To come home and do a few minutes' worth of chores and then turn to homework or the Internet. Like puppies or any other severely underchallenged organism, adolescents will often live *down* to the demands placed upon them. Understanding their hard-wiring may indeed be key to giving them environments that bring out their potential.

WHAT WAS SHE THINKING?

So how might we use this knowledge of adolescent brains to revisit and rethink our approach to adolescent problems? Let's start with a problem that seems to almost cry out for a hormone-based explanation: risky sexual activity.

No discussion of adolescent brains, and the effects of hormones on these brains, would be complete without considering the role of sexual development and the behaviors that often follow from it. It so happens, though, that even in this area of adolescent behavior that seems most obviously hardwired and biological, the drivers are less clear than they first appear. The very timing of a young woman's first period, for example—something most would assume is a purely biological function—has now been found to be partly linked to psychosocial factors ranging from the amount of physical contact with one's parents to the presence of a male stepparent. But more important, the onset of sexual *activity* appears far more determined by social environments than by biology. The age at which a person begins dating or first engages in sexual inter-course is far more closely linked to the norms of his or her local peer group than to measured levels of sex hormones. Adolescents' intense interest in sex clearly reflects hormonal changes, but what adolescents *do* with those interests appears at least as tied to their social interactions as to their hormones. Such was the case with Ellen, the eighth-grade lacrosse player we met in Chapter 1.

Ellen's sexual acting out—which started out in the back of the bus during school trips and snowballed from there—seems at first glance like a textbook example of the effects of the raging hormones and impulsivity we've come to associate with adolescence. "What could she possibly have been thinking?" her mother asked with tears welling in her eyes during one of our early sessions. In many ways, Ellen was a sitting duck for the brain/hormone write-offs of her behavior. But a closer look reveals just how facile an explanation this is.

For one thing, Ellen's behavior wasn't mainly about the sex. In fact, she was quite clear she didn't even find it all that enjoyable. Nor was it even just impulsivity. Her parents would have liked to believe these were just impetuous acts, but after the first time, Ellen typically knew in advance exactly when and with whom an opportunity for oral sex would arise.

So if Ellen wasn't displaying the results of raging sex hormones or an immature brain, what *was* she doing? We'd argue that she was engaging in a quite different endeavor, though one that appears equally rooted in biology, and is universal to adolescents across cultures and history—she was trying to be a grown-up. Ellen was very clear that she wanted to do what adults did—call her own shots, make things happen, and take actions that had an impact. In this way, yes, she was displaying results of her brain development, but it was development that appears better viewed as movement toward adult autonomy than as simple adolescent immaturity. She was also looking for some excitement in her life and a way of doing something that mattered to someone else. Something that would draw upon some of her remarkable adolescent energy, which the lacrosse field barely dented. Something beyond the boredom of six hours a day sitting in school followed by a few more hours of sitting at her desk doing homework.

Upon reflection, Ellen's problem seems less that her brain was immature than that it had been rapidly maturing and she badly needed an environment challenging enough to match her newfound capacities, energies, and strivings. Recognizing this would ultimately be the key to helping her.

BUILT TO THRIVE

We hope by now we're getting across the idea that perhaps we've massively underestimated just what our teens can do. Further, teens' biological immaturity isn't going to provide a good excuse if we're not happy with our teens' attitudes or behaviors. Once we stop to think about it, this shouldn't be so surprising. Most scientists believe that nature and the forces of evolution don't tend to waste a lot of time imbuing members of any species with useless impulses and erratic behavior. As humans evolved over the millennia, it's highly doubtful that survival pressures would have offered much room for the mythically hormone-crazed, biologically driven irrational teen behavior described in the popular press. Given far shorter adult life spans and the work that needed to be done to survive, it seems far more likely that teens' brains evolved to allow them to rapidly gain independence, self-sufficiency, and competence in the larger world.

Would it make sense that humans would have evolved in any other fashion? We can watch animals in the wild mature to adulthood without ever being tempted to ascribe to them a long period of erratic, senseless, and self-destructive behavior. Do we need to believe that if we see such behavior in our teens, it's simply an inevitable part of their biology? Yes, teens are immature. Yes, they need scaffolding around them as they learn and grow so the mistakes they make in their explorations won't be too costly. But they also need to be given real opportunities to grow and develop.

Neuroscientists are continuing to learn and be impressed by just how much brains can be influenced by their environments. Experiments have shown, for example, that actions as simple as teaching a person to juggle can create readily detectable changes in the very *structure* of their brains in just a matter of weeks. If a few weeks of juggling practice can change the brain, what can years of passivity and overprotection do? It may well be that the parts of the brain that handle risk-taking and recognize danger in our teens will fully develop *only* to the extent that we give them experience in a real world with real consequences for their actions. Holding back on this experience to wait for such development to occur seems akin to barring all physical activity for children until their bones and muscles fully mature. Not that some limits aren't warranted in both cases, but with an overly protected, infantilizing approach to our teens, we certainly run the risk of inhibiting the very development we're waiting anxiously to see.

We'll talk about some specific ways to speed teens' development along these lines in Chapter 8, but for now we simply want to get across the idea that coddling, restricting, and excusing our teens' behavior because they are "immature" may often bring about the very problems we most fear.

CRITICAL PERIODS, CHIPS AND BOULDERS

If adolescents appear hardwired to be active, autonomous, and adventurous, what are the consequences of putting them in an environment that fails to capitalize upon these traits? One of the interesting facets of the development of many advanced organisms is that there appear to be critical periods for learning certain kinds of information. During these periods, information is learned with ease (think of a child learning a first language from scratch in just a few years). Miss these periods, and it may be difficult to ever fully catch up. We can certainly conjecture that establishing oneself as an independent and competent actor in the world has been a primary task of the teen years throughout much of human history. What is it doing to teens to spend this period in a state of enforced passivity and dependence that goes against almost all of their instincts?

Sam, for example, ultimately made it, as we'll describe in Chapter 6, but she carried many scars into adulthood. While some people have a chip on their shoulder whenever they feel their autonomy might be threatened, Sam had a boulder she lugged around with her constantly. "I'm *never* gonna let anyone push me around again . . . *ever* . . . no matter what!" is how she put it. She was hypervigilant about any threats to her autonomy, including, unfortunately, threats that existed mainly in her own mind.

Yet other teens may in some ways be even less lucky. Sam at least saw herself as a fighter; many teenagers just come to accept their passivity. They come to accept that they lack competence to make decisions on their own, that they need adults to handle basic tasks even well into their twenties: that this is just who they are and how the world works. It doesn't take much speculation, or even much insistence on this critical-period theory, to recognize that years spent in such a state at the outset of one's maturity are likely to take their toll.

In contrast, the closer look we've taken at teens' brains in this chapter suggests the existence of a tremendous amount of energy and potential just waiting to be channeled. It's not that the teen brain books are wrong about how much is going on inside adolescents' brains. Indeed, some of these books, such as *The Primal Teen* by Barbara Strauch, are thoughtful and balanced, and are fine sources for following up on the points touched upon in this chapter. But the quick-and-dirty summary of their message in the popular media can lead us to write off adolescents at precisely the time when we need to work to bring out their full potential. And it's this potential we should be loath to give up. How many adults, after all, would pay dearly to have a few years back in which they felt the boundless energy of adolescence, the ability to think more quickly, and the increased willingness to try new things even if they might not work out?

We not only waste much of this potential currently, we frustrate and alienate our teens in the process. How and why is this happening on such a large scale? If we're going to suggest that teens' environments have become aversive in ways that drive many of the attitudes, behaviors, and values that concern us most—and more important, if we want to ultimately *change* those environments—then we need to understand just what exactly is happening within them. From the outside, we can see how teens' environments may be a bit problematic, but to fully appreciate just how and how much they undermine our teens' development, we need to take a look at them from the inside, the way our teens do.

Inside the Bubble

So just what does the Endless Adolescence look like to those stuck within it? It was one of my undergraduate students who helped me understand the experience when she introduced me to the concept of "the bubble." I was teaching a course on adolescent development for psychology majors at the University of Virginia, and we were talking about the ways in which adolescents interact with society at large. It was a big class with more than a hundred students, only a handful of whom were brave enough to regularly ask questions and make comments. The short, brown-haired young woman who raised her hand was not one of the "regulars." Her comment was simple, but probably captured the essence of the Endless Adolescence as well as any other single comment I've heard: "Most teenagers really just live in a bubble," she said. "It's just their room at home, their classroom at school, the shopping mall, the television, and the telephone." (The Internet hadn't yet come on the scene.) As she elaborated and her classmates nodded and chimed in with their own observations, it became clear that virtually nothing that she or any other teenager did within this bubble would have any significant impact on anyone in the larger society. The bubble was in some ways more like a cage or prison, albeit one well-gilded with material goods.

It's easy to underestimate just how much living inside the adolescent bubble undermines our teens' development. Over and over again we've seen life in the bubble affect teens in three critical ways: It cuts them off from meaningful roles in the adult world, it cuts them off from close day-to-day contact with adults, and it hyperexposes them to peer relationships, which then become their primary socializing influences. Let's consider these effects one at a time.

THE BUBBLE BOY

What happens when a human being is cut off from all chances to meaningfully contribute to and participate in the larger world? We use the concept of the adolescent bubble figuratively, but for one young man, the bubble was all too real. David Vetter was born on September 21, 1971, with a disease that would make him tragically famous. David suffered from severe combined immunodeficiency syndrome—a rare genetic disorder that left him completely unable to fight off even the most minor infection. The illness is usually quickly fatal, but David's doctors took on a heroic effort to save him by fashioning a plastic bubble world in which he could live, protected from all sources of infection.

David's plight and his doctors' response attracted national attention. David quickly became known as the Bubble Boy, and was nurtured like few other kids have been before or since. There could be little doubt that he had many people who loved and cared about him deeply. More than a million dollars was spent on his daily care, creating a unique and safe environment filled with all sorts of entertainments and distractions. Trained staff devoted extensive time to his well-being, and his parents rearranged their lives to accommodate his needs. He was featured in numerous films and documentaries, and now even has a school named after him.

Yet, according to multiple accounts, as he approached adolescence, David increasingly became profoundly dissatisfied not only with his existence, but with himself. For there was very little he could actually accomplish within his bubble. At age six he used a specially constructed space suit to walk down the hall of the hospital where he lived and was able to get a glass of ice water for a nurse—the first act he'd ever performed for another human being. But beyond such minor acts, there was little he could do for anyone or for himself, and he knew it. As the years passed, David remained well cared for, but completely unable to take on any meaningful role in the world. Increasingly this compliant boy came to be described as surly, obnoxious, and difficult. His sense of uselessness and frustration ultimately became so great that at twelve he made a valiant effort to try a procedure to allow him to live outside his bubble, but he ultimately succumbed when it failed.

David's bubble was literal, of course, and critical to keeping him alive. While it would be profoundly disrespectful to him to say that teenagers today have the same experience he had, there are certainly many elements of his life that are echoed, at least in minor keys, in the typical adolescent's life: from the vague guilt over the resources poured into one's existence and the lack of any way of justifying them, to the sense of uselessness and powerlessness, to the disconnection from the adult world. These factors came together in extreme fashion in David Vetter's life; unfortunately, many teens today experience something only slightly less demoralizing.

A FAILURE AT EVERYTHING

Fourteen-year-old Austin didn't live in a literal bubble, but the limited opportunities of his adolescent life had similar effects on him. Most people find adolescence emotionally difficult; Austin found it almost unbearable. He kept searching for venues where he could be a success, or at least be of use to someone, but within his world there was only a very limited number of options, none of which seemed to work out for him. Austin's academic work habits were weak, and he was not a natural student in any case, and thus school was constantly on the verge of turning into a minor disaster. For some young people grades can be a positive motivator—it feels good to get an A—but what about those for whom A's are likely to be few and far between? Does working hard to get an average (or even below-average) grade provide much motivation? It certainly didn't for Austin.

Austin was also not at all a natural athlete, and could only envy those youths who, whatever their grades or other failings, could dazzle on a football field or even just in a pickup basketball game and feel good about themselves in that way.

Nor was he popular. Not that he was unpopular, but rather, a bit of an introvert, and social interactions did not come naturally to him.

Being popular, a good athlete, or a strong student: These were the main venues to success in Austin's world, and they weren't going well. Actually, this whole adolescent thing wasn't working out so well for him. "I suck as a teenager," was how he described it. He'd become convinced he was, in his words, "absolutely a failure at everything." He wasn't a failure at everything, of course. In fact, he had a number of talents that would likely serve him well someday in the adult world. He had a real way with computers. Not just playing computer games (of which he did plenty), but setting up his home network, building an impressive Web page for himself, and tinkering with the innards of his dad's old PC. He also had a strong, if quirky, sense of humor, and a pleasant, self-deprecating manner. But within the very limited realm of social and academic roles available to most adolescents, Austin wasn't doing very well. He found this adolescent world incredibly frustrating, and more than once expressed the feeling that he wished he were just dead, so he wouldn't have to face it anymore. "But then if I tried to kill myself, I'd probably just screw that up too," he added in a way I found anything but reassuring.

Austin and I had a number of not terribly fruitful discussions about his sense of himself as a failure. "I'm not any good at anything," was his constant refrain, and he believed it. As I tried pointing out some of his stronger traits, his rejoinder was consistent: "How does that make a difference to anyone? My grades still suck. I can't play sports. I'm not rich. Face it, there's just nothing that's important that I'm good at."

UNIQUE, JUST LIKE EVERYONE ELSE

One of the problems with the bubble in which teens are growing up is that it leaves so little room for each adolescent's unique areas of competence to emerge. The resulting crisis of confidence has been thought to be part and parcel of adolescence, but perhaps that's more a reflection of the severely restricted range of venues in which teens can shine than anything innate to the age. Much has been made of the adolescent's search for identity. Psychologist Erik Erikson has cogently made the point that locating oneself in social and historical context is essential to healthy identity development. We gain a sense of identity by comparing ourselves to others. How are we similar or different? Where are we more or less competent? What makes us each unique?

Austin's situation suggests just how the limitations of the bubble in which teens live contribute to this crisis. We place kids like him in schools together with hundreds, and sometimes thousands, of other kids typically from similar economic and cultural backgrounds. We group them all within a year or so of one another in age. We equip them with similar gadgets, expose them to the same TV shows, lessons, and sports. We ask them all to take almost the exact same courses and do the exact same work and be graded relative to one another. We give them only a handful of ways in which they can meaningfully demonstrate their competencies. And then we're surprised that they have some difficulty establishing a sense of their own individuality. "Remember, you're unique, just like everyone else," the bumper sticker proclaims, and its irony isn't lost on teens like Austin. Ultimately, he was lucky and got a glimpse of life beyond adolescence that pulled him through, as we'll describe in Chapter 5, but many of his peers aren't so lucky.

A SIMULATED LIFE

Victor Frankl has written eloquently about his experiences in Nazi concentration camps, describing the uplifting conclusion that humans can deal with almost any hardship, provided they can find or create some sense of meaning within it. His principles apply well to adolescents like Austin and explain a second aspect of Austin's problem.

Watching his fellow prisoners, Frankl realized that who survived and who didn't, aside from some obvious physical factors, was most determined not by how difficult a situation the prisoner had, but by whether a prisoner had a sense that his or her suffering had some meaning. Those who had someone to care for or a task to which they badly wanted to return tended to survive; others, lacking such meaning, perished even if they began in better shape.

Our modern teenagers are living in a world where such meaning or broader purpose is largely lacking, and where the chances to do something for others (or even for themselves) are minimal. David Vetter was physically constrained from doing anything to help anyone else, but most teens like Austin, Perry, and Ellen don't necessarily do anything more than David did. If Frankl is correct that "meaning" is a fundamental human need, then we've put these teens in a very difficult situation indeed. It's not surprising that they don't feel good about themselves.

At first glance this idea that most teens have too few meaningful roles, though it might fit the teen who mainly lies in bed or plays on the Internet, seems to fly in the face of the caricature of the hyperstressed, overscheduled teen seeking to get into a top college. The key word here is *meaningful.* A fundamental aspect of the adolescent bubble is that the realms within which even talented kids can succeed—from grades to soccer to Spanish club to managing peer demands—almost all seem somewhat hollow and meaningless in the larger world. Teens are taught to care about these manufactured tasks and even to become stressed about them, yet in the larger world they don't matter all that much to anyone else, and most teens sense this.

We've found that a simple thought experiment helps get this idea across: Imagine how adults' work motivation and satisfaction would change if instead of doing their regular jobs each day, they were told to engage only in simulated versions of those jobs. Teachers would teach only to a video camera recording their behavior, plumbers would work only on simulated water leaks, lawyers would argue only mock cases, surgeons would operate only on well-constructed dummies. And these simulated "jobs" would continue day after day for years on end, with only five or six letter grades every few months as indicators of progress. The importance of being graded highly? Well, it would be tied very loosely to some relatively indeterminate career options many years in the future.

When we ask most people how their motivation would change under such circumstances, the answers come quickly: "I wouldn't really care what I did." "Why bother going to work?" Or, "I guess I'd keep doing it, but I think it would seem kind of pointless and boring." These, of course, are precisely the responses we hear from teens as they describe their schoolwork.

In terms of "real" experience, we often give teenagers even less intrinsically meaningful work than these simulated jobs, all in the name of preparation for a workforce role that could easily lie a decade or more in the future. Many teens, like Austin, just force themselves to jump through the hoops in front of them, though without the enthusiasm or energy that have historically characterized this stage of life. But others, like David Vetter, ultimately decide to do whatever they can to get out of their own bubbles, whatever the long-term costs.

NEEDING TO SAIL

Tim ultimately followed a course closer to David's. When Tim came to see me as he was finishing his junior year in high school, he had achieved phenomenally good grades for years and was in line to be class valedictorian at an extremely challenging school. By all accounts he was remarkably accomplished, and even in the hypercompetitive college admissions scene, Harvard, Yale, and the like were all very much on his radar screen. But the Endless Adolescence was poised to strike.

Tim had been pushing himself hard. Really hard. And he was exhausted. "I'm up till one or two in the morning at least once each week, and in exam weeks, I'm up that late almost every night," he told me. "It just never seems to end. In the summer, I've got this huge reading list, and then I'm going to band camp, because my band director says that if I get good enough, it will help me get into a really top college. It's okay I guess; I'm just really, really exhausted."

But Tim's problem wasn't just exhaustion. He was troubled by the sense that his life had turned into one huge grind pointing toward college. And unlike Perry, he didn't just suffer quietly. He was outspoken about his concerns, and I think it must have been something in the way he talked that led Tim's parents to push him to come see me.

As he voiced his concerns with me, it became harder, not easier, for him to push himself through his studying ritual. Tim didn't even start his homework most nights until eight—not because he was catching some downtime, but because that's when he'd finish his dinner and shower after coming home from cross-country practice. And that didn't even account for the days when he had a band performance in the evening, or a theatrical play practice, or trumpet lessons.

Tim was hanging in there and his grades never slipped, but he was getting ready to make his break. Finally, one day, he announced it. He wasn't going to college the following year; in fact, he wasn't even going to apply. Maybe he'd go to college someday and maybe not. Instead he was going to take some "time off" to try his hand at comic book drawing. Drawing was one thing he enjoyed in his daily grind, and he wanted to do something that was fun for a while.

As the weeks and months went by, and despite immense pressure from his parents and my own discussions with Tim about the possible downsides of his choice, he held steadfast. He was feeling increasingly dug in about his decision and was moving toward ending therapy.

In one of our final sessions, I was looking for ways to talk to him about the benefits of being well-prepared before venturing off into the work world. I had just seen Tom Hanks in the movie *Cast Away* and recalled for Tim how Hanks's character spent many days building his first boat to get off the island on which he was stranded, only to find that he hadn't made it sturdy enough as it got quickly swamped by the rough incoming surf. Yes, I wanted to see Tim escape to something that was less about drudgery and more about passion . . . but preparation was also key.

After thinking about it for a bit, with some hesitation, but with real emotion, Tim replied, "Yeah, I can see what you're saying and that may be right. But I just feel like I've been building my boat and polishing it and building and polishing it for so long that I just want to sail it, and I don't even care all that much exactly what happens or how well it goes. I just want to be trying it out and not just spending my whole life getting ready to try it out."

He left therapy soon afterward, and I don't know if he ever did make it to college. I found it deeply unsettling that I wasn't able to tell Tim much more than being well-prepared was indeed a good thing. Over time I realized I was unsettled because I understood this seventeen-year-old's reasoning all too well. Tim's new course was fraught with the risk of throwing away many of the benefits of his strong academic effort and could well lead to a life of disappointment over lost opportunities, yet it was the one escape route he could see from a life that had indeed become mainly dull and pressured. I could take some comfort in knowing that he had given a great deal of thought to his choice, but what an unfortunate choice to have to make at seventeen.

Tim's predicament is not unusual among high-achieving students, of course. Just last year, after I recounted his story in a lecture on teenage stress in my undergraduate course on adolescence, a young woman approached me after class. "You know, the kid you described in class today is just like a *huge* number of students here at U.Va.," she said. "You just can't imagine how many people are just running flat out all the time and feel like they can never quite do enough to keep up. People do extracurriculars just because they feel like they're supposed to. Everyone's stressed about their classes. And most of the kids I knew in high school were a lot like Tim." Whether Tim ended up happier than these other students who'd gone on to college is a question about which we can only wonder.

If you're having trouble seeing the force of Tim's reasoning about not wanting to wait years for the payoff for his hard work, changing the context might make his reaction easier to understand. Most adults find it tough to follow diets where the results show up in weeks or months; the efforts are challenging and the gains often seem small and far removed from the temptation at hand. Yet we're asking our teens to take on even harder tasks for which they won't see results that make a real difference in their lives for *years*. Perhaps the only thing worse than living in a bubble is feeling like you'll never get out. David Vetter, of course, had plenty of contact with adults while living in his plastic bubble. Most teens currently not only are stuck in a bubble, but find themselves far removed from meaningful adult relationships at the same time. Let's turn to that issue next.

LORDS OF THE FLIES

William Golding's 1959 classic, *Lord of the Flies*, spins out the wartime story of a group of British schoolboys marooned on an island with no adult supervision following a plane crash. In graphic detail the book traces the rapid devolution of these five- to twelve-year-old boys from socialized and proper British youths into a half-naked, cutthroat, anarchist society—one with rules and practices not unlike those found in gangs of adolescents on the streets of our cities. When the book was written, it was received not as a story about youth, but as a parable about human nature when societal constraints are removed. Unfortunately, adolescence today in many ways *is* a parable come to life in which societal constraints and intensive adult contact are—if not removed—at least placed off in an adult world that appears almost as remote and irrelevant as the mainland did to the stranded boys in Golding's book.

We wish that adolescents would just "become socialized," but we seem to have lost sight of the obvious truth that socialization requires an engaged socializing agent. The boys in *Lord of the Flies* didn't have one, but neither do many teens today. It is as if we're just hoping that adolescents will absorb our social mores and values mysteriously through the airwaves. In the end, we get our wish, in a manner of speaking. Values *are* transmitted to our teens through the airwaves, not via magic but through signals from television, radio, cell phones, and wireless connections to the Internet. The values they receive through these airwaves, however, are not our own, but reflect instead a distorted picture drawn by the demands of advertisers and the imaginations of Hollywood writers striving to reach the largest market by hitting the lowest common denominator.

Teens' relative isolation from the adult world creates a tremendous burden for those few adults who do have sustained contact with them. And in many ways, parents are as trapped by the adolescent bubble as their teens. Along with embattled high school teachers, they are often trying to manage almost all of the socialization of teens who previously were socialized by larger communities of adults. The problems with this arrangement are twofold. First, teens are in the midst of trying to establish their independence from their parents; hence, parental influences in some ways are already under siege. Second, teens are gaining in strength and capacity at about the same time as parents are passing their peak capacities in many realms, from physical to mental and even to their earning capacity. Thus, parents often appear to their teens as somewhat bedraggled and besieged individuals just trying to hold on, rather than as forceful role models with desirable lives to be emulated.

Adults other than parents have a critical socializing role to play for teens. "You've got to stop being late all the time" can be a call to battle between a parent and a teen, but a teen who gets this same message from multiple adults outside of his or her family is more likely to eventually recognize its validity. The problem is, most teens have few opportunities to get these reinforcing messages. Nor do they get the chance to get the kind of warmth, support, and eager ear from other adults that might make them want to take these kinds of messages seriously.

INEFFICIENT EFFICIENCIES

In some respects, the isolation of adolescents from adult society began with the move toward mass education of adolescents in the late nineteenth century. This movement required adolescents to spend an increasing amount of time in school, and correspondingly less time engaged in activities that required intensive interactions with the adults around them. And as the numbers of teens in school increased, school itself was also changing. Education moved from the one-room schoolhouse in which students and teachers commingled year after year, and could form long-term relationships, to the assembly-line efficiency of the modern, thousand-plus-student high school, in which each teacher is often responsible for the education of anywhere from 150 to 200 students on a given day. It is a testament to teachers' motivation that they even learn all their students' names under such conditions. This high school system virtually guarantees that teens will spend relatively little time in close interactions with adults. "Without high school, there would be no adolescents," cultural observer Thomas Hine has stated, noting that even our development of the concept of adolescence closely parallels the educational changes that have segregated teens from the adult world.

The movement toward greater efficiency in raising our adolescents is largely reflected in terms of reducing the number of adults needed to "manage" a given number of teens. Rather than asking teens to work closely with, learn from, help, or even play with adults, we send them off to clubs, teams, church groups, and camps where the ratio of teens to mature adults often *begins* at 15:1 (for most sports teams) and can extend upward to 80:1 at expensive summer camps that rely heavily on late adolescents as counselors. These practices not only reduce teens' access to meaningful adultlike roles in society, they also cut them off from almost all close adult interactions from which they might learn.

This process has its efficiencies, to be sure, but it has produced an adolescent cohort that is one of the most highly segregated groups in our society—segregated by age. Corporations engaged in outsourcing to increase efficiency have learned through trial and error that a downside to such streamlining of social interactions is its potential to eliminate the subtle, informal human interactions that are critical to engaging and acculturating a workforce. The call center operator doesn't fully understand (or care about) the goals of the distant corporate employer. Similarly, many adolescents in the United States might as well be phoning in from Antarctica for all they experience or appreciate adult culture and values.

Even outside of school, the disconnect of adolescents from adults has occurred not so much because adults willing to take on mentoring roles have disappeared, but because society has become structured in ways that tend to minimize this contact. As extended families have become geographically scattered, the one most ready source of such interested adults—every family's "Nana" or "Uncle Bob"—has so little routine contact with teens that their roles shrink into guest spots and cameo appearances. Similarly, in the typical teen workplace, true adults (not just nineteen-year-old supervisors) have become an endangered species.

WORLDS MOVING APART

The isolation of youth from adults and their consequent lack of social-ization become key elements in a vicious circle. As our teens fail to become socialized, they are less and less desirable to be around. A wife's suggestion to her husband, "Let's go out to dinner with the family," is often met with, "How about we just go out alone? The kids will just complain and argue and be rude anyway." A similar process unfolds with all sorts of activities: adult get-togethers, family dinners, weekend trips. It's often easier for parents to just go it alone. But when that happens, there's no one there to do the socializing, and what might otherwise be small teen problems has a chance to grow large. And as teens find themselves cut off from the adult world and have only one another with whom to interact, entitlement, surliness, and at times even rage and destructiveness can settle in, sometimes directed at the adult world, but often directed at one another.

In contrast, across history and in societies beyond the modern West-ern world, teenage youth have for the most part spent a good deal of time in their daily lives in activities that involved interactions with adults. In those relatively rare societies where they didn't, anthropolo-gists have found teens were far more likely to display levels of violence and destructiveness more akin to what we see with adolescents in our society today.

We also see the self-perpetuating effects of the teen-adult discon-nect on the adolescent's side as well. One rejoinder we often hear when we talk to adults about their role in teens' lives is, "But our teens don't want us to be involved!" This point of view isn't completely wrong, but it's only half the story. Having never learned how to live well in the adult world, our teens find themselves constantly struggling to gain their footing. They are criticized in restaurants, stared at at parties, and ignored by otherwise polite and sociable adults. Teens are often unable to recognize that in many cases their own behavior is bringing on these responses. Worse yet, they don't get the chance to *change* their behavior by learning from repeated interactions with adults. The end result is that we often have teens who can only look down and mumble when introduced to adults—teens who are as eager for such conversations to end as the adults themselves are.

But there's a second issue as well, and one that leads to a good deal of misunderstanding. Teens are hardwired to seek their autonomy, but this doesn't mean they need to shun adult connections to do so. It just means that they aren't as likely to want to look or feel dependent by seeking out adults. We've seen many parents respond to this apparent distancing by pulling back themselves, leaving teens even more disconnected than they would otherwise be: missing the relationships they once had, but not knowing what to do about it. The result is unfortunate for all involved and makes the adolescent bubble all the more suffocating.

THE CREEPING ADOLESCENCE

When we give our teens so few ways to display adultlike engagement with the world, we not only leave them frustrated and impatient, we also leave them looking for other ways to obtain a glimpse of adulthood. Some approaches, such as Tim's pursuit of comic book drawing, may or may not end up successful, but at least aren't destructive. The same cannot be said for other young people.

Cultural observer Thomas Hine has noted, for example, that crime is one of the few pursuits that allows young people to reach economic maturity at around the same time that their bodies reach physical maturity. If we extend Hine's notion from economic maturity to social maturity, then having sex and babies, and using cigarettes, alcohol, and drugs, can also fill similar functions. These behaviors are attractive in part because they offer the appearance of maturity for teens for whom the real thing seems far off. No doubt Ellen was seeking this appearance of maturity in her sexual exploits with Jake and his friends.

This push for the trappings of maturity is directly related to a question we commonly get from parents when we discuss the Endless Adolescence. "But aren't kids growing up too soon?" we're often asked. What about the eleven-year-olds who want to dress in explicit and provocative ways? The twelve-year-olds who can (and do) curse like sailors? And the thirteen-year-olds who know more about what R-rated movie is hot than their parents? How does all of this tie in with the idea of the Endless Adolescence?

The tie-in is that adolescence has been expanding in *both* directions as it's increasingly become unmoored from any connection with the adult world. We give our young people too few ways to reach real maturity, and so instead they seek out behaviors that provide the appearance of adulthood without the substance. And if adolescence doesn't actually involve taking on real adultlike tasks and responsibility, if it's become just an extended form of childhood, then of course nine-, ten-, and eleven-year-olds might want to join in the fun. Adolescence has come to be associated with drinking, smoking, having sex, and acquiring material goods, legally or otherwise. These activities provide the veneer of adulthood, but with none of the underlying demands or responsibilities (like holding a real job) that would otherwise make adolescence unreachable for most preteens. Because pseudoadult activities like drinking or watching R-rated movies don't require much if any real maturity, they are often accessible and desirable even to children who aren't even within sight of their teen years. They come to define adolescence.

We've worked with young people who were incredibly sexually active but didn't have a clue how to successfully shop for groceries to make a meal; or kids who engaged in adult-level criminal behaviors but didn't have the first idea how to take care of themselves physically; or adolescents who could buy clothes at the best stores, but lacked even a glimmer of a sense of what it takes to earn the money to pay for them. These young people were desperately seeking at least the appearance and trappings of adulthood before getting any responsibilities that would let them truly function as adults. It's a pseudoadulthood, and it serves young people poorly at whatever age it begins.

Interestingly, juvenile crime represents one of the few domains in which we've moved toward seemingly treating teens more like adults, increasingly transferring young delinquents into adult courts and correctional systems at earlier and earlier ages. In reality, of course, we aren't giving these juveniles any more freedom, responsibility, autonomy, or respect than in the past—we're simply punishing and restricting them in harsher ways. Thus, some young people take on the false trappings of maturity at earlier ages with their delinquent activity, and we treat them at earlier ages with the punitive, infantilizing restrictions that we apply to adult criminals. In either case, real adulthood is nowhere to be found.

THE PEER EQUATION: SIXTEEN AND SIXTY

The adolescent bubble lacks opportunities to perform meaningful work, and it prevents sustained contact with adults and the adult world, but adolescents do have one social element in abundance within their bubble: They have one another. And while adolescents have no doubt always been primed to learn from their peers, the current structure of the adolescent world almost guarantees that peer culture and norms will take on outsized importance for most teens.

Adolescents today spend approximately sixteen hours each week interacting with adults in one-on-one or small-group interactions, and about sixty hours in similar kinds of interactions with their peers. Although adults without teenagers of their own may find these figures surprising, most parents don't. What comes as a bit of a shock to almost everyone, however, is knowing that not that long ago in our history— and indeed for most of human history, as far as we can tell—these numbers were almost exactly reversed. Teenagers used to spend far more time in close interactions with adults and far less time off hanging out with one another. Adults used to be the prime socializing force, but they've been replaced by other teenagers. These adolescents aren't always the best socializers of one another, but they're often all they have.

TONY AND VICTOR

Tony, a sandy-haired, wiry young man from a local family, first came to me in his sophomore year of college, experiencing symptoms of depression. He was a talented musician, highly intelligent, and particularly skilled in the hard sciences. He struck me from the outset as remarkably well-educated, even within a selected pool of undergraduates, as he referred easily to topics ranging from neural functioning of the brain to the intricacies of global warming. Much of what Tony had learned he attributed to the boarding school he'd attended—one of the top schools on the East Coast—but I was even more struck by the things he hadn't learned. In academic terms, his parents' decision to send Tony to boarding school—following some tumultuous early adolescent years at home as his parents went through an ugly divorce—seemed to have worked out wonderfully. But in terms of Tony's social development, his story reminded me of a quite different tale I'd heard years earlier, about a strange boy named Victor.

Victor was first discovered running naked on all fours in the woods outside of Aveyron, France, at about age twelve, in the waning days of the eighteenth century. He was not only unclothed, but spoke no language, uttering only wild-sounding grunts. By all appearances he had been raising himself in the woods with wild animals for a number of years, and his origins were never uncovered. What was striking about Victor was that physically he was only slightly worse for wear; in terms of simple conditioning and skill, he could probably have easily surpassed most of the French schoolboys of his time. But he simply had no preparation to live in the larger society. Indeed, contact with other humans seemed mysterious, and more than a bit frightening and alien to him, and the first few times he was found, he quickly escaped back to the world in the woods he knew best.

We don't know when Victor began living away from adult contact, but for Tony, the demarcation was clear. Beginning at thirteen, he had been "raised" largely by other boys his age. Naturally shy, his angry battles with his divorcing parents had left him even more wary of adults, and in the boarding school he attended, it was possible for a boy who followed the rules like Tony to fly under the radar and get little attention from the adult proctors. This left mainly other boys to act as parental figures for Tony, and the lessons they provided were harsh. He came to school feeling shaky, uncertain, and vulnerable, and like a wounded gazelle on the Serengeti, quickly fell prey to those around him. Though a physically tough kid, he was frequently bullied. But it was the emotional humiliations that left the deepest scars, as Tony was repeatedly taunted and mocked by his peers for real and manufactured faults. For a critical five years of his adolescence, he learned a great deal about physics and biology, but almost nothing of the adult world, or even of the ways that civilized people were supposed to treat one another. Not how to stand up for himself, talk to adults, or resist temptation. Much of what he did learn of the social world from his peers was frightening, disorienting, and infuriating.

When Tony arrived at college—still a protected environment, mind you—even the modest choices he faced befuddled him. Lacking the structured study time of a boarding school, his previously fine grades plummeted. He moved off campus his second year with a group of "friends" from his first-year dorm who took advantage of him financially. Tony survived much as he had in boarding school—by lying low and shying away from adult contact. He developed a drinking problem and mainly just kept to himself. Though this handsome, intelligent young man looked from the outside like he was ready to take on the world, on the inside he knew virtually nothing about how to make it as an adult in society. Even when he left college, he still often felt dazed, bewildered, and fearful about his entry into the larger world beyond. "I feel like I'm all of a sudden sitting for the final exam when I've never even been to the class," was the way Tony described it.

Victor eventually got cleaned up and learned to wear clothes and walk upright. But he never learned more than a few words of French, and never joined society. His experience provided some of the earliest evidence that there was a "critical period" for language acquisition, after which language could never be acquired as easily, regardless of the effort expended. Given human resilience, one would hesitate to suggest that Tony wouldn't someday fully recover from his adolescence. But the loss was clearly there.

THE POPULARITY PROBLEM

Tony's story suggests the problems that can arise when teens are left to be socialized mainly by their peers. He is in some ways an extreme example: a vulnerable teen in an unusual environment subjected to a particularly challenging peer group and lacking the skills to manage its demands. What we've been learning, however, is that even far more socially adept teens still show the effects of being socialized primarily by other adolescents. Sometimes even hanging out with the "right" crowd can be highly problematic.

As we've studied thousands of teens over the years, one of the more surprising findings illustrating what we mean has arisen from our studies of well-liked kids. We started our research in this area simply to document something that most of us had long intuitively known: that doing well with one's peers in adolescence was an important marker of the extent to which one was doing well generally in life as an adolescent. It's what we refer to in psychology as a "grandmother" finding, as in, "Your grandmother could have told you that!" But then we found a wrinkle that we're not sure Grandma would have known about.

We learned about popularity by surveying large numbers of teens in a school and asking who in the school each teen liked. We didn't focus on the "high-status" kids, but rather, on asking about who students would like to actually spend time with. And then we identified these well-liked kids—the kids who showed up on many people's lists of desirable friends—and we stayed in touch with them over time. These were not necessarily the most visible kids in school. They may not have been the football team captain or the homecoming queen, but the kid who managed equipment for the football team (and was well-liked by almost everyone on it), or even the quiet, friendly kid who was just a good listener.

Much of what we found was unsurprising: These well-liked kids tended to get along well with their parents, they had strong and close best friendships in addition to their general popularity, and they were good at delaying gratification when they needed to and at balancing their own needs with the needs of those around them. In short, these kids looked remarkably well-socialized, just as we might have expected. So far we're in "your grandmother could have told you this" territory.

When we first began following these kids, when they were thirteen, we also looked at more problematic behaviors like alcohol use and minor delinquent activity, and at first found little of interest—these well-liked kids were no better or worse than their peers in this regard. Again, not a huge surprise. But when we caught up with these kids a year later, the picture that emerged caught us by surprise. Our popular, well-socialized teens had started using alcohol at almost three times the rate of their less-well-liked peers! We obtained similar findings when we looked at minor forms of delinquency, such as vandalism and shoplifting. By age eighteen, the gap in the likelihood of using alcohol between the popular and less-popular groups had grown to more than thirty percent.

Maybe they're just social drinkers, we thought. What happens if we continue to follow them? Well, we've followed them up through age twenty, and so far two conclusions emerge: First, they continue to drink at much higher rates than their peers who were less popular back at age thirteen. Second, even when we look not at drinking, but at significant problems related to drinking—things like drunk driving, fights, arrests, and lost time from work due to drinking and the like—our popular and "well-socialized" thirteen-year-olds have grown up to look like they aren't doing so well in this regard. Similar research by other colleagues has confirmed that even when followed into adulthood, these kinds of well-liked, friendly, popular kids continue to display significant problems.

So had these "good kids" suddenly turned bad? It wasn't that. When we looked at other measures—for example, whether teens were seen as hostile or aggressive by their peers—we saw that our well-liked thirteen-year-olds looked steadily more sociable and less likely to lash out at others over time. Finally it hit us. We had sought to study well-liked kids, and hoped and expected to find that these kids were well-socialized. And indeed, that was just what we had found. The problem wasn't that our popular teens weren't well-socialized, it was that they were being well-socialized *by a bunch of thirteen-year-olds*!

In some ways we've come to think of our popular thirteen-year-olds as being like mini-politicians. They're socially successful and good at reading crowds. While they seem to be leaders—and in some ways they are—they're also experts at discreetly checking out the "opinion polls" of their peers and putting themselves in the forefront of peer trends. The problem is not with these teens, though; it's with the particular electorate they're following. As we interviewed late adolescents to try to understand these findings better, it became clear that the problem was simply that many teenagers *value* drinking and other minor forms of misbehavior. Not universally, to be sure, but as we noted above, there's an element of coolness and adultlike appearance to these behaviors that makes them attractive to many teens. Our popular teens were simply being well-socialized into these values.

These values—that getting "wasted" is fun, that smashing mailboxes is a kick, that shoplifting is cool—have sprung up like weeds on fertile soil left untended. And while drinking, vandalism, and shoplifting appear minor in some contexts, they are far from trivial. Large numbers of teens, as well as innocent bystanders, are killed each year in alcohol-related accidents. Recent evidence suggests that early use of alcohol has long-term effects on brain development, and may predispose at least some young brains toward a greater lifelong risk of substance-abuse problems. Homeowners, consumers, retail shopkeepers, and others bear tremendous costs from both vandalism and shoplifting. In short, so-called "minor" adolescent problem behaviors may reflect a passing stage in adolescent development for many, but they create huge short- and long-term costs to society and to many of the adolescents involved. But these are just symptoms of the larger problem: By isolating teens from interaction with adults, we've let a peer world grow up that resembles the jungle island in *Lord of the Flies*, a place where adult norms no longer apply, even for otherwise well-adjusted kids.

TRAINING DELINQUENTS

Once these peer norms take root, they can be difficult to trim back. We've had to learn this lesson the hard way in our efforts to treat delinquent youths. One of our colleagues, psychologist Tom Dishion, is an expert in the prevention and treatment of juvenile delinquency. He's also interested in peer relationships in adolescence, so it was probably only natural that among the myriad programs targeting teen delinquency, Tom would end up focusing on those that sought to use peer relationships to enhance their impact, though what he found wasn't what we might expect.

When peer-based treatment programs for delinquent teens were first created, the idea behind them was considered novel and appealing: Peers are an incredibly powerful force in adolescence, so why not make delinquency-prevention programs peer-focused? Kids would rather sit with groups of other teens than be lectured by an adult any day. The idea had such appeal that programs sprang up all over the country. Some were residential—dealing with teens already incarcerated, or at least assigned to live outside the home, based on their behavior. Others were run in schools. Some targeted highly delinquent kids; others targeted those who simply showed early risk factors for future delinquency. All of the programs began with high hopes.

Over and over again, however, evaluations of these programs kept arriving at the same unsettling results. These programs consistently had small effects in the direction of making delinquent behavior *worse* among the youths who participated in them. It was Tom who figured out why. He pieced together what was happening by conducting two carefully controlled studies in which he showed that the solution was in fact the problem: Putting together groups of at-risk youths consistently tended to increase their likelihood of becoming delinquent over time because teens formed their own miniculture, and it wasn't a miniculture adults would feel good about. As long as the peers were left mainly to interact with one another, there was little the adults in these programs could do to change this culture.

The conclusion we want to draw is not that peers are inherently bad as socializers—indeed, our research has also shown that normal groups of peers can have positive socializing effects on behaviors such as aggression. When teens are removed from significant socializing contact with the adult world, however, norms that are disturbing from the vantage point of that larger world are likely to spring up. The problem isn't with popular teens or their friends, any more than it was with the British schoolboys in *Lord of the Flies*. It's the fact that all need the larger socializing influence of the adult community to develop well. Whatever problems our society has accumulated over the years, it has also accumulated much knowledge and much that's good in terms of our values—but these values will not get passed on to our teens unless we interact with them.

WHAT PEERS PROVIDE

The interventionists who wanted to bring kids together to prevent delinquency did have one thing right: The peer world *is* interesting to young people. But as we've talked with teens over the years, we've been struck that one of the reasons the peer world is so interesting today is that it provides feedback to teens in a way that's real and immediate, and that the rest of their lives simply cannot match.

Don't study for a test, and your parents might realize and get annoyed eight weeks later when your report card arrives. But wear the "wrong" jeans to school, and you'll know about it before homeroom ends. In addition, other teenagers are particularly attractive to adolescents as associates in part precisely because they treat one another as peers. Teens don't have to constantly look up to their agemates as higher-status individuals. Their peers take them seriously. Where adults rarely ask teens for their opinions or expertise, their friends ask them for help, advice, and opinions all the time. And like all of us, teens relish being in a position to hold forth and have others listen with interest. Our experience has been that on those occasions when adults do happen to treat teens with interest and respect (that is, as peers), teens eagerly soak up such interactions. This just doesn't happen all that often.

And so we're brought back full circle to the other essential elements of the adolescent bubble. The peer world is driven in part by its allure when compared to the lack of meaningful roles or connections adolescents have with the larger adult world. We know much of this intuitively, and we remember some of it if our own teen years were relatively recent. What we are less likely to realize is just how much this peer world has grown in importance in recent years, as the adult world has receded far into the distance for most teens.

THE BUBBLE, ZOOS, AND THE PERFECT STORM

Though many of the elements of the adolescent bubble result from efforts to keep teens nurtured and safe (just like David Vetter), in the end the bubble has the opposite effect. Over the past few decades, zookeepers have learned a similar lesson that may have put them ahead of adults and parents of adolescents in this one respect. Initially, zoos were designed so animals in them were simply kept safe and had little to do to get their food. Over time, however, zookeepers realized that with little to do, the animals became lethargic and anxious, and sometimes dangerous and erratic, regardless of how safe and "nurturing" their environments were.

It may not be a coincidence that we use terms related to zoos and domesticated animals to describe our adolescents at their worst, whether referring to their antics in *Animal House* fraternities, or to the pigsty-like quality of their rooms. Life in the bubble doesn't match teens' biology, any more than life in a confined zookeeper's cage matches the needs of most wild animals. Interestingly, what defines more modern zoos now is an effort to make enclosures better mimic the challenges and stimulation of the animal's natural environment.

Unfortunately, the elements of the teen bubble—from isolation from adult work and contact to hyperexposure to the unmoored values of the peer world—don't just appear one at a time; they come in clusters, and they often exacerbate one another. Teens frustrated with the lack of meaningful places to put their energy can all too easily find peers in parking lots with vandalism on their minds. Teens who seek to move beyond the narrow confines of the peer world encounter few opportunities to connect with adults. And as the teen world drifts further from the values of the adult world, adults are less and less willing to take the time to interact with teens, to invite them into their lives and their workplaces to apprentice and socialize them. The end result is that the elements of the teen bubble combine and build upon one another to create a near-perfect storm that can blow even the most conscientious teens off course.

So how can we change this? Well, a good place to start is to recognize that problematic adolescent attitudes and behaviors aren't inevitable, and that adolescent brains bring tremendous promise and capacity. But before we get to the positive things we can do to help our teens grow and mature, we'll have to work to *unlearn* some important behaviors that keep them stifled. For one of the greatest ironies of the Endless Adolescence is that it is often precisely in our efforts to *help* our struggling teens develop their potential that we make things worse. It's a widespread phenomenon, and one of the driving forces that's led to the creation of the Endless Adolescence. We call it the Nurture Paradox.

4

The Nurture Paradox

MEGAN AND LARRY

Eighteen-year-old Megan was racked with anxiety in what should have been the best days of her high school career. "I'm a basket case," she told me, and her description struck me as odd at first. Megan came to see me soon after committing to her top choice for college and just a few weeks away from finishing high school. To that point she had seemingly navigated past many of the shoals of the Endless Adolescence, and her life had been filled with the typical successes of a high-achieving student from a well-to-do background. For the past year and a half, though, Megan hadn't been able to enjoy any of it. The problem: leaving home.

Home was truly special. Megan's mom was a gifted cook who also gave great advice and didn't freak out over minor problems like some other parents did. Her dad was a whiz at managing life's details: From college-application tricks to selecting the perfect cell phone, Dad could handle it all for Megan, and did so with relative ease. Megan had her room (well-furnished by Mom), her car (picked out by Dad), and her MacBook, which could run Windows (again set up by Dad). In many ways, her parents had given her what seemed like the ideal adolescence, and they'd worked quite hard to do so.

The problem was, all of this was threatening to come to an end. Worried about facing life on her own, Megan had spent much of her senior year so anxious that even the modest stress of socializing overwhelmed her. As her friends chatted about SATs and the college search during lunch, Megan found herself avoiding the school cafeteria, eating alone in a classroom, and telling herself she was overwhelmed with schoolwork and needed to study during lunch. Halfway through volleyball season, a varsity player, she dropped off the team for fear that she wouldn't get her college applications done. In the end Megan's dad had to pull together her college essay, because she was paralyzed with worry. What if college turned out to be too hard? What if she hated her roommate? How would she choose good classes? What if she got homesick? Good questions, to be sure, but to Megan they felt less like questions than ticking bombs that she had no clue how to defuse.

Fifteen-year-old Larry lived a few miles from Megan in a neighborhood of subsidized housing. Larry's mother was on food stamps and had been for most of Larry's life, though she often worked overtime in the stockroom of a local department store. In spite of his mother's modest income, Larry did not go wanting for material goods. He had a Nintendo Wii, an iPod, a cell phone, a top-of-the-line backpack, and expensive clothes. Take him out of his tiny apartment and stand him next to Megan at school, and the two wouldn't look much different, a comparison that would have made Larry's mom beam with pride. Except that Larry was rarely at school.

Larry was a bright and appealing kid who had impressed his teachers as promising, at least up until the past year. By the time I saw him, though, halfway through tenth grade, he was failing two classes and had missed forty-five days of school. Because she took two buses to get to work, Larry's mom was already gone when he was supposed to wake up and get to school. Not surprisingly, that just didn't happen very regularly. "He just won't get up, no matter how much I tell him it's important," his mother explained. What was surprising, however, was her response when I asked whether she could rearrange her schedule to be at home more in the mornings.

"Well, I *could* cut back my hours, I suppose," she started hesitantly, "but then we'd be so tight for money, I wouldn't be able to give Larry any of the little extras that make life worth living." Larry's mom had already cut her other expenses to the bone. She bought her own clothes from Kmart, and the family ate on a large, old packing box rather than spend the money on a kitchen table. But she'd given Larry a great Christmas, which her friends and extended family all acknowledged was no small feat given her financial situation. In doing these things, Larry's mom felt she was doing everything possible to help her son succeed. "We may not have much money, but at least Larry doesn't go wanting," she said.

"Okay," I acknowledged. "But how about if Larry gets a part-time job after school to help make up the difference if you cut back a bit?" We had already discussed her frustration that all he did after school was watch TV. "That way you get to be home a bit more and he might get some good experience." Larry's mom looked annoyed. "He's *not* going to have to work while he's still in school," she stated firmly. "I had to do that, and I promised myself my kids wouldn't have to. It's a parent's job to provide, and a kid's job to go to school. He just needs to do his part."

But that wasn't happening.

From opposite ends of the socioeconomic spectrum, Megan and Larry were both going badly off track on their journeys to adulthood. Both lacked any sense of what the larger world was going to expect of them. Neither had any confidence that they would make it. Megan had everything external in place, including her schoolwork, but felt completely unready. Larry's academic career was in grave danger, and he had little idea how to motivate himself even to get up in the morning. Different as these two were, they were both overwhelmed and prone to giving up when the going got tough.

Megan and Larry have plenty of company. In a sense they could be poster children for the "failure-to-launch" generation. And as we've thought about what these two young people have in common, what we're most struck by is the deep similarity in their *parents'* goals and attitudes. Both Megan's parents and Larry's mother were desperately trying to nurture their children in the most lavish ways they could in order to provide them with the best possible adolescence. And in significant ways, both were succeeding. But they were seriously undermining their teen's development in the process.

PROBLEMS OF PLENTY

Our physical worlds are filled with problems of plenty. Overeating, for example, paired with inadequate exercise, leads to illnesses ranging from obesity to diabetes to heart disease. Even outstanding food and wine, expertly prepared, can lead to painful episodes of gout, as unfortunate fortunates from Henry VIII to Sir Laurence Olivier to Pope Clement VIII have learned. One of the nutritional lessons we've absorbed over time is that while good food can be a real boon to health, too much good food can literally poison the body, especially if it's not accompanied by exercise.

A similar phenomenon seems to be unfolding with our young people, but we're only just starting to catch on to it. Instinctively, we believe that if we can just provide sufficient nurturance, our kids will thrive. But when we don't put a check on our nurturing instincts and learn also to *ask* some things of our teens, we end up poisoning their character just as surely as an excess of sugar and fat in their diets can poison their bodies.[1] Megan and Larry were both suffering this fate, and their parents were unaware that they were bringing it about.

So how did these families get to this point? The short answer is that they got there with the best of intentions.

---

[1] The one important exception, of course, is the population of teenagers who lack parents who are able or willing to provide *any* significant nurturance, whether as a result of severe poverty, mental illness, substance abuse, or the like. Although even these youths may experience and suffer from other aspects of the Endless Adolescence, such as seeing meaningful adult roles closed off, clearly the problem of being overnurtured is not one that applies to this unfortunate group.

Let's look at Megan first. Of course, we don't know for sure if her *grand*parents were as nurturing back when they were raising a family as Megan's parents were to her. But tighter finances back then, fewer time-saving devices at home, larger families, and an emphasis on a family's establishing itself with some security in the world would have likely prevented them from focusing as intently on their children. Megan's parents, in contrast, had few natural checks on their nurturing instincts. They were secure in their jobs and their home. They only had Megan and her brother to care for. They had found numerous classes and clubs to round out their children's days. And they'd thrown themselves into raising their children as fully as they had once thrown themselves into their careers.

With every choice about whether to do something for Megan or teach her do it, they were struck by just how *easy* it was to do it themselves. "It's really no strain for us to help her out when she needs it," is how Megan's dad explained it. It was certainly easier for Megan that way—and with a nicer outcome, for sure (she'd have missed half the features on her MacBook if her dad hadn't set it up for her). But it was also more gratifying, and often quicker, for Megan's parents. Dad could intensively edit—okay, let's be honest, he could *write*—sections of Megan's college applications far more easily than he could review multiple drafts and nag her to revise them again and again. "I was just punching it up a little," he explained, only a bit sheepishly.

Megan's parents loved her deeply and were trying to give her the best possible life a high school senior could have. But in doing so, they were giving her almost none of the opportunities she would need to feel competent away from home the following year. Her high school world was indeed near perfect, but as she reached each new milestone in the college-selection process, this "perfect" world came to look ever more fragile, and Megan's mental state came to mirror this fragility. Her parents, meanwhile, grew increasingly worried and dismayed as they watched their oldest child flounder in spite of all the attention, energy, and love they were showering upon her.

It would be tempting to write these problems off as only affecting spoiled rich kids, but what we've come to realize is that parents across *all* income groups are increasingly trying to "nurture" their teens in ways that ultimately hamper their development. Larry's mother faced severe financial constraints, yet still managed with great strain to shower Larry with material goods, even at the expense of his development. And even though the bills piled up by the end of each month, she would not consider pushing Larry into the workforce, even part-time, and even though he lacked after-school activities. She took great satisfaction in knowing that he wouldn't know the material deprivation she'd experienced as a child and was still experiencing.

Larry and Megan came from quite different neighborhoods and backgrounds. But what both of their parents shared was the unstated assumption that good parenting is reflected in what we *provide* our teens, rather than in what we *expect* from them.

THE NURTURE INSTINCT

In our combined forty-five years as therapists, researchers, and parents, we've almost never met a parent who didn't truly love their adolescent. We've seen plenty of parents who were frustrated or angry or estranged from their offspring, but underneath it all, either deeply buried or just below the surface, the love is almost always there. Hardwired into our biology and our humanity, this love leads us to do everything we can for our offspring. Who would have thought that it could also lead us to undermine our teens' development at the very time this development matters most?

Our instincts to nurture and protect our teens know few bounds, and through much of human history have had only the constraints of severe environments to keep them in check. As these environmental constraints have faded, however, our capacity to nurture our teens has grown without limit. From before our children are born, we're trained as parents to nurture and protect them in every way possible. From Dr. Penelope Leach to *What to Expect When You're Expecting,* we are drilled in the best ways to meet our children's needs. Our society and market economy rise up to help us meet the challenge, providing all manner of camps, lessons, iPods, computers, cell phones, enrichment activities, CD-ROMs, and Wiis to keep our teens stimulated and entertained. Affluent parents like Megan's are the most natural targets of these forces, but even parents like Larry's mother find themselves deeply affected and struggling to keep up. The desire to do what's best for one's children knows no income boundaries.

Both Larry's and Megan's parents fell prey, however, to a confusion that has become all too common recently. Across human history, parents have been primed to make all manner of sacrifices to give their teens what they needed to thrive, but of late a subtle but crucial shift has occurred. Parents today no longer just sacrifice to give their teens everything they *need,* they sacrifice to give them everything (or almost everything) they *want.* The shift is subtle, but the effects are not.

For our teens, we've defined nurturance largely in terms of the things we can do for them, the stuff we can buy them, and the experiences and opportunities we can provide. In reality, what most teens need is neither more stuff nor more lessons, nor do most teens even need more tender, loving care or quality time. While young children need a great deal of parental nurturance in the form of direct assistance geared toward meeting their needs, adolescents need something different. Unlike children, teens' growing bodies and brains most need nurturance of their developing capacities to *function on their own* in the world. This means expecting things *of* them, not just giving things *to* them.

Megan could easily have learned to handle almost all the tasks her parents picked up for her along the way. Similarly, a teen Larry's age could well handle getting up on his own, but only if he'd had the experience of being pushed to learn to do this. Adolescents' competencies don't simply develop; rather, they need challenges and demands to nudge them along. This requires a significant change in mind-set for parents, but it's not one that usually comes naturally. To many parents, however, making these demands—whether requiring Megan to do some work for her car or expecting Larry to go to school before he gets more electronic goodies—seems more like denying their children than nurturing them.

FROM CONTRIBUTORS TO CLASSROOM CLOWNS

What took place in Megan's and Larry's families is neither rare nor unique. We've seen similar tendencies in almost all the families with whom we've worked, and have come to realize that this Nurture Paradox actually has roots far deeper and broader than the psychology of individual family relationships. In fact, the story of the development of this paradox is closely tied to the progress of our society over the past 150 years. It's a story that begins with changes to the landscape of our economy, and ends with dramatic changes to the landscape of adolescents' lives.

The onset of the industrial revolution began eliminating the workplace venues teens had formerly inhabited. The farms that for generations had so reliably harnessed teens' energy and physical skills needed them less and less, and the solo craftsmen who employed apprentice teens were also gradually vanishing from the economic landscape. As families moved into cities in search of manufacturing jobs, adolescents went from supplementing the efforts of their parents on farms, where their labor was in great demand, to competing with adult strangers for the chance to work in highly uncertain urban economies. Keeping adolescents productively involved in the adult labor force thus came to be seen by at least some adults as detrimental to their own interests. It is no coincidence that some of the strongest proponents of child labor laws during this period were labor unions, for whom keeping young people out of adult factories was one of the surest ways to protect adult jobs and wages.

As these workplace changes progressed, something else was also occurring. There grew a widespread and accurate perception that the *pace* of change itself was increasing. After generation upon generation in which teens could be raised to do as their parents had done, a new world was dawning. The awareness came slowly, but parents, educators, and others gradually realized that it wasn't at all clear what kinds of experience would be needed to best prepare teens to live in the world of the future.

These economic, demographic, and cultural forces all came rushing together to bring about one of the most massive transformations to the activities of any age cohort that's occurred before or since. The response to these forces was, in a word: education. What better way to address both the problem of teens' competing for adult jobs *and* the need for more preparation and flexibility in future careers than by sending teenagers off to high school? The gradual lengthening of the human life span across this period also seemingly reduced the cost of poaching a few years from the beginning of adulthood and devoting them to further academic preparation. There was a tremendous increase in the number of high schools in America in the twenty years prior to the publication of G. Stanley Hall's *Adolescence* in 1904, but this change was just the beginning. In 1900 eleven percent of teens in the United States attended high school—a dramatic increase from the experience of prior generations. But by 1930 the percentage had increased almost fivefold again, to more than fifty percent.

Let's be absolutely clear: A great many of the changes that followed have benefited adolescents. Factory labor was often dangerous work, and farm labor had been only marginally better. Giving youths' broad-based knowledge and skills applicable across a range of contexts was a huge boon to our society. And increased education of our young has been one of the keys, if not the key, to the rapid advance of our economy, and indeed of our entire society. But progress often brings with it new problems and challenges, and this brings us straight to the roots of the Nurture Paradox.

The one big unintended consequence of all of these changes was a dramatic shift in the roles of adolescents: from contributors to their families to beneficiaries of others' efforts. From active helping hands at work to passive recipients of knowledge in school. Over just a generation or two, teens were literally stripped of the meaningful roles they'd previously held, and in its stead, offered time spent mainly in classrooms and free time with their peers. Teens gradually came to recognize their new role, or lack of one. The effects on their behavior and their attitudes were profound. As Austin, the teen in the last chapter who felt so incompetent, described it, "I'm no good to anybody and I just cost my parents money."

And as these changes unfolded, adults also came to view adolescents differently. Our goal became not to utilize teens' energy and abilities to help their families survive and thrive, but rather to nurture their future potential. Adolescents who had previously been seen as competent and productive junior adults were now increasingly viewed as highly dependent and incompetent large children. Adolescence shifted from being a time of *doing* to being a time of *preparing*.

As part of this change, the environment in which the typical teenager lived evolved from a slightly watered-down version of adulthood into a well-padded holding zone. The teen bubble was born. Life in the bubble became almost entirely one-dimensional, focusing intensively upon formal education while jettisoning the implicit forms of preparation that had previously been part of the teenage years. Just as parents "nurture" their teens with an abundance of material goods, so too our educational system came to provide them with an incredibly rich diet of intellectual experiences. This would generally be considered a good thing, but it provided few opportunities to exercise teens' newly developing capacities in ways that were meaningful outside the classroom. Teens' diets thus became increasingly rich, but highly unbalanced.

These social changes outside the family dovetail with the changes occurring within families. The problem is not just tied to the tasks we perform for our teens, or even just to the material goods we provide. Many well-off parents, for example, realize their teens need more than just material goods. Their response is to shell out huge amounts of money for an endless variety of "enriching" experiences. Piano lessons, dance lessons, horseback riding lessons, you name it. Then there are the camps. Soccer camps. Lacrosse camps. Music camps. "Just hang out and have fun" camps. All this in families with parents running flat out to manage full-time jobs to pay for all these experiences, not to mention the work of providing transportation to them.

This becomes a vicious cycle. Families with parents working hard to earn the money to provide all these activities end up feeling guilty for not spending more time with their teens. The response to this guilt: Send more "stuff" the teens' way, whether it be material goods, enrichment activities, tutors, or even just cash. The stories of the sumptuous banquets afforded to Henry VIII almost pale in comparison to the smorgasbord of activities offered to many teens today. But as with Henry VIII, the opportunities for exercise to work off and digest this smorgasbord all too often seem lacking. Where are the real demands placed upon teens that might help them use all they've been given, in order to grow in their capacities to manage successfully as adults?

For example, the college graduate from Chapter 1 who applied to work as one of my research coordinators, but who worried in the interview, "Will I have to be bored?" had no doubt been exposed to many settings, from camps to lessons to youth groups, that were designed to be as interesting and engaging to him as possible. This student had absorbed the expectation that any setting he was going to enter was there to meet his needs. He'd clearly had far less experience in arenas that simply needed and demanded his hard work and conscientious effort. Compared to teens of prior generations, he may have been bored less often while growing up. His implicit sense of entitlement might even be understandable. But he still didn't get the job.

SUCH A NICE BOY

Teens' entitlement also routinely seeps into family interactions in ways that set them up for harsh experiences in a larger world that is unlikely to give them the same deference as their parents do. Such was the case with Lee and his family.

Lee was a big, outgoing, red-haired kid who even as a teenager carried more than 250 pounds on his six-feet-four-inch frame. He usually aimed to please, though both he and his parents acknowledged he had "a bit of a temper." Both of Lee's parents had grown up in extreme poverty but were now, through diligence and sheer grit, managing a modest but stable working-class lifestyle. Lee had more than his share of material goods, but the amount wasn't the issue. Rather, the problem was that his parents were simply unable to turn him down when he asked for something from them, whether it was staying out after curfew or financing his school trip because he hadn't participated in any of the fund-raising opportunities the school had provided.

Whenever his parents tried to turn him down, Lee's temper and the desperation of his pleas brought back memories of their own real deprivation as kids, and whatever their initial thinking, they almost always ultimately caved and gave him what he wanted. "He's a good boy, and we want him to have a better childhood than we did," his mom noted. They saw doing so as part of good parenting. It never occurred to them that having their son near tears at the prospect of not getting his way was a sign that something had gone badly awry.

Lee's teachers, in contrast, had no trouble at all seeing the problem. "I can't believe they can suspend me just for getting mad!" was the way Lee explained his most recent school problem to his parents. His teachers saw it otherwise. Yes, in some sense Lee was right—he was being suspended for getting mad—but what he didn't realize was just how intimidating a figure he cut to the teacher who had to watch this strapping young man loom over her, red-faced in full tantrum, as she insisted on enforcing a basic classroom rule. It was *how* Lee got mad, and how mad he got, that was the problem.

His parents' reaction to all this was at least as disturbing as Lee's. "But Lee's just such a *nice* boy. If the teachers would just take the time to understand him, they'd see that he doesn't mean anything by it," his dad explained. He went on, "Lee just really thought what the teacher was doing was unfair, and it sounds to me like it was unfair, at least a little." Lee *was* a nice boy, and his parents were more than willing to go to bat for him. They were even able to get the suspension reduced a bit, which left everyone feeling better. Until the same incident happened again, and then again one more time, and Lee found himself looking with his parents for another school to attend.

Alas, Lee's parents' reaction was that since he had now "been through so much," they would need to be especially careful not to upset him further. The cycle continued.

TURNING TO FEAR

In addition to social and economic changes, there is one other huge factor that has grown up over just the past generation to drive the Nurture Paradox. That factor is fear. In less than a generation, parents have become increasingly uneasy about their children's well-being. No matter how much we try to do, nothing fully takes away the fear that perhaps we're not taking good enough care of our teens and that something ill will befall them as a result.

This fear is no doubt partly bred in our bones. A hand-painted plaque on the wall in our close friends' house says, "Having children means forever becoming accustomed to having one's heart wander around outside one's body." That about captures it for us, and we think for many parents. The parental fear for the well-being of their offspring may be woven into our DNA, but like other aspects of the nurture instinct, without other checks to keep it in balance, it threatens to strangle our teens' development.

Left unchecked, these fears rapidly morph into mild phobias. The difference between a fear and a phobia is not that a phobia has no basis in reality. Acrophobics are right, for example, when they say that falling from heights can be deadly and that falls can happen even to those who are careful. No, what defines a phobia is not that it has no possible basis in fact, but rather that it goes so far overboard that it creates problems of its own. With our adolescents, the real danger is that our fears are leading us to behave in ways that cause problems at least as bad as those we're trying to prevent. Teens like Barrett experience this firsthand.

EMERGENCIES, PHYSICAL AND OTHERWISE

Barrett had been brought to the emergency room four times for acute stomach pains that each time made the E.R. doctors think appendicitis, but in each case, all the tests had come up negative. Nor had follow-up appointments detected any signs of a physical problem. It was on his fifth trip that one of the doctors sent him over to us. While too much exposure to the world's hard knocks is no doubt a problem for some teens, Barrett's difficulty was of a completely different nature.

He had been homeschooled since second grade, after he came home reporting some nasty words he'd heard from other kids and his parents decided they could do at least as good a job as the school in educating him. And no doubt they had, as Barrett did well on all his tests and was now working well above his nominal tenth-grade level. But his world was his home. Period. Other than his cello lessons, he had little reason to stray outside. He was protected from drug use, sexual predators, bad peer language, and even the Internet. But he was also kept away from much of the work of growing up.

I found Barrett to be remarkably articulate from the outset—he'd been doing a lot of thinking. "Emotionally, I'm a six-year-old," he said in one of our first sessions. "I know my mom just wants what's best for me. And I know I could never handle a regular school." He was a bit breathless as he went on, "And I know that there are a lot of really dangerous things going on out there. And they've said I can live with them for as long as I want."

But it was only later that Barrett was able to put words to his most paralyzing fear: "What if I'm *never* ready to make it in the world? I just don't know how I'll get there." At night, after his parents had gone to sleep, Barrett lay awake in bed trying not to think these thoughts. But as they snuck into his consciousness via all different routes, he could feel his stomach tightening. As the pain got worse and worse, he knew he needed help. He knew his problem was far more serious than a simple stomachache, and more than his parents could possibly know how to deal with. The E.R. was clearly his best shot.

GERMS AND ANTIBODIES

Barrett's parents were right to be afraid, but they had focused on the wrong danger. For Barrett was raised with good values in a loving family and in all likelihood would have traversed the temptations of the adolescent world reasonably well, even without their protective measures. But in their fear, his parents were literally keeping him from growing up.

There's a physical analogy here that's apt. Parents of young children often seek to provide their offspring with as sterile an environment as possible, one that's free of stray germs, microbes, allergens, and toxins. It seems like a good idea, but immunologists have now learned that it backfires. The children who are least likely to develop allergies in adulthood turn out to be those who are actually exposed to microbes and dust and pollen and dog hairs and the like. Kids raised on farms, for example, fare far better in terms of later healthy immune functioning than kids raised in far more sterile environments. The moderate stress of exposure to some germs and allergens seems to prompt their immune systems to develop in a healthy fashion.

With adolescents, it seems likely that a similar process operates. Bumps and bruises (both physical and emotional) are painful, but they also build tolerance for the larger stressors of adulthood. Others have pointed this out successfully; most recently, Conn Iggulden made the case compellingly with respect to younger children in *The Dangerous Book for Boys*. Without exposure to some risks and some failures, we risk developing hothouse flowers—beautiful in their mastery of the cello, but subject to wither as they encounter the first cold frosts of adult life. The irony of our approach is that the more we protect and shelter our teens, the less ready for adulthood they become, and the more we have reason to fear for their abilities to cope without our oversight and guidance.

SCARY MOVIES

Our fears for our teens are readily stoked by the media. Study after study has shown that most individuals estimate the risk of falling victim to crime to be about ten times greater than it actually is. No doubt this results from seeing so much crime on TV and in movies. But when it comes to our youth, the overestimates get even more outlandish. The specter of having one's child snatched by strangers, for example, strikes to the heart of most parents' deepest fears. But it turns out to be as remarkably rare in real life as it is common on weeknight TV. Each year the actual odds of a true abduction of a given child by a stranger, the kind that occurs almost nightly on TV, are less than one in 40,000.

Our fears might just be a recurring irritation if it weren't for a fundamental problem: The desire to protect our teens from the world's dangers is in many ways antithetical to what it takes to prepare them to successfully navigate in that world. In seeking to avoid real, extreme dangers, we bring about more mundane but equally debilitating problems, like Barrett's.

Ever since the terrible tragedy at Columbine High School in 1999, for example, parents have never felt quite the same sending their children off to school. The anxiety has been, if anything, even more crushing for school administrators, held responsible by entire communities for keeping thousands of kids safe. Yet, a closer look at the underlying reality suggests how exaggerated these fears have become.

Soon after the Columbine shootings I was asked to consult with our local school administrators as they were considering all manner of safety precautions they might take. Metal detectors. Visitor badges that magically faded after a few hours, presumably so they couldn't be sold or given to others. Doors that only opened for students moving between buildings if they had the right ID cards (as if students ever did). These were all costly, intrusive steps that would inevitably compete with other uses for scarce financial resources. "Okay, but isn't it worth taking almost any steps to prevent what happened in Columbine from recurring?" a principal asked me. "Even though I know it's not all *that* likely, what if it happened here?"

The answer, as doctors and medical ethicists have known for years, is that in a world with limited resources, we must always be deciding which are the most important dangers to try to prevent. I presented the dilemma to our school administrators with a simple question. Based on our national experience over the past very difficult decade, how likely was it that a shooting death would occur in the local area schools if no new action at all were taken? To put it more concretely, how many years would go by before there was a 50-50 chance of having a single student killed somewhere within the school system? Five years? Twenty years? Fifty years? Administrators' answers varied widely, as one might expect.

The actual answer: two thousand years.

But wouldn't we still want to reduce that risk? Of course, but at what cost? Consider that in those two thousand years—again using national base rates—the local school system would lose not one, but three hundred students to suicide, not to mention *hundreds of thousands* whose lives would be forever impaired by dropping out, becoming pregnant, or getting hooked on drugs. And what would be the cost of placing our teens in an environment that came to resemble a locked ward more than an open school? Would they feel protected, or would they just feel that the adult world "out there" was even scarier than they'd realized?

THE AVAILABILITY HEURISTIC

Why do we have such a strong fear of events that are so unlikely? Two Nobel prize–winning psychologists, Amos Tversky and Daniel Kahneman, found a key piece of the puzzle while studying how the human mind processes information. Their idea seems simple in retrospect, although it was enough to set them on their way to the Nobel prize. They coined the term the "Availability Heuristic" to describe what they'd observed.

Humans, unlike computers, do not evaluate probabilities with mathematical precision, but instead use certain shorthand approaches called "heuristics." These approaches work reasonably well for events that happen with some regularity, but they tend to go awry when applied to very rare events. It seems that if we become aware of a very rare event occurring *anywhere* at any time, then in our minds we are likely to dramatically overestimate the odds of this event occurring again. The more we can think about it, and the more it is *available* to our consciousness, the more we assume it is at least reasonably likely to recur, whatever the actual reality of the situation.

Combine the availability heuristic with the twenty-four-hour cable news cycle filling its airtime with rare but horrific tragedies befalling young people, and it's a minor miracle parents are ever able to sleep at night. Fifty years ago if an abduction or child murder occurred in a small town in rural Idaho, few people knew about it outside the immediate area. Parents knew abduction was theoretically possible, but there was no specific example broadcast repeatedly over the airwaves to trigger the availability heuristic, and we thus gave such events no more weight in our planning than they warranted. Now, however, such an event would be repeatedly broadcast in grisly detail on cable news networks. The availability heuristic kicks in and parents' fears skyrocket. The result: We end up raising our children in a culture of fear in which parents vastly overestimate the risks of rare but horrible events, even while underestimating far greater, though less-publicized, risks that are likely to strike far closer to home.

We see Perry's parents, whom we described in Chapter 1 with their high-achieving anorexic boy, stubbornly insisting that playing tennis in an "isolated" area may be too risky. This, even though moderate physical activity turns out to be a surprisingly effective treatment for the kind of anxiety and depression Perry felt. And given that anorexia at Perry's level of severity has very close to a ten percent lifetime mortality rate, it's worse than ironic that Perry's parents were more worried about the one in 40,000 chance that he'd be abducted while hitting a tennis ball against a wall at his high school. One in 40,000 vs. one in ten. Clearly, it's going to pay for us to learn to keep our fear in check and our nurturing instincts from running wild. Yet even those among us who are tasked with thinking most analytically about the risks facing our teens can be swept up in the raw fear. For the fearful side of the Nurture Paradox can affect our laws and public policies as well.

UNSAFE AT ANY SPEED?

Recently, for example, I was invited to give a talk on adolescent development to a panel convened by the National Academies of Science on the risks of teenage driving. During the break, I had a surprising conversation with a colleague who studies teen motor vehicle crashes. We were talking about how to decide the "right" age to allow teens to begin driving. His view, which he readily acknowledged was influenced by having a teen just approaching driving age, was that the longer the delay, the better. Beginning drivers have high crash rates, he said.

True, I replied, but isn't that at least partly because they are beginners . . . and won't they still be beginners at whatever age they start? Our family had recently taken a trip to Ireland and experienced driving on the wrong side of the road from the wrong side of the car with a manual transmission requiring use of a different hand, so I had firsthand experience with just how hard driving can be when everything about it is new. Wasn't a good part of the higher teen crash rate due to this newness, and not just to youth?

My colleague readily acknowledged this point. In fact, he noted that teens who for whatever reason begin driving a few years later than their peers also had strikingly high crash rates in their first year of driving, so age maybe wasn't even the main issue. I thought we were on the same page, but what he said next startled me: "But even if we just delay their driving by a year and they are just as dangerous when they start driving a year later, at least we'll have saved them a year of risk."

I wasn't sure I'd heard him correctly. Even if much of their risk was going to be the same whenever they first learned to drive, why not just put that risk off as long as possible? I'd heard right but was having trouble believing what I was hearing. Yes, we'd save teens a year of risk, much the same as we'd save a year of risk if we forbade all thirty-year-olds from driving for a year—but at what cost?

I've had a pretty clear sense of just how dangerous teen driving can be ever since my best friend was killed in a drunk-driving accident during my own adolescence while riding in a car with another teen who'd been drinking. And if there's anything that brain immaturity is likely to affect, it's impulse control and decision making about risky behaviors. But what I was hearing was not a judgment about teen risky behavior. It was a judgment that said in essence: Let's protect our teens from a key part of adult life, even if it means removing them from it. Or as one parent put it to me, "They'll have their whole life to drive, but at least I won't have to worry about them for another few months."

But driving provides the independence to go to a job, to the library, or to visit with friends. And allowing this driving does not automatically imply allowing late-night driving or driving with large groups or party hopping. We know as parents ourselves that it's scary, indeed *incredibly* scary, to let our teens grow up, and the world is indeed dangerous. For the one in 3,500 teens who will die in a motor vehicle crash each year, there can be no greater danger; I know firsthand that it happens. But for the other 3,499 teens, is simply delaying this step toward adulthood truly going to make things better? Is it even going to keep them safer in the end? There *are* better ways to handle this problem, and we'll outline some of them in Chapter 6, but only if we can get beyond our fear.

BIG FEARS, LITTLE FEARS

It's not just our big fears that threaten to undermine our teens. Smaller fears, left unchecked, can be almost as damaging. Many parents fear their teen won't get into a good college, for example, and the frenzy around college admissions has been well-documented. But the effects of this fear start well before college applications are sent in. As I was discussing this book with a colleague and friend recently, she told me about a dilemma she'd faced that morning.

Her daughter Caitlin came down to breakfast in a panic because she'd forgotten that she had a major test in French that day. Caitlin was a reasonably good student, though also a bit lazy and careless. She was supposed to have memorized a poem, a bunch of vocabulary, and read a story—none of which she'd done, as she'd been thinking the test wasn't for a few days yet.

Her grade in French was in the middle B range, but this unexpected test could move her from a shot at an A for the quarter into the high C range. But Caitlin had a plan. Her mom could simply write her a note explaining that a "family emergency" had prevented her from studying and asking that she be given an extra day. Reluctantly, and with much complaining ("This better not happen again"), Caitlin's mom wrote the note.

Later that day Caitlin's mom explained her dilemma to me.

"Well, right now she's hanging in there in this class, but if she bombs this test she could end up with a C, which would really hurt her chances for college." It was anxiety that Caitlin might cost herself some future opportunity that led her mom to bail her out. And that of course only increased the chances that Caitlin would fail to learn from her mistakes, and that she would make them again in the future.

Our ultimate goal with our teens shouldn't be to get them into a good college, but rather to have them learn to be successful on their own in their future lives. We've only got so many opportunities to teach them what the world will and will not reward, and Caitlin's mom had just passed one up. The easiest way to explain this to her was to ask whether she'd prefer to have Caitlin learn just how painful and costly it was not to keep track of assignments *now,* or not to learn this until she was in college. Caitlin's mom's replied somewhat feebly that she hoped Caitlin would have learned better by then. And maybe she would. But ultimately Caitlin's mom was falling into one of the thought traps that have made the Endless Adolescence possible: that time and age alone will bring maturity, rather than experience confronting the consequences of one's actions. I've seen far too many college freshmen on the verge of dropping out of school—kids who obviously had enormous talent and had done quite well in high school (though perhaps with a bit too much of their parents' help)—but who just weren't ready for even the relatively modest independence of college life. This was the message I tried to convey to Caitlin's mother, but I'm not sure it got through the anxiety I could hear so clearly in her voice.

Another friend described her ninth-grade daughter's outburst one night a few days after a school trip, when, with extensions granted by her teachers running out, she was having trouble getting caught up on the work she'd missed while on the trip. The daughter asked her mom for help, but when her mom could only sympathetically suggest staying up a bit late, prioritizing as best she could, and planning to work harder later to make up for any poor grades now, the daughter was furious.

"You're supposed to be able to know how to fix these things!" she said. "You keep track of everything in my life, why haven't you kept track of this? I don't know how to fix this. *You* tell me what to do!"

The biggest problem with our fears, and with letting our nurturing instincts run wild, is that our teens have come to depend upon us not just for things that only we can manage (providing shelter, etc.), but for handling the basic tasks in *their* lives. Our fear that they will miss out, experience setbacks, or just not have the optimal adolescent experience leads us to take care of them in ways that stifle their chances to learn to handle life's challenges on their own. What parents don't realize, and what we'll describe in more detail in Chapter 8, is just how easily these "setbacks" could be turned into growth experiences for teens.

What happens instead is that our fears threaten to take over not only their lives, but our lives as well. We create surly, entitled prima donnas when we act like teen life is so demanding and central that we rearrange adult lives around it. Most teens won't complain if their parents take on worrying about and tracking teens' to-do lists. But we've talked to many parents of teenagers who feel totally exhausted trying to do so, and well they should: They are trying not just to manage the complexities of their own lives but of their teens' lives as well.

GENDER AND THE NURTURE PARADOX

Both Caitlin and our friend's ninth-grade daughter may have had one advantage, though. Most of what we have to say in this book applies equally well to both adolescent males and females, but there is one way in which the Nurture Paradox has had a lesser effect on girls than on boys. To the extent that female adolescents have continued in caretaking roles in our society, their lives have been a bit less affected by the Nurture Paradox. Work inside the house has diminished over the years, but not as much as work outside the house. Child care, for example, is one of the tasks of adolescence that still provides a slightly scaled-down version of its adult equivalent. While teenage boys' lawn-mowing efforts have largely been replaced by the efficient machinery of lawn services, babysitting by teenage girls remains in high demand.

The result is that we often see girls helping out in caring for younger siblings, or helping out in the kitchen while their older brothers are up in their rooms playing computer games. These roles are stereotyped and sexist and something to be moved beyond, to be sure, but they also leave adolescent females with at least some adultlike roles that aren't that different from what female teens had in the past. And these different roles may well contribute to how differently males and females fare as they progress through adolescence.

In childhood, for example, boys and girls perform about equally in terms of overall academic achievement, with girls slightly ahead in reading and boys in math, but by the time they leave high school, males' average academic performance has begun a precipitous downhill slide. They not only have lower grade point averages at the end of high school and are more likely to have dropped out than females, they are also much less likely to go on to college. For every hundred young women entering college, there are only eighty-three men who enter. Worse yet, for every hundred women who complete a bachelor's degree each year, only seventy-four men receive degrees.

A good friend recently described to us visiting her daughter in her college dorm room at eight-thirty one weekday morning. The campus shuttle bus stop was outside the window, and at first our friend was surprised to see it populated almost entirely by girls. Then, as the time got closer to the bus's arrival, the boys began to arrive, half-clothed, inconsistently showered, scurrying to catch the bus, with several arriving just after it left. The girls clearly had their acts together in ways many of the boys did not. We've seen the same effect replicated in our teens' high school. The girls tend to "take care" of the boys. Reminding them of things. Picking up cell phones left behind. Cajoling them to get moving, etc. And the strongest students academically are, not surprisingly, mostly those same girls.

This is emphatically *not* an argument for maintaining gender-based stereotypes. Quite the opposite. The problem is not with the tasks girls are taking on, it is that *only* girls are taking them on. If our assessment of the situation is correct, then teenage boys would benefit greatly from taking on more of these tasks. This gender difference in outcomes for teenage boys and girls in adolescence is just one more piece of evidence that the lack of adult roles may be critical to understanding how our adolescents are faring. More important, though, these differences also suggest that even subtle changes in roles may lead to significant improvements (or deficits) in key outcomes for our teens.

THE WORLD WE'VE CREATED

Left unchecked, our nurturing instincts lead us to treat our adolescents in ways that are ultimately harmful to their long-term development. It is those instincts, based in part on low expectations of teens whom we falsely believe to be severely constrained by their brains and hormones, that give rise to many of the worst features of the "bubble" in which we place our adolescents.

But enough about describing the problems with the adolescent world as it is. Many years ago psychologist Kurt Lewin said, "If you want to understand something, try to change it." It's time now not only to reach for the deeper understanding of which Lewin spoke, but also to focus directly on ways to begin improving our teens' lives. Let's turn, then, to our most important task, which is looking at ways we can begin to get teens out of their bubble and into more productive lives that move them toward maturity and adulthood.

PART TWO

ESCAPE ROUTES

In the first half of this book we've seen how teens like Perry, Ellen, Megan, and Austin have become trapped in the End-less Adolescence. Now we'd like to look at the ways we've found to help these and other teens begin making their escape. Individual teens' problems differ, of course, and their escape routes will vary, but ultimately we're going to suggest a single overarching refrain to guide all of our efforts: *Let's put the adulthood back into adolescence!*

In the following pages we'll describe a whole host of ways to introduce, or reintroduce, major elements of the adult world into our teens' lives. Progress will require attending to some different signposts than those we've been used to following, though. Instead of asking, "What will keep our teens out of trouble?" "What will make them happy?" or "What will get them into college?" we need to switch our focus to a different set of queries: "How can we introduce realistic elements of adulthood into their worlds?" "What activities best provide real feedback about their effort and skill?" and "Which other adults can we recruit to help pass our values on to them?" In short, we need to switch our focus from activities that reflect living happily *as a teenager* to activities that let our young people actually use their energy, connect with adults, and make choices that matter in order to begin *moving successfully into adulthood.*

Not that these tasks are mutually exclusive. The adulthood-centered tasks we'll emphasize are indeed intended to support the growth needed to help our youth stay out of trouble and pursue their education and careers with gusto, and we find that teens who see themselves moving toward adulthood are indeed happier teens. But the adulthood focus is going to be the key. Without it, anything else we might do—from adding more standardized tests and tutoring to implementing stricter curfews to providing more laptops, lessons, and gadgets—is just tinkering around the edges.

We want to acknowledge from the outset that the task of putting the adulthood back into adolescence is a work in progress. The societal changes that have led to the Endless Adolescence are broad and have been building across multiple generations; we're not going to reverse them in a single stroke. But the good news, as we'll see below, is that even modest changes are often sufficient to radically transform our teens' attitudes and behaviors. The stories we'll recount highlight just a few of the routes by which teens can escape the Endless Adolescence. We describe these pathways not only so that others may follow, but also in the hope that they will aid others in charting still more additional routes to maturity and to a productive adulthood for today's adolescents.

"It's a Good Thing I Was There!"

Many mystery novels begin with audacious crimes or unexpected deaths. The mystery we'll be describing in this chapter began with a group of adolescents who met with outrageously *positive* outcomes from a modest little program that just didn't seem to amount to all that much.

It was a gray, cool fall morning when I first met Tonya. I had driven about ninety minutes from my home in Charlottesville, Virginia, to talk with Tonya and other students taking part in a program—Teen Outreach—that kept popping up in our evaluations with some surprising and remarkable effects in changing young people's lives. I made my trip that morning to try to understand those effects, and didn't realize at the time that my trip would be the beginning of a change in my view of what really matters for helping adolescents grow up.

Years of work evaluating programs for youth had turned me into something of a skeptic about even the most well-intentioned approaches. Many (indeed most) promising new programs for youth simply wilt under the harsh glare of stringent evaluations, but the Teen Outreach program hadn't. Quite the opposite. Under the most rigorous evaluation conditions we could establish, this program—which did little more than engage kids in a few hours each week of voluntary community service and adult-led, small-group discussions about this service—had been consistently and repeatedly producing reductions in dropout rates of more than *fifty percent*!

Even more astounding, the program had also been producing reductions in teen *pregnancy* rates of fifty percent, even though teen sexuality wasn't even its focus. This was strong stuff for a program begun by a single teacher with no funding, taking on problems that had withstood the best efforts of dedicated service providers for years, if not decades. A bit of volunteer work and discussions with an adult leading to fifty-percent reductions in pregnancy rates? When we published the initial evaluation results, pregnancy expert Doug Kirby was quoted in the *Washington Post* describing our findings as "the best evidence to date that social programs can prevent teen pregnancy." But the question I'd been asked many times since and had always struggled to answer was, "Why?" Why did such a modest program have such huge effects? I was making the drive that morning in search of the answer.

I'd been conducting the formal evaluations of Teen Outreach from a distance—analyzing numbers coming in from around the country—for several years. Together with my good friend and colleague Susan Philliber, we'd done everything we could to assure ourselves the results were real: We'd compared participants to well-matched members of a scientifically selected control group—teens who had wanted to participate but who ended up on a waiting list as a result of a coin toss. We'd waited to see if the program effects could be replicated, and found that they reappeared consistently across thousands of kids and hundreds of schools. Though I found the results intriguing and certainly encouraging, I was also increasingly puzzled and even frustrated because, though I worked with adolescents for a living, I had no idea how such a simple program for teens could achieve such powerful results.

I met Tonya in a classroom at her school during a free period. She was a smallish, shy student with large brown eyes who'd been struggling to make it through the tenth grade. Her older sister had dropped out in twelfth grade after giving birth to her first child. Tonya wasn't pregnant (yet), but she saw little in school to interest her, and was finding it hard to get up in the morning to go. But when she began with Teen Outreach, the program got her working in the Early Start Childcare Center for an hour or two a week, and then discussing this work with her friends and a facilitator back at school during a weekly health class period.

Tonya wasn't a star student, nor was she even particularly well-spoken, but she had no trouble conveying her enthusiasm about her work. As she did, the profound power of this simple experience began to shine through. Though we were meeting early in the day and Tonya was clearly still waking up, her face lit up as she described what her work at Early Start meant to her. Three things stuck out, and all were new in Tonya's life.

First, she loved working with these kids, and they felt the same way about her. "It's just so cool to see their little faces light up when I get there. I've got a few favorites but all the kids are really cute, actually." Her enthusiasm was infectious, and the kids took to her as much as she'd taken to them. To these preschoolers, Tonya—who'd never felt like she'd made much of an impression on anyone—was a rock star.

Second, Tonya learned from the adults working there. For example, she now understood that different roles came with different levels of responsibility (and pay), and that who got what depended in part on how far one had gone in school. She realized that one could make a modest but satisfying career out of caring for little kids. For the first time, she could envision a future for herself in the adult world.

Finally, Tonya saw that she actually could do something for others that made a difference. This child care center, like many, was chronically understaffed. Once the adult workers realized that she was reliable, they started turning to Tonya more and more each week, recognizing her talents. This had never happened in school, where her B's and C's were acceptable but far from noteworthy. Though sixteen and reasonably bright, the experience that her presence and skills were *actually needed* was a new one for her.

Conversations with Tonya and other youths who have participated in Teen Outreach helped us glimpse the first outlines of what we have come to call the "Adult Work Effect," something far more powerful and effective than simply telling teens to "get a job!"

In contrast to the adolescent bubble, what Tonya and her peers described was a sense of having a place where what they did mattered. Tonya is typical of many youths with average grades in school who find that there are few places in their lives where they can stand out. Pulled out of the high school environment, placed in a child care center, and given real challenge and responsibility, Tonya becomes central to the lives of several of the toddlers at the center. They await her arrival. She makes them laugh. She can sometimes soothe them when they are distressed. She *matters*. Not in a competitive way. Not as an achievement for a college application. But to others she is helping.

It's one of the simplest and most powerful of human experiences: the gratification that comes from helping another human being. It can inspire anyone, but to teens who have so few ways to contribute, it can be life-altering. Others may have had more skill than Tonya (even at child care); others may have had more drive. But on the mornings when Tonya was in Room One at Early Start, no one else was there helping these particular children. She realized that whether or not she showed up each week actually mattered to these children, and even to the teacher she assisted. She realized that when she pushed herself to smile and lead a song (even when she was tired and grouchy), it actually made the toddlers smile. Meeting these challenges also changed Tonya's sense of herself. Someone wasn't just mouthing the bromide to her that she was special. To these children, she *was* special. And that reality makes all the difference. Tonya's experience, and those of thousands of teens like her, have led us to conclude we've hit upon a significant path toward helping teens escape the Endless Adolescence: *doing work that matters to someone.*

But we need to be very clear about what this path does and does not entail. Since we first published the results of the Teen Outreach Program more than a decade ago, the push for youth volunteerism has burgeoned, but with this growth also comes the need for a major caveat. For example, soon after the Teen Outreach results began streaming out to the public, we had a challenging conversation with an aide to the governor of New York about why simply *mandating* "volunteer" service—while enticingly cheap and appealing from a political standpoint—was unlikely to be effective. The problem is that much volunteer work that teens do actually matters little to anyone. The teens know it and gain little benefit from going through the motions of meeting quotas for volunteer hours. It's not only useless, but discouraging and demoralizing for teens to show up to volunteer where they mainly stand around feeling in the way or doing busywork. Similarly, we've seen too many teens helping their dads clean out the garage to rack up their "volunteer" hours for school mandates. We can structure teens' work in ways that do or do not foster development toward independent adulthood—and the difference this makes is huge.

Adults typically feel good when they see teens keeping busy doing volunteer work, but Tonya's experience was having a far more profound effect. School dropout and teen pregnancy are two of the most destructive and expensive problems facing our teens; clearly, Teen Outreach is doing something much more than just keeping teens busy or giving them something good to do. Rather, as teens see themselves able to help others, they simultaneously come to see themselves as having a real future role in the larger adult society. This vision, in turn, translates into a willingness to take care of themselves and to prepare for that future. "The best contraceptive is a future you believe in," is how Marion Wright Edelman, head of the Children's Defense Fund, has put it in talking about preventing teen pregnancy, but the "doing work that matters" principle clearly has an impact even well beyond teens' sexual behavior.

We would also be missing the most important lessons of Tonya's story if we simply concluded that what all kids need is Teen Outreach. Let's instead ask ourselves about the broader lessons embedded within this mysteriously powerful program. Does this approach work only for "at-risk" teens? Does it always require a formal program? Or can we find key elements of the Adult Work Effect that we can apply in broader ways to help our teens? Taking a look at teens from backgrounds quite different from Tonya's helps us begin to capture more of the essence of this mysteriously powerful effect.

Our close friends the Lamberts had heard us talk about Teen Outreach and were struggling to find useful activities for their firstborn son, Will, in the summer after his first year in high school. On the April evening when they were going over possible volunteer activities they'd found for him on a United Way website, this talented, though somewhat lethargic young teen was anything but enthusiastic. "Why am I doing this?" "Do I really have to?" "Why can't I just spend an extra few weeks at camp or relaxing at home?"

By the end of that evening, the Lamberts had given Will several choices of activities, but the only one in which he displayed even marginal interest was working at a nearby outdoor camp for kids with serious physical illnesses (Will liked the outdoors). When the Lamberts told him the next day that they'd signed him up for four weeks of full-time work at the camp, he was underwhelmed, to say the least. The Lamberts relayed this to us and skeptically wondered if the Teen Outreach folks perhaps knew something they didn't.

A few weeks later, though, the Lamberts dropped their sleepy fifteen-year-old off for his first day working at the camp. When they returned to pick Will up that afternoon, they were eager to find out how he liked it, but Will simply couldn't stop talking about the work itself. "It's a good thing I was there!" this thin, athletic boy exclaimed with a mixture of pride and concern. "They really needed help!" He went on to recount the various tasks he performed, from sweeping out the mess hall between meals to shepherding around a boy in a wheelchair over the bumpy camp paths for several hours in the afternoon. "I don't know how he would have gotten to any of the activities, because there was no one else there to help him!" The energy and excitement of these few weeks of post-ninth-grade volunteering charged Will up through the rest of the summer, and he started school the following fall with more energy than usual. Will eagerly signed up to go back to the camp the next summer and was welcomed just as eagerly by the staff.

Now, Will probably did as much cleanup work in a few weeks at camp as he'd done the entire previous year at home. But knowing it mattered to real adults (parents don't always count in this regard), and being treated like an adult in the assignment of tasks, made a huge difference. He truly didn't seem to mind the hard work. It was particularly interesting how the experience seeped into other areas of his life. Though Will's academic motivation would wax and wane across his high school years, his new-found motivation for work that made a difference to people grew steadily. By his junior year, this young man who found waking up in the morning difficult would often get up early, and instead of waiting to take the bus, walk and jog two miles to school in order to arrive before school started to tutor a recent immigrant girl who didn't speak English. "She's really bright, but she's just learning English and she's trying to read poems that anyone would find tricky to read!" Will recounted. He was struck by the hard fact that there would be no way this bright girl could possibly keep up in school without considerable help. The girl didn't want to fail, and Will didn't want to let her down. He was less willing to miss a tutoring appointment than almost any other obligation in his week. As with his experience over the summer at camp, he had caught a glimpse of real work that mattered in his tutoring, and its draw was powerful and lasting.

Will's story is a hopeful one, since it suggests that we don't necessarily need a formal program to inspire teens. It still leaves many questions unanswered, though, in explaining the mysterious process by which simple work can sometimes change teens' lives. Are the effects we've seen just a matter of getting kids working, and if so, why aren't more teens feeling these effects? What about paid work? It might seem that just having teens get a job would fill the bill of helping move them into adulthood. Perhaps at one time it did, but teen jobs are different now, and most work available to them does not inspire in the way Teen Out-reach or *work that matters to someone else*—paid or volunteer—does.

Sixteen-year-old Jim's first job provides a good example of the ways work can turn out differently than we might expect. Jim's parents had been encouraging him to find a job for months, and when his best friend told him about an opening at nearby Sal's Pizza, where the friend had been working, he was happy to apply. Jim's parents were equally enthused and even filled out his application for him. Jim's natural charm (plus his friend's recommendation and the manager's desperation!) were sufficient to land him the job, and for a while things seemed to be great. Jim found the work easy, enjoyed the socializing when his friends came in, and got more than his share of free pizza. He worked hard at it and enjoyed it, and so things progressed.

Jim got his first paycheck and was, at least briefly, richer than he'd ever been. After not that many weeks of work, he was able to buy himself all manner of great stuff—a car stereo, an iPod, a leather jacket, and a new cell phone. His schoolwork slipped a bit, as he often eagerly picked up extra shifts when someone failed to show, but he reassured his parents that he could make that up easily. Over time the work got easier, but not necessarily because Jim had mastered the requisite tasks. His nineteen-year-old manager took him aside one day and let him know that he really didn't have to work quite so hard. It just made everyone else look bad. Jim didn't have to be told a second time, especially when he noticed that the manager often gave himself credit for more hours than he'd actually worked. Plus, unlike school, much of his time at work involved talking and joking with kids his own age when business was slow. Working was easier than he'd thought!

It wasn't until Jim held the job for three months that his parents recognized the problem that had been developing. School had fallen to last place on Jim's list of priorities, and it now showed unmistakably in his grades. What little control Jim's parents had over his behavior had also slipped significantly, partly because instead of depending upon his allowance from them, he could now use his own money to buy himself almost anything he needed aside from a place to stay. Food, of course, was not a problem, and in fact Jim often brought his friends to Sal's, where he slipped them free food with his manager's tacit wink of approval.

So what had gone wrong?

Well, while it seemed like Jim was taking a big step into adulthood by working, the reality was far different. For one thing, he was still being socialized by other teens "in the bubble." And in fact, most of the socialization was coming from the nineteen-year-old manager, who had few ambitions in his own life and had little to pass on to Jim, save for his questionable work ethic.

Jim's paycheck also exposed him to a far-from-realistic world. The term coined for what he experienced financially is "premature affluence." What it meant was that Jim had free spending money in amounts that no adult working such a job and having adult financial responsibilities would ever be likely to have. Jim had no way to realize that the extra couple of hundred dollars a month he had to spend on whatever he wanted was far more discretionary income than even his parents, with far better jobs, typically had. We've worked with family after family like Jim's, in which parents struggled to pay the bills while their teens were pocketing hundreds of dollars a month in pure spending money. Very often these are exactly the teens still living at home in their twenties, as they are not used to using earned income to actually survive, and are not asked to contribute to their family's expenses.

This premature affluence fed directly into Jim's attitude toward his schoolwork. Sal's seemed like a fine job, and by working more, he could buy even more stuff he wanted. And he could buy it *now*, not down the road after college. What was the point in working hard at school when there wasn't any payoff he could see? Jim's parents tried talking to him about the future and the need to do well in school so he could move up to better jobs. In a vague way, Jim knew what they meant, but he also knew that he had a job that left him feeling quite well-off already. What was there to worry about?

Jim's situation illustrates why helping teens move into truly *adult* work requires more care and thought than might first appear. At first glance, just taking on a paying job seems like one of the best ways to move teens toward adulthood. In the past it often was, but, to rephrase the old Oldsmobile car commercial, "These aren't your parents' jobs." While jobs for teens used to involve demanding work supervised by adults, today's "McJobs" often involve mindless, noncareer-oriented labor, supervised primarily by older adolescents. Teens aren't given any responsibility to think independently, to decide how to handle tasks, or to meet challenges. Indeed from an employer's perspective, the ideal teen work setting is one designed to run well even when populated and directed by uninspired teens.

We might hope that Jim's situation is just an anomaly. Unfortunately, the systematic research done on teen work suggests it is far more typical than we might wish. Our colleague Larry Steinberg has done much of the pioneering research in this area, tracking what happens to teens who work for varying amounts of time in their high school years.

While small amounts of work appear relatively harmless, once teens hit fifteen hours per week of paid work during the school year, they experience negative effects in a whole host of areas.

Poorer grades and a greater likelihood of dropping out of school perhaps aren't so surprising, given the amount of time paid work can drain off from schoolwork. But higher levels of alcohol and drug use? Yes, these are also associated with longer hours of adolescent employment, along with more cynical attitudes toward work and toward behaviors like workplace theft. We can see these effects in what Jim was learning from his supervisor. We also find that as teens take on more work, their parents feel that they have less control over them at home. Again, that's not surprising given the financial pseudo-independence work provides.

In some ways the money provided by these jobs functions almost like drinking and smoking to teens. It can provide the trappings of maturity, but with none of the responsibilities of real adulthood—no bills to pay, rent to meet, or car repairs to manage. Teens come home feeling like adults and expecting adult prerogatives. The jobs themselves are often designed to be minimally taxing, and thus provide a poor model for real adult work. All of these effects lead us to add a second, cautionary principle as we map out the ways teens can use work to move into adulthood. At the risk of alienating those who didn't like math in high school, we offer a simple equation to make our point:

High financial reward + Low demand $\neq$ an Adult job

So what exactly does it take to get the "It's a good thing I was there!" effect from teens' work? Does it have to be volunteer work to be helpful? Is paid employment always a bad thing? Not at all. Set up poorly, volunteering can and usually does devolve into another McJob. By the same token, paid work with the right components can provide an outstanding path to adulthood.

Pete Worrell, Claudia's older brother, tells of going to work as a teenager in the 1970s in a men's clothing shop in Manchester, New Hampshire, where he was the youngest employee by about twenty years. Pete describes folding some shirts in his first week at the shop, putting them out on a shelf, and then going about other business. Half an hour later one of the older men approached Pete. "What in the hell do you think you were doing with those shirts?" he huffed.

"They told me to fold them," Pete answered somewhat defensively.

"Are you kidding? You consider those shirts properly folded? That's not how you fold a shirt." This was quickly followed by, "Come here. Let me show you how you do it *right*."

And after watching, Pete realized that his folding job, though following the same basic pattern he'd initially been shown, wasn't nearly so careful, and would in fact leave the shirts more wrinkled. This kind of lesson in how to do a job, even a small job, with thought and care, was repeated over and over in his first weeks at the shop. But how do we get a teenager to take these kinds of work lessons seriously? Pete himself, who now runs a boutique investment banking firm, offers several clues.

"Even at age fifteen I knew that folding shirts was kind of trivial," he recalls. "Whether or not I flicked the cuffs in onto themselves just right to make them lie flat, I knew was not a life-changing event. What *was* a life-changing event was that I realized that these 'men's men' weren't going to consider me one of their club until I knew how to do it correctly, and I demonstrated that I could be relied upon to do it correctly again and again, because to them, even though they knew they were working in a relatively inconsequential job, this was the way that they demonstrated their pride, their *craftsmanship*. They let me know it was important that I shared this focus, or I would never be trusted to be in the club."

Pete had two parents who were every bit as motivated as most parents to see him learn to do a job well. They had instructed and corrected him many times. But every former teenager knows that he or she often learns more from other adults than could ever be learned from one's parents.

Being on time, for example. "This job also made me see that it was important that, every day, I show up, and on time," Pete notes, "because these guys were waiting to take their own break until I covered one of them in the store. So my being there was not some silly after-school job. It was, I began to see, a small cog in what made that place successful. I mattered to them. They kidded me a lot, but they began to like me, and I still think a lot about the guys there.

"For me, that first job was a permanent character builder. It taught me: Show up on time. Do what you say you are going to do. Finish what you begin. No matter how trivial the job seems or how little you are paid"—$1.60 per hour—"you can do it with a sense of craftsmanship, and screw the rest of the world if they don't understand that—nothing can take that away from you."

These adult men had become Pete's peer group. After working at the store for a while, he remembers, "I lost a bit of interest in gaining acceptance from my peers and realized that it was much more fun and more interesting to gain acceptance from people who you can learn a lot more from." And these men were more than willing to apply peer pressure to get him to change his behavior. But unlike the peer influence within the typical adolescent bubble, these adult peers were intent on socializing Pete in a way that would serve him well in the larger world (and get their shirts folded properly at the same time). Part of Pete's motivation was that he very much wanted to join the world of competent adult workers. He wasn't just hearing another random adult lecture; these men were telling him the rules for working in the adult world he was eager to enter.

Imagine how the scenario would have played out differently today at a local fast-food restaurant with a high school student working with friends and supervised by a nineteen-year-old manager. The supervisor would be far less likely to be intent on teaching forcefully about a job well done (for, unfortunately, such an intense focus on pride and excellence is not what typically leads most young people into careers in fast food). And even if such a lecture were delivered, would it have the same impact if accompanied by quiet snickering in the background from one's peers?

Finally, one other implicit element was crucial in Pete's story. These men *cared* about him. They liked him and wanted to see him do well. They were gruff as could be, but didn't hesitate to take the time to show him how to do good work . . . how to grow up. If there were an antithesis to the *Lord of the Flies* scenario we painted in Chapter 4, it might well be the workroom of the Men's Shop in Manchester, New Hampshire, circa 1970. "Working with adults who care" thus becomes another of the prominent signs we look for as we map out routes into adulthood for our teens.

Pete's parents also had a simple solution to the premature affluence problem we described above. It was called, quite simply, "expecting your teen to pay for some of their own stuff." They asked him to pay for most or all his own clothing and recreational activities, and that request was more than enough to make clear that low-wage jobs, however engaging in other respects, are not the ticket to adult prosperity.

BILL-GATES-IN-WAITING

It should now be clear that the "It's a good thing I was there" effect is not a matter of simply expecting our teens to get a job or volunteer. Rather, we want our teens to be doing work that *matters* to someone, entails real *challenges,* involves *interacting with adults who care* about the work, and comes with *reasonable (not excessive) financial compensations.* Finding or creating this kind of good work for our teens is going to take some effort, but when we succeed, we've taken a major step toward moving them out of the adolescent bubble. And just as the bubble has effects on a multitude of levels, so too does good work go a long way toward undoing some of those pernicious effects.

Identity issues, for example, seem to have become a taken-for-granted aspect of life in the adolescent bubble. In our self esteem–obsessed culture, adolescents struggle to feel good about themselves no matter how many trophies and certificates we present to them or how much we tell them we love them. The problem is, we've viewed teens' self-esteem as though it's going to be dependent upon what we say to them or do for them, instead of upon the things they learn to do for others. The Adult Work Effect suggests one antidote.

Austin, the teen in Chapter 3 who felt like he was a "failure at everything," ultimately learned this lesson almost by accident one weekend when the computer network crashed at the office of his dad's small business. The network support people said they could come in first thing the next week, but his dad had to get a project out by Monday at nine. As

Austin heard his dad worrying about it at dinner Friday night, he thought to himself that the problem didn't sound so hard. Finally, he spoke up and told his dad he thought he might be able to fix it. With some wariness, and after many warnings to be careful, his dad decided he had little to lose and let Austin take a look. The problem wasn't as easy as Austin expected, and he spent five hours trying different things (while his dad was wondering if he'd made a mistake). Finally, just before eleven that Saturday night, as his dad—who'd been working by hand on stuff at the office—was about to call it quits, Austin had a breakthrough and got the network back up. The project would now make its deadline.

That Monday, when the "network guy" came in, he said the problem was relatively minor, and only a thirty-minute job if one had seen it before. But regardless of how long it took him, Austin had provided the help when it was needed, and he spent the next several months beaming quietly whenever he heard his dad recount the story to others.

Following one of these recountings, one of Austin's neighbors mentioned that his computer was "acting weird" and that he couldn't get his printer to work, and asked Austin if he'd be willing to take a look at it. Again, Austin took a good amount of time but ultimately solved the problem. When the neighbor insisted he take thirty dollars for his time, Austin was thrilled . . . partly about the money, but even more because he'd done something that mattered that much to someone. Word got around, and with his dad's help Austin ultimately got a summer job working for the networking guy his dad had on contract. The work mainly involved simple stuff—swapping in and out hard drives, installing new memory, and the like—but the clients were grateful, and to Austin it was heaven. He'd eagerly recount his day's work each night at dinner, and though to his parents much of what he said seemed to be in Greek, they were delighted to listen to their now-happy son.

I can't say that Austin's grades took any remarkable upswings—they improved a bit, but he simply wasn't cut out to be a star student. The essential change, though, was that he now no longer saw himself as a failure; he knew he had something he could contribute. Even more important, he felt he had something to look forward to in his life. He eventually got more heavily into Web design in a freelance way locally—

enough that he made more money than his friends who worked at fast-food restaurants. He'd begun to carve out his niche in the adult world—a world far larger and, for all its hard edges, in some ways far more accommodating to his adolescent interests and talents than most of what existed in his large public high school. Austin was no longer waiting for the gates of adulthood to magically open. He had found a way to do something that mattered to others, and his path to adulthood became more clear.

Though his self-esteem skyrocketed, he also gained something even more valuable. He gained a sense of his own self-*efficacy*. Self-efficacy refers not just to feeling good about yourself, but to having confidence in your ability to master tasks that actually make a difference in your life. Austin had previously seen himself as a failure because in many ways he didn't fit into the narrow fast-track slots we lay out for teenagers; he wasn't popular or good at sports or school, and thus couldn't find those places where his talents could fit into his adolescent world. But once he started to get out of the adolescent bubble, this young Bill-Gates-in-waiting was on his way. And his self-image problem largely vanished in the night.

HOW PSYCHOLOGISTS ARE MADE

We tend to naturally understand the practical lessons of work—being on time, contributing, etc.—but we ultimately underestimate just how much pure inspiration the right kinds of adult work can provide. Good work can convert adolescent aimlessness into focused movement toward a career, and greatly reduce the likelihood of spending years in one's twenties casting about for the "right" job. I'd experienced this myself as a late adolescent, although it wasn't until thirty years later, in a conversation with some young U.Va. students, that I remembered just how important the experience had been.

I was approached recently by a group of college students from a local program called "Helpline," who asked if I could meet with them. Helpline is a confidential hotline for callers who are experiencing almost any sort of distress, and it's almost entirely student run. Long ago, I had worked on a prior incarnation of the hotline during my own years as an undergraduate at U.Va., and the students were interested in meeting with me to learn more about the program's history. The only time I had in my schedule during which they were all free was at 8:30 A.M. on a Friday morning. (They all had this time free largely because students at U.Va., as at most universities, desperately seek to avoid both early morning classes and Friday classes.) I offered the time apologetically, but they instantly snapped it up, and all six students—the leadership team of the program—were there, eager and waiting, as I arrived at my office that morning.

Why? I asked myself.

They got nothing material out of their participation. No pay, no special status, no perks. And while participating in the hotline program might help their résumés, visiting me certainly wouldn't. It was only as I began to reflect with them about my own experiences, thirty years earlier, that I realized why they had all shown up at a time when most U.Va. students were fast asleep. And that's when I realized that I had also been the beneficiary of the "It's a good thing I was there" effect.

I was in my second month as a seventeen-year-old first-year student at U.Va. When I registered for classes that September, I bypassed the "activity fair" that followed the registration process. While I'd always been a good student, I was reasonably lazy otherwise, and already feeling overwhelmed by my first days at college. It seemed that classes were going to be more than enough to manage, and extracurriculars were not something I was seeking. It wasn't until six weeks later, when a roommate mentioned he was going to a meeting of a hotline that was being started in Charlottesville, and asked if I wanted to come, that this changed. I hesitated, as I had work to finish that night and I didn't need or want extra stuff to do, but my roommate wanted company and was incredibly persistent and so I went.

The first night was fascinating. Almost right away we began learning what it took to help someone in crisis when speaking on the phone with them. And because the hotline was just getting started, it needed every volunteer it could get, so we were told directly that we mattered a great deal to its chances of success. Bottom line: This wasn't busywork, it seemed important, and it was kind of fun. And it got more fun the longer I stayed with it. Eventually I became part of the early student leadership group for the hotline, and we spent endless hours planning, dealing with crises, fund-raising, and chatting. It was enjoyable and engaging, but it was also real. In fact, that was why it was so much fun. I'd taken a psychology course in high school and was taking one that first semester in college. But to be honest, I'd found both a little boring, and looking back, I have no doubt that it was this volunteer experience—not theoretical course work—that ultimately guided me toward my career as a psychologist.

So, as a seventeen-year-old, I discovered there were tasks that were "work," that were "extra," and that paid nothing . . . and could be the high points of my day. As I spoke with these fourth-year college students in my office that Friday morning, I realized they'd been learning much the same lesson. And upon sharing this story with many friends since, I've been struck by just how many recounted similar sharing tales of how the most meaningful experiences of their college careers happened far from the classroom.

We worry endlessly about how to motivate and direct our teens. What we forget sometimes, though, is that the chance to do real work where we're needed tends to be inherently engaging. Teen Outreach had actually been teaching us that lesson for years before we caught on. If we'd been alert to it, the very fact that this young program was already oversubscribed enough to allow us to assign students to a waiting-list control group would have given us an early clue as to its power: Adolescents—that allegedly laziest of all age-groups—were *eagerly* signing up in large numbers all across the country to take part in a program where they voluntarily worked for others. There were no mandates or requirements, just good work and enthusiastic teens. This was certainly a testament to the people running the local Teen Outreach programs, but even more to the intuitive appeal of this kind of work to young people.

THE WORK OF A VILLAGE

Once we've identified some of the key ingredients and the beneficial effects of good-quality work for teens, the question naturally arises as to how we can best build these experiences into their lives. In the two decades since we first learned about Teen Outreach, for example, we've found only one consistent limit to its growth, and that's the challenge of finding enough volunteer sites to accommodate youth who are interested in volunteering. From the vantage point of a businessperson, or even a social service agency manager, the problem is easy enough to understand. Who wants a bunch of teenagers running around their workplace?

To be honest, setting up and supervising this kind of volunteer placement *does* take adult time. But it's time that we used to routinely spend helping teens grow up. No doubt, craftsmen of yore used to sometimes roll their eyes at the young apprentices who were their charges. But two things were different then. First, there was an implicit recognition that part of almost every adult worker's role was to train the generation of youth coming behind. There wasn't yet a temptation to outsource this task to our schools, forget about it, then complain about the end result. Second, there was the recognition that these young people could actually be of at least some use with a bit of training.

One of the approaches communities often take toward including teens in the adult world is setting up teen apprenticeships. The impulse is a good one, although as with other types of work, apprenticeships can be done well or poorly, and we're going to have to look beneath the surface appeal of the apprenticeship to understand the difference. For example, on her high school spring break, Caitlin, the high school student in Chapter 4 who "forgot" about her French test, got to shadow a local lawyer for several days—a real privilege, according to her school guidance counselor, and an experience her parents had pushed hard for Caitlin to get.

The shadow apprenticeship model has its interesting aspects, but it also has several fundamental flaws, as Caitlin soon discovered. First, contrary to the principles of the Adult Work Effect we've been outlining, Caitlin wasn't doing anything to actually be helpful to the lawyer (who had offered the apprenticeship to the local high school simply as a way to be helpful to the community). We've come to call this model the "Disneyland apprenticeship" because it reminds us of those rides where one gets to pretend to be an astronaut without actually doing anything astronauts do, or anything at all, really.

In fact, Caitlin was not only not providing help to the lawyer to whom she was assigned, she was a bit of a drain on his time. Having to think about what she was doing, and whether it would be interesting enough, was one more task on the lawyer's to-do list each morning. The lawyer knew this, and more important, Caitlin knew it too. Rather than sensing that she was becoming a contributing adult, she got an even more stark reminder of just how useless she was in the adult world. "I just didn't want to look bored or like I didn't have anything to do, because I didn't want to bother Mr. Smathers," was the way she described the experience to her mom. And because she was mainly following the lawyer around and watching him do his work, the work she was watching seemed clearly beyond her.

Caitlin got little sense of how she could someday gain the skills needed to take on such a job, and when she asked, she was just told, "Do well in school." These Disneyland apprenticeships no doubt have their role—they give teens at least a passing view of what a real job in an area might be like—but there's also little doubt that there's a reason they're typically limited to a few days or a week at a time.

We can engage teens successfully with an apprenticeship model, but it's likely going to mean restructuring the typical approach. Three-day apprenticeships just aren't going to cut it for teens or for employers. But what if instead of Caitlin's three days just following a lawyer around she'd instead spent a semester volunteering for five hours a week after school? Could a law firm use an eager tenth grader's time? Yes, if the focus were upon teaching Caitlin to do some useful tasks. At first that might involve little more than making photocopies, opening mail, and pulling law books from the library. Not the stuff of TV legal dramas, to be sure, but these tasks are necessary, indeed critical, in the adult world. Might Caitlin then graduate to some simple cut-and-paste tasks with legal documents? Given most kids' computer skills, that certainly doesn't seem like too much of a stretch—and some challenge and stretching is a very good thing for teens. Of course, Caitlin could also take some time to simply observe what happens in court—the exciting part—but now she'd also have a fuller picture of what legal work involves. Whether she could do enough work to completely pull her weight and balance the time spent training and supervising her is an open question. But the burden would be modest at most, since Caitlin's time would still be free to the lawyers, and what she gained would be potentially huge.

Although arranging these kinds of experiences entails up-front investments of time, the right volunteer or work environment can almost effortlessly teach lessons that parents and schools often struggle to convey: the importance and satisfaction of a job well done; the benefits of taking on real responsibility; the need for consistency and focus. Parents and teachers alike often lecture, nag, and fret endlessly about how to convey these lessons, and spend inordinate amounts of time making teens redo jobs poorly done, often to little avail. But if we can put teens in the right environments—environments that can, with just a little planning, function as well as the growth-producing environments of old—we can stop struggling to drag teens into adulthood with lectures and complaints, and instead simply watch those environments do the honing and shaping work that they've done naturally for generations.

One thing that makes the task of finding good work for teens a bit easier is that once the lure of lots of pocket money is taken out of the picture, teens appear quite adept at identifying for themselves the work that will be rewarding. We spent several years with the Teen Outreach program, for example, trying to identify the best types of volunteer work for teens. We used all sorts of questionnaires and asked about all sorts of experiences. Ultimately, we found one factor that consistently separated volunteer experiences that did versus did not predict positive future teen outcomes: A good experience was one the teens felt that they had gotten to choose, instead of having assigned to them. Much as Will Lambert continually gravitated toward meaningful volunteer work (and had a choice about what kind of work to do from the outset), and Pete hung in there in what might have seemed like a tough, boring job folding shirts, so too other teens seem to have an intuitive ability to recognize when such work has a payoff.

Although we've focused our own research efforts on evaluating formal volunteer placements and programs, once parents, teens, and community members become aware of the power of the Adult Work Effect, the opportunities to employ it begin to appear all around. Helping a neighbor build a deck. Spending regular time at a parent's place of employment and finding ways to help out. Volunteering in one's church. Helping a teacher after school. Tutoring a neighbor or a little brother or sister. Making recordings for Reading to the Blind. Walking dogs at an SPCA. And beyond that, there are dozens of volunteer organizations in most communities that not only make a difference, but see value in inspiring others to volunteer. Perhaps it should be a part of *every* volunteer organization's mandate to bring young people into the fold.

Once we begin to think along these lines, the possibilities are limited only by our imaginations. The rubric for developing these ideas is a simple one. It's not so much a matter of racking our brains to dream up activities for our young people. Instead we simply need to consider *every* meaningful adult task performed each day by parents, friends, and colleagues and think about how one might engage a teenager in it.

HAVING FUN WITH WORK

"Putting the adulthood back into adolescence" might at first glance seem just another step in the increasing pressurization of adolescence, but we'd argue that when it's done well, it has the exact opposite effect. By giving teens real work that matters to others, instead of just manufactured hurdles like standardized tests, class elections, and athletic team tryouts, we find we often *reduce* their level of stress. Knowing one has something to contribute to the larger adult world and a productive way of spending one's time in it tends to be an antidote not only to the self-esteem issues of adolescence, but to much of its anxiety as well. That was certainly what Tonya, Pete, and Austin found. And yes, there's still plenty of time to have fun in this adolescent-becoming-an-adult world. Indeed, relaxation rarely feels better than when it follows a period of hard and productive work—a lesson we find teens are often delighted to learn. It's another one of the reasons we find teens more than willing to choose good work when it's presented to them.

Fortunately, helping our teens engage in good work is just one of the ways we can begin to put the adulthood back into adolescence. To uncover others, however, is going to require making some fundamental changes in how we think about our teens. We began that process in

Chapter 2, as we challenged the idea that teens were biologically confined to immature behavior, and we tried to push it further in Chapter 4, as we challenged the "nurture assumptions" parents make about their teens. Now let's take these ideas a step further and begin considering just how we can identify and draw out the developing maturity that all teens actually do possess.

Finding the Inner Adult

BEYOND THE INNER CHILD

Making fundamental changes in how we think about our teens is going to require revisiting the ways we understand many of their behaviors. In this chapter we suggest a specific approach to this rethinking process: a shift in focus that we call "Finding the Inner Adult." This new focus is a deliberate play on the recent "find your inner child" fad, which implied that adults sometimes simply need to let go of responsibility and return to the freedom and whimsy of their childhood dreams. Not surprisingly, we take quite the opposite tack regarding adolescents.

The overarching principle of finding the inner adult begins with a rather bold assertion: *Beneath it all, adolescents are almost always pursuing adult goals even in their most disturbed behavior, and we help them most when we uncover and draw out those goals.* This principle suggests that even though teens' approaches may be highly problematic or even downright disturbed at times, their underlying goals are not so different from those of any of the rest of us: whether it's maximizing a sense of control, competence, and connection in life, or minimizing pain and discomfort. The problem lies not in teens' goals, but in the ways they sometimes pursue them.

We can use this perspective to redirect our approach to some of the most challenging, destructive, and seemingly irrational behaviors teens can throw at us. Our goal is not just to understand these behaviors, and certainly not to excuse them, but rather to change them. So let's take a look at what this means in practice.

PSYCHOLOGICAL JUDO

When I first present the principle of finding the inner adult to doctoral students in the Adolescent and Family Therapy course I teach each year, their initial reaction is usually skepticism. *All* adolescent behaviors are intended to reach positive, adultlike goals? That sounds like a stretch. But then I begin by challenging my students to come up with behaviors that wouldn't fit this principle, and our discussion begins.

"What about teens who smash windows or drive around knocking down people's mailboxes with a baseball bat just for fun?" someone inevitably asks. "Surely there isn't any 'inner adult' driving behaviors like that." I then ask my students to draw upon their relatively recent memories to think about just why kids smash windows.

Two reasons emerge. The easiest is also the shallowest: because the kids are angry. And certainly this is often the case, but in these discussions, another student usually quickly pipes up, "Yeah, but lots of kids who do this really don't seem that angry. It's more just something to do when they're bored. I remember doing some stuff like this as a kid and it was more of something we did for excitement."

"So what's exciting about it?" I ask.

"Well, a few things," the student answers somewhat sheepishly. "Partly I know *other* kids who said it was just really cool to see a huge plate-glass window shatter. Then there's the excitement of trying not to get caught."

As we discussed these behaviors further, their link to life in the adolescent bubble became increasingly apparent. There were very few places in teens' lives where they could have a real impact on the larger adult world; part of the satisfaction of seeing the plate glass smash or of writing graffiti was the sense of having such a strong impact, even if it was primarily destructive. Getting lots of adults to take action, seeing an effect on the physical world that was nontrivial—these are things that *adults* are able to do, albeit usually in far more constructive ways. One student even recalled hearing friends excitedly describe seeing a bunch of people out the next day repairing the damage these teens had wrought the night before. Clearly we were onto something with this notion of teens' destructive behavior partly reflecting their hunger to have an impact on adults and the adult world.

To this point my students often counter, "Okay, in theory there might be something to this, but it's pretty awful behavior and certainly not something we want to condone." That's true, of course. So how, then, does this viewpoint help us?

Well, it helps because it gives us a tool to engage in a sort of psychological judo with our teens. Their destructive energy can be tremendously powerful and at times almost impossible to restrain. Just ask any janitor responsible for keeping high school bathrooms free of graffiti. But what if we don't try to stop this energy, but instead work to redirect it? Might we be able to not only reduce behaviors like vandalism, but also to replace them with something more constructive? Remarkably, the answer is yes, under the right conditions. The staff at the Youth Action Project had this kind of judo down cold, and were able to employ it while working with some of the toughest youth in our society.

ADOLESCENT JUDO

Before the summer of 1982, I'd never been to East Harlem. This was a period in U.S. history when crime rates were still on their long upward spike, and gangs were a prominent feature of the urban landscape. I was working on a research project based out of Columbia University across town, and even though it was a bright summer morning, as I walked across 110th Street to the headquarters of the Youth Action Project, I was feeling a bit uneasy.

My colleague and friend Bonnie Leadbeater and I visited the program to speak with the youth workers who had set it up. The aim was to reach kids who were potential gang members before they got fully absorbed into the gang world. As we entered the project's headquarters building, the impact of the program was literally spread before us. We saw young people hard at work in a huge building-renovation project, handling power tools, hammering, carrying drywall, painting, pushing brooms.

"How did the program get kids so engaged?" we asked the staff. "We get to know kids on the streets a bit over time, and as they get to trust us, we ask them what they want to do. And they typically give us all kinds of outrageous, unrealistic, and crazy answers," one staff person explained. "Our job is to find a way to say 'Yes!' to their requests."

The idea sounded a bit off the wall, or at best like a catchy slogan, but the results were certainly impressive, so we asked them to explain further. These counselors had begun a year or so earlier with a group of kids who said they wanted a fort or clubhouse (or perhaps even a future gang hangout, though no one had voiced this out loud). A place where they'd be in charge and no one could bother them. The youth workers' reply after giving the matter some thought, was, "Sure. But if you're going to do it, let's do it right. Don't just have some spot under a bridge or in an alley that is all crappy. Let's do something cool."

And so began the Youth Action Project. What happened next was that these kids (with plenty of adult guidance) decided to try to renovate a small building that had long sat abandoned on their streets. The workers found out how to send in an application for permits, but were told that the city didn't care about buildings like this and it might well take years to get a reply. The kids weren't surprised. "No one has done anything with that building for years. No one ever even looks at it."

Finally, one of the kids said, "Let's just fix it up anyway. I've got bolt cutters, and it's just one stupid padlock on the front door that's in our way. No one even cares if we smash windows in buildings like this; they certainly won't care if we fix it up!" And so, with a bit of trepidation on the part of the adults, that's exactly what they did.

The staff was nervous at first, but quickly realized that whatever risks were involved in this project, they were far less than the risks the kids faced out on the streets. And it was true; no one cared about the building. So the staff and kids jumped in. The results were gradual in coming, but remarkable nonetheless. The "foreman" on the job, a nineteen-year-old named Jamal, explained the plans with pride. The Youth Action Project parent agency had obtained modest donated supplies (yes, it sometimes takes adults committing resources to help kids pursue their adultlike goals). "We're going to make the first floor into a youth center that kids can come to whenever they want," Jamal explained. "The next floor will be offices, and the top floor will be a residence for kids who can't stay at home." They also got adults to donate some time to help the teens learn basic construction skills and make sure they were working safely.

So what eventually got produced? Well, as you might expect, the project took longer than expected. And, to paraphrase Joni Mitchell, it lost some of its grandeur coming true. But they did get at least one of the three floors renovated and into quite solid shape, and many months later the city permit did in fact come through. More important, though, numerous teens got engaged in a project that made a real difference in their own neighborhood, all the while learning adult skills. Several had learned a good deal of carpentry. Their "inner adults" were able to emerge, rather than being shunted into smashing windows or forming yet another gang offshoot. It was a small step, but it showed just how eagerly the inner adult lies in wait among our teens. And interestingly enough, this increasingly "new"-looking building had almost no problems with vandalism in an otherwise very rough neighborhood.

The youth workers looking for a way to say "Yes!" to these teens may not have articulated it, but they were doing a masterful job of finding the teens' inner adults. They took a strong adolescent urge, looked beneath it, and helped teens recast it in the most mature way possible. And the teens were with them every step of the way. For finding the inner adult is not some gimmick for tricking teens into behaving as we might want. Rather, it is a way of taking teens' deepest motivations and allowing and encouraging these motivations (and teens' budding adulthood) to come forth. Done right, teens are almost always on our side in this process. We call this principle "Adolescent Judo." The idea is that if we directly oppose teens' energies, we're bound to fail. If we simply try to tamp them down, we'll at best create low-energy, apathetic teens. But if we flip these energies back in the direction they were originally designed to go—toward making an impact on the world—we can use teens' own drives to move them more rapidly toward maturity.

ELLEN ESCAPES

Closer to home, our efforts to understand Ellen's motivations in her sexual exploits with Jake and his friends, as we described in Chapters 1 and 2, provide another example of the value of finding a teen's inner adult. Ellen's frustrations and motivations became clear over a number of weeks after that first cold February night. The issue wasn't so much sex as that she wanted desperately to be able to act and be treated more like a grown-up and find ways to use her near-boundless energy. She had few healthy ways to make those leaps. We chose to address her problem behaviors not by focusing on her precocious sexual behaviors, but on the inner adult strivings they represented.

Our continuing refrain, "Let's put the adulthood back into adolescence," applied in spades here. While Ellen had previously spent her summers hanging around the house, her parents, using all the wheedling, cajoling, and persuasive skill they could muster, were able to convince a local stable owner to let Ellen work as an unpaid intern that summer (Ellen loved horses). The owner agreed on the condition that the job be taken seriously (nine to five, and no skipping because other opportunities came up). The owner followed through on her intention to make the job real, and when Ellen arrived the first day, she found herself mucking out stables, grooming horses, and learning all sorts of tasks that she'd never even known went into the upkeep of the horses she loved to ride. But she was a quick learner. She was engaged and challenged (exhausted, actually), her work was valued by those around her, and she was truly *acting* as an adult in the tasks she quickly learned to perform.

Ellen ended up loving this farm . . . and why shouldn't she? It was providing a good deal of what she'd been seeking so desperately, and so destructively, in the backseats of buses and cars. "I feel like they treat me like the other adults when I'm at work," is how she described it. Her parents noticed the ways that Ellen seemed almost like a "new kid" when she returned each day from work. "In some ways," they said, "it was actually more like they'd gotten the old Ellen back," the one with a gleam of excitement in her eyes, at least when she wasn't too exhausted to keep them open!

This was only a start, of course. The school year brought new challenges and more boredom and passivity with which to contend. Sitting in school only exacerbated Ellen's desperation to feel more grown-up, and her parents had to really keep their eyes open for ways to put the adulthood into her life: handing over Ellen's clothing and entertainment budget in quarterly chunks to help her learn to manage it as an adult would; encouraging her to accept a neighbor's request to tutor her third grader; and moving Ellen to the adult table at Thanksgiving (three years earlier than when her older brother had made this move). And yes, Ellen's parents kept a close eye on any potential unsupervised time alone with boys; but frankly, Ellen's trip to the doctor probably made more of an impact, when her doctor privately explained just what *adults* need to know to keep themselves sexually healthy.

Often we've found that drawing out a teen's inner adult isn't even a matter of making huge changes in what he or she is doing. Sometimes it's a matter of shifting perspectives (ours and theirs) about the tasks they already face. Simply showing a teen that there actually is an adulthood to be had out there can often make the difference. It did with Sam, the teen we described in Chapter 2 who had held out so long against the idea of even talking in therapy.

SILENT SAM'S SOLUTION

So just what happened with Silent Samantha? She clearly wanted autonomy. Blowing her way through twelve residences in twelve months was pretty good proof of that, not to mention her four weeks of elective mutism with me. But the ways that Sam was trying to establish her adult autonomy weren't working very well, and even she could see that. When asked why she had stayed at her most recent placement for five months, when she'd gone through so many in the prior seven, her reply indicated that she was already starting to think about a more mature approach to her life.

"You know, I get really tired of just changing places all the time. And half the time I just end up somewhere worse."

Sam had the drive to become autonomous (and then some), and she had the recognition that the ways she'd been pursuing her autonomy weren't working. What she needed now was some vision of a truly workable alternative route to adulthood that would allow her to use her autonomy drives. That became the task of our therapy.

"So Sam, you hate where you're living now, is that right?"

"Yeah, it's stupid, it's dirty, the counselors don't care, and I just want to get out." She had a point on all counts, I'd learned, even regarding the "counselors" who were paid just over minimum wage and tended to last less than a year in the job.

"So would you be interested in getting out for good? To a place that you chose?"

"Absolutely."

"Would you be willing to really work hard for it?"

"I've never been afraid of hard work," Sam replied matter-of-factly, but with just a hint of defiance and pride.

And with that we began. I spoke with her social worker, who had two initial reactions to my suggestion: One, yes it was possible to request a change of residential placements; but, two, Sam would have to show she could actually try to make something work before this social worker was going to jump through any more hoops for her. Burning through twelve placements in twelve months, while brutal for Sam, wasn't easy on her social worker either. And so Sam began trying to work within the system to change how it treated her.

What's remarkable is how much this one change in how she approached the problem left her viewing her life differently. Following the rules at her current placement was no longer a matter of giving in to "the Man." Rather, these rules were just a minor hurdle, almost a stepping-stone, toward Sam getting *to choose* where she lived and say good-bye to this place forever. Sam no longer saw running away as a step toward freedom, but as a kid's way of avoiding problems and giving other people an excuse to take charge of her.

Interestingly, after Sam complained for months about her placement, she ultimately didn't appear all that eager to leave it. Once she tried following the rules, SafeHaven turned out to be less inhospitable than she'd thought.

"My social worker says I could go somewhere else now," she confided quietly to me one day, "but if I just stay here for another few months, I'll be eighteen, and my social worker says then she'll set me up in an independent living house where I can have my own room and come and go whenever I want. It just makes more sense not to make another big switch when I don't have to."

Sam was growing up.

The key to understanding the progress of Sam and Ellen and the teens at the Youth Action Project is recognizing that adolescents *want* to grow up. Once we recognize this, and let teens know we recognize it, we stop being seen as adversaries and start to appear more as allies. We gain still more trust and credibility with our teens when we then start outlining paths by which they can fruitfully pursue their desire to become grown-up. Both we and they are often surprised to find that these paths—whether they involve renovating a building, working on a horse farm, or just viewing the rules from a different perspective—can actually leave them satisfied and productive at the same time. Teens come to realize that these adult-centered approaches are ultimately more gratifying than smashing windows, joining gangs, seeking sex with multiple partners, or trying to fight the world.

PLUS OR MINUS FIVE

Often, though, we find it difficult to communicate clearly enough with our teens to get even a glimpse of their inner adult. One of the things that makes it harder to understand teens' underlying intentions is just how confusing their behavior and efforts at communication can be. At times they can sputter irrationally and behave in remarkably childlike ways that make it hard to see the adult-in-waiting that lies hidden within. For all of our emphasis on finding the inner adult, we aren't naive: We fully recognize that teenagers are not yet adults and that most of them make this clear to us almost every day in their behavior.

We've often told parents that they should think of their adolescent's age as the teen's chronological age in years—plus or minus five—to reflect the variability in how they often function. A fifteen-year-old, for example, on a good day behaves very much like a twenty-year-old, and on a bad day behaves in a way that can't be readily distinguished from a ten-year-old. An eighteen-year-old sometimes acts twenty-three and sometimes acts thirteen. And so forth. This fluctuation may well be partly brought about by living with developing capacities that are near adultlike, while moving about in a world that on a day-to-day basis treats one largely as a big child. For whatever reasons, though, such variation is very much the norm for adolescents today, and any attempt to communicate effectively with them needs to take this into account.

The problem with teens' immature talk and behavior is that it often draws out instinctive adult responses and teen counterresponses that lead down a discouraging path of arguments, criticisms, insults, and tantrums. The inner adult gets lost in the process. Inevitable as this might seem at times—and we've fallen into it ourselves more often than we'd like—there is a different way. Let's start with an example of the sort of dialogue most parents of teens have had on numerous occasions.

A simple reminder, "Don't forget you need to do the dishes," is followed almost instantaneously by an angry tirade. "Why are you always nagging me? You can't just control my every move, you know. I don't even have to live here if I don't want to."

What do we do when our teens act almost like little children, objecting irrationally and raising the stakes to even the most reasonable requests? There are many ways one could respond here. Taking the bait that is being offered. Getting into a power struggle. Reasserting parental authority. Walking away. We've tried most of these at one time or another, and rarely do they go very far. The frustration is that we know our teens have a more mature perspective inside them somewhere because we see it at times, but this greater maturity sometimes disappears completely when we need it most.

TALKING TO THE INNER ADULT AND
AVOIDING WORLD WAR III

There is a way, however, to handle these confrontations and negotiations much more effectively. Perhaps the best way to illustrate it is to use an incident from what may have been the highest-stakes negotiation the world has ever known. Parents often feel like they are on the edge of World War III in their households, but not that long ago the threat was not just figurative.

President John Kennedy faced a negotiating dilemma in 1962 that in some surprising respects was similar to the power struggles many parents face daily with their teens' erratic behavior. More important, he found a way around it. The dilemma arose during the Cuban Missile Crisis—a nuclear standoff with the Soviet Union that historians have called the single greatest threat to mankind's survival that we've yet faced. The crisis was a classic battle of wills. The Soviets didn't like the United States having nuclear missiles in Turkey and so wanted to put their own missiles in Cuba. Kennedy felt he couldn't allow that under any conditions. The negotiations that followed crackled with tension and danger.

After nine fraught days of strategizing and negotiation, a glimmer of hope arose when Kennedy received what appeared to be a personal letter from Soviet Premier Nikita Khrushchev suggesting a reasonable basis for resolution and a step back from a path leading to nuclear war. Before the United States could reply, however, a second letter arrived that was far more strident and bellicose, one which offered the United States few options other than military confrontation.

The Kennedy team was distraught and frustrated upon receiving the second letter, fearful that a chance for a peaceful resolution had been lost. Then they hit upon a brilliant response. Why not just respond to the reasonable offer and tone of the first letter and completely ignore the bluster and threats of the second? After much debate, this course was pursued; soon afterward, the Soviets accepted the response and also chose to ignore the second letter. The rest, as they say, is history.

Kennedy's approach to the Soviet Union provides a lesson we can and should apply daily with our teens: Sometimes responding to the more mature and reasonable side of those with whom we interact pays off and brings that side out, even if it isn't always visible at the moment. Fortunately, the stakes are usually much lower in discussions with our teens, but the way out is similar. So, leaving our history lesson for now and returning to our far-more-mundane (but equally contentious) dialogue about the dishes, the approach we suggest is to *not* reply to the childlike portion of what's being said, but to respond as though we've just heard an adult put forth a far-more-reasonable version of what we'd guess our teens might be feeling. We respond to the more reasonable "first letter" statement from our teens, even if we haven't actually heard them voice it yet.

So when our ears hear, "Why are you always nagging me? You can't just control my every move, you know," we try to translate this into something that an adult might say if they felt as our teens appear to feel: "You know, I just don't feel like doing the dishes right now, because I'm in a really horrible mood."

And so, we respond with, "You sound miserable. Is there any way I can help you out here?"

More often than not we find this kind of reply takes some of the bluster out of teens' sails in a way that we and they both seem to appreciate. Better yet, they often end up responding in a way that is far more adultlike: "No, I just *hate* all these chores and I've got so much to do and I'm really tired."

The dishes usually end up getting done (or sometimes we help them out as a favor), but in either case, the conversation proceeds far more productively. And teens appreciate being treated in an adult fashion and often rise to the occasion and raise their game in the conversation, in order to keep this (far-more-gratifying) adult dialogue going.

Humans are creatures of habit and script, by and large. If we present our teens with an adult conversational script, they are likely to follow it. President Kennedy seemed to recognize this implicitly. Of course, part of the trick is to recognize that we parents are also creatures of habit and script. The first task for us parents, then, is to avoid falling into the childlike bickering script that our teens are initiating. Keeping the inner adult in sight when we're talking to our teens is crucial, but it's not always easy. Our refrain over and over to parents in this regard is simply:

Remember, there's an adult in there! Once we remember this, it's easier to direct our conversations to that (often well-hidden) adult, in an effort to bring him or her to the surface.

SPOKESPERSON NEEDED

Particularly during arguments, teens are often verbally overmatched and can be easily made to feel foolish and irrational. Their actual positions may not be so unreasonable, but the ways they've learned to argue often leave them looking far more immature than they are. Even if teens ultimately give in, they end up feeling not so much persuaded as unheard. In these cases, finding the inner adult means making the effort to help teens voice their position as clearly as possible. The staff at the Youth Action Project understood this implicitly. We've found that at times we need to act almost as a spokesperson for our teens, to help them articulate the reasonable goals that may be hazily formed in their minds, lest they come out poorly and be ignored.

Let's apply this principle to what may be the most shopworn parent-teen conversational routine of all time. It goes as follows:

PARENT: How was your day at school?
TEEN: Fine.
PARENT: Can't you say anything more than just "Fine" each day?
TEEN: . . .

Need we say more? You know this line of conversation almost always goes nowhere, no matter how many times it's repeated.

Many teens don't quite have the articulation skills, self-possession, or even mental energy to simply say what's most often on their minds when they hear this question.

If they could clearly articulate what they were thinking, it would probably be something like: "It's been a long day. I don't feel like talking right now. Maybe we can talk later." Or perhaps, "I don't like having to give you a report card at the end of each day about what went on at school." But most teens aren't able to voice their feelings this clearly.

So we have a choice. We can either beat them up over what a lame response "Fine" is, or we can help them put better words to what they're thinking, even if it's not what we want to hear at the moment.

When we try to help them voice their feelings more articulately—acting as their spokesperson might—things almost always perk up:

PARENT: You don't really feel like talking right now, do you? Maybe later?

TEEN: Sure, I guess. It's just been a long day. Do we have anything good to eat?

Interestingly, once teens realize they aren't going to get boxed into a corner and badgered over not wanting to talk, they are often a bit more willing to talk, although still not necessarily right after school. Over and over again in our own household, we've found that when we don't badger our teens at three-thirty, around ten that night they'll often walk into whatever room we may be in and start talking about their day. Now at first we found these drop-ins—just as we were about to drop *off* for the night—exasperating (perhaps equivalent to how our teens felt at three-thirty). Then we realized what a gift we were being given. Our teenagers were *volunteering* thoughts about their day and their lives. They were just doing it—as adults are wont to do—on a schedule that best suited their own moods. We quickly realized it was worth losing a bit of sleep to engage in these often-animated conversations.

LISTENING TO A FOREIGN LANGUAGE

When communication breaks down with our teens, it's particularly easy to then see their behavior as irrational and capricious, even when it isn't. This is a common human reaction to words or behaviors we don't understand. Long ago, the popular TV show *Bonanza* used to occasionally feature interactions of the Cartwright family on their Nevada ranch with their Chinese cook, Hop Sing. In moments that were meant humorously (though with racist overtones that were largely overlooked at the time), Hop Sing would experience some unfortunate kitchen pratfall and go into a tirade in Chinese. The Cartwrights all laughed, as did the audience. Hop Sing just looked so silly and childlike ranting in what sounded like gibberish in a high-pitched voice. Of course, if Hop Sing had been speaking English, the scene wouldn't have been nearly so funny.

When we don't understand someone, it's easy to belittle their complaints and their feelings. We see them as childlike and capricious, silly even, simply because we don't understand. As a society, we've (mostly) learned not to do this with those who speak a different language than we do, but we haven't made nearly as much progress in listening to teens whom we have trouble understanding.

How easy it would have been to misinterpret a teen's afternoon reply to, "How was your day?" as "just" adolescent obstinacy. We would have been viewing them as fundamentally immature and unhelpful when in reality they were just acting as fledgling adults learning to negotiate when and where they wanted to engage in conversation. Further, by getting angry, we might well have poisoned the atmosphere and made those later-in-the-evening conversations impossible. Alternatively, by looking past the *way* our teens talk and the language they use, we can glimpse the more mature, reasonable side of their thinking and their behavior. Such glimpses not only change our views—and provide some real basis for optimism to parents in the trenches of adolescence—they also tend to bring out the best in our teens, who appreciate someone recognizing that they're trying to pursue reasonable goals with their actions.

NEGOTIATING ADULTHOOD

This idea of finding, guiding, and aligning with a teen's inner adult also suggests a different way of handling battles over rules and privileges.

As parents, it's hard not to be drawn into protracted battles about when teens are old enough to get which privileges. There's a way around this, though, and it doesn't involve just *talking* to our teens differently, but *thinking* differently about what we ask of them.

Antonio's parents were engaged in a classic argument over curfews, for example, and as we worked with this family of strong-willed individuals, they provided a great illustration of what we mean. The conversation in our office began as follows:

"Look, guys, my friends all get to stay out till twelve on weekends, so I really think my curfew should be later."

"Sorry about that, big fella, but your curfew's eleven. We've told you that when your birthday comes around in nine months, we'll raise it, but till then, you're stuck."

"Why do I have to be in by eleven? That's just lame! What's so bad about being out a little later on a weekend night?"

"Because it's too late at your age, and we've been through this a million times and we're not going to go through it again."

"You guys are just impossible!"

The parents here are certainly not unreasonable in having a curfew, sticking to it, or even in limiting debate about a topic that has clearly been debated much before; yet clearly things aren't going well. It's a bind many good parents find themselves in.

What Antonio's parents are not yet doing, though, is trying to find and talk to the adult lurking beneath Antonio's angry complaints. Let's replay this as Antonio's parents eventually learned to do:

"Why do I have to be in by eleven? That's just lame!"

"Okay. You hate being in by eleven. We get that. And we know that in not all that long you'll be off at college and won't have any curfew. So we want to be helping you not need a curfew as well."

Sounds good, but where do we go from here? Well, at this point it's not just a matter of how we talk to our teens, but of how we're actually going to treat them. Moving away from strictly age-based rules and limits turns out to be a great place to start. As we've taught many parents over the years, to draw out and indeed to reward the inner adult means to stop tying limits and rules to specific ages and start tying them to *demonstrated* signs of maturity (that is, to becoming an adult). With Antonio's parents it worked as follows:

"So here's the deal. Instead of saying we'll raise your curfew by an hour at your birthday in nine months, let's talk about ways you can show *now* that you're responsible enough that you can handle being out later."

"Like what?" Antonio asked uncertainly, but with increasing interest.

With a little prompting, they all quickly agreed on several things:

Adult responsibility meant meeting basic commitments. In Antonio's case this meant getting at least all B's in school, doing chores almost all the time without being asked, staying out of trouble, and managing the existing curfew successfully.

Teens are usually willing to come on board with these ideas, but are typically most eager to hear about the time line. The time line is simple . . . as soon as the changes happen and have shown they are going to stick, the curfew can change, *but no sooner.* Framing a later curfew as a reward to be pursued can be quite motivating to teens. Putting this in place, though, requires keeping our nurturing instincts in check. For there's a temptation to set this plan up as an agreement going forward ("Okay, we'll raise your curfew but you have to promise to get all B's"). Adulthood rarely works this way, though. Paychecks come after work has been done, and meals don't get eaten until after they've been cooked. Further, if we give our teens the reward before they've shown the adult behavior, then we're forced into a monitoring/punishing role, because all that's left is the option to take the later curfew away if they don't follow through. Whereas teenagers tend to like to think about future rewards and like working toward them, in contrast, punishments often breed anger, resentment, and a desire to focus attention elsewhere. This is actually a human principle more than an adolescent principle, but it's one that's worth taking full advantage of here.

"But what about safety?" parents usually ask. "It just isn't safe being out and about really late in our town."

Here again our overarching goal of getting our teens to engage in the world of adulthood helps chart our course. Most teens, like most adults, have no inherent interest in being unsafe. And, as we explain to teens, even if they don't agree that being a bit safer is worth coming home early for, in the adult world people often have to negotiate with other adults who have different opinions than they do.

And so the negotiation proceeds, but the tone has become far more reasonable, allowing for some thoughtful give-and-take.

"How about if I come home at eleven if I'm going to be out at a party or something, but if I'm at Andy's, or Tyler's, or Steve's, I can stay till twelve? Because there's really not anything dangerous going to happen at their house and it's a short drive home."

"Okay, but can you call us by ten-thirty to let us know what the plan will be?"

Both teen and parents have bought into a good deal. The parents are only offering to partly give up a bit of a curfew that they were going to give up in nine months anyway, in return for better grades, better chores, and a more responsible teen. Their teen may or may not follow through, but at worst, the parents have now gained a simple lever—framed in the language of adulthood—for getting their teen to take school and chores more seriously.

Are the parents simply giving in? Not if the adulthood conditions they set are real. Most parents base their rules for their teens at least implicitly on their sense of how their teens are managing their lives. If we'd asked Antonio's parents at the outset how they would feel about a later curfew if they were raising a teen who was getting good grades in school, not getting into any trouble, handling the existing curfew well, and being responsible around the house, most likely they would have felt much better.

Teens, on the other hand, are getting a chance to gain what they most want—freedom—and all they have to do is follow guidelines that they know are probably good for them anyway. And they can always choose not to do it and be no worse than they were. But now the choice is theirs. And choices are a powerful thing to have! We give the teens the adult freedom they want, but do it gradually, with supports and with the expectation that they acquire adult-level maturity in the process.

We've got years of research findings showing that when parents use this negotiating approach, the results extend well beyond the home. For example, in a long-term study we conducted looking at peer relationships in adolescence, parents who used the approach we just outlined had teens who were viewed as the most socially competent within their peer group. Similarly, our own research as well as that of our colleagues has found that these effects extend to improved academic performance as well. Teaching teens to negotiate like adults, while still respecting parents' ultimate decision-making role, pays many dividends.

The signpost we ask parents to follow here is quite simple: *Freedom should be linked to behavior.* Once one starts down this path, numerous routes begin to open up and tense negotiations tend to become less personalized and based more on the objective realities of adulthood. Privileges come not with parental whim and not because other teens have them, but based on mastery of adult tasks. School, for example, is viewed as a trial form of adult employment. Yes, it's boring at times (far too often, actually, but we'll get into that later), but so is work sometimes, a fact the college graduate who asked, "Will I have to be bored?" when I was interviewing him for a job had never learned. And chores and homework and similar tasks need to be handled well because in adulthood the analogous tasks such as paying bills, doing taxes, and meeting work deadlines all leave little margin for error. Adults need to learn to manage such tasks, and adolescence provides a place to gain practice and experience when the stakes are still relatively low. Being treated like an adult should go hand in hand with learning to function well as an adult.

SCAFFOLDING

A big part of the parenting approach we're describing relies upon a clever principle that's been studied with younger children but hasn't yet been much applied to adolescents. It's called scaffolding. The concept was first identified by Lev Vygotsky, a marvelously creative Soviet developmental psychologist from the early twentieth century who sought to challenge the notion that there were ironclad, intrinsic limits on what youths of a given age could and could not master. Vygotsky noted that even young children could often manage complex tasks that seemed far beyond them if adults provided what he called "scaffolding" to support them. Like the scaffolding that surrounds construction sites for tall buildings, Vygotsky's notion was that adults could and should provide just enough support to allow youth to reach otherwise unattainable heights through their own efforts.

Scaffolding is perhaps our single best answer to the question of just *how* we can bring the adulthood back into adolescence while still recognizing that our teens aren't yet fully mature. We can easily imagine, for example, contexts in which our teens would be all too likely to fail to behave maturely and potentially meet with catastrophic consequences, from work in life-and-death medical settings to 4:00 A.M. curfews. And given the "plus or minus five" rule, even far more modest tasks appear outside the reach of our teens at times. But with proper guidance, limits, safety nets, and support—that is, with scaffolding—it turns out that there is little that teens can't do. To treat them otherwise is to massively underestimate their capacities.

So how does this work in action? To find out, let's return to the argument about teen driving described in Chapter 3. It's been our experience that while most parents with whom we've spoken recognize that teens used to take up driving earlier and with more eagerness, they also wonder whether we fully appreciate what's at stake. The answer is that we appreciate it all too well, which is precisely why we argue for trying to give our teens their licenses *earlier* than we do now, but with more scaffolding. Before we set off a panic among parents of midteens with this statement, let us explain what we mean.

When I had my discussion awhile back with my colleague who did research on teen driving, it turns out there was one solution on which we could both agree. And this solution involves scaffolding. The answer—the "graduated license"—is already being implemented more and more widely, but we believe it could be extended even further with good effect. In this approach, teens have to begin by spending significant amounts of time driving with an adult in the car with them. The idea is to let them gain driving experience while piggybacking on the greater experience (and extra set of eyes) of a knowledgeable adult. Remarkably, while accident rates for unsupervised teen drivers are frighteningly high, rates for teen drivers operating under a restricted license with an adult in the car look much closer to rates for older, experienced drivers. We're simply arguing for extending this period by getting teens to begin it a bit earlier.

This approach could address the one consistent problem with the graduated license as it's currently implemented: Parents don't always take advantage of it. The Commonwealth of Virginia, for example, requires forty hours of driving with an adult over a nine-month learner's period before a teen is allowed to drive alone. But our experience is that many parents don't use this time to drive with their teens. Rather, they let their teens drive occasionally, but often as not do the driving themselves. Having been through the process ourselves, we understand the temptation. It's easier for parents to drive: less stressful, quicker, and theoretically safer. And there's a threshold effect. Until our teens become reasonably adept, we don't want them handling more-complex drives; yet our daily lives don't always provide much natural opportunity for the easier drives necessary to gain this skill. We don't have hard data, but anecdotally our sense is that many parents who sign the form documenting the forty hours of supervised driving time have spent far less time than that with their teens behind the wheel.

So why not start a bit earlier and let teens drive with their parents longer? The idea of teens behind the wheel at fifteen certainly gives us pause, but not that long ago fourteen-year-olds could get unrestricted licenses in cars that were far less safe. And yes, the roads were less crowded then, but what if we use the scaffolding principle to mimic that? What if fifteen-year-olds (or even younger teens) drove with their parents, *but in daylight, in good weather, and only on uncrowded, easy roads?* This could happen gradually, with little pressure to "get practice time in" before a real license loomed. Our own experience is that after enough time driving with parents, many driving habits become firmly engrained, and many rare but dangerous hazards have been handled, thus puncturing adolescents' sense of invulnerability while still keeping them safe. We are not saying teens should get their *unrestricted* licenses any sooner than they do now, only that this approach might make them more ready for those licenses when they do come.

An equally important type of scaffolding is emotional in nature. Teens, for all their independence, very much need adults' support, encouragement, and even cheerleading as they take on new task after new task. Learning to manage adultlike tasks is not just cognitively challenging, it can also be emotionally trying and leave even competent teens feeling discouraged at times. Close, supportive relationships are crucial to bucking teens up under these circumstances and allowing them to reach their full potential. In the next chapter we'll consider in more detail the kinds of relationships that can maximize the healthy support we can provide teens, but for now we just want to make clear that the kinds of scaffolding teens require are not just practical but emotional.

Day-to-day examples of scaffolding abound, and indeed our principle of putting the adulthood back into adolescence couldn't be applied without it. Ellen could not have handled her work on a horse farm without the owner taking time to show her exactly what she needed to do and looking over her shoulder the first few times she did it. The young people at the Youth Action Project would have gotten nowhere without adults willing to set up a reasonable, doable plan for their building renovation and providing guidance and training along the way. Sam needed and used our therapeutic interactions to overcome her angry impulses enough to see the path to adulthood and freedom that was before her. Antonio would still need limits on his curfew in order to manage it safely.

It would have been far too easy to just decide that each of these young people was simply not ready for the tasks they were taking on. Or to simply get tangled up responding to the immature rants of each teen's inner child and not even consider sending these tasks their way. But with a combination of heightened expectations for our teens, a willingness to look not just at the "minus five years" behavior, but at the "plus five" potential, and some scaffolding, we can bring out the best our teens have to offer.

This leads to our next escape tip for teens and their parents: *With enough support, anything is possible!* A few generations ago we had no choice but to take this approach with young teenagers. An extended adolescence was a luxury few families could afford, and so parents naturally saw their fourteen-year-olds as individuals who should be well on their way toward handling adult tasks and responsibilities. And by and large those teens managed reasonably well. The good news is, if we adopt some of the same attitudes, we can also move today's teens into adulthood far more quickly and effectively. We might even find ourselves more often enjoying the time we spend with them.

Hardwired to Connect

A man among children will long be a child.
A child among men will be soon a man.

—THOMAS FULLER, 1732

WALTER AND JOSH

Walt was fed up. He'd been really trying to maintain a decent relationship with his fifteen-year-old son, Josh, but had little to show for
it. "Nine out of ten things I invite him to do, he just says no, and he's always got some excuse as to why he can't or doesn't want to. He acts like
he couldn't care less!" Dinners out together, shooting baskets, renting a
movie, taking a hike—Josh casually turned down almost all of Walt's
invitations, and though Walt knew adolescents were known for this, he
still felt a sting of rejection with each new rebuff.

Up until Josh was twelve the two had enjoyed a close relationship.
Typically back then, Josh could scarcely get enough time with his dad:
playing football, going to sporting events, or just hanging out. But times

142 · Escaping the Endless Adolescence

had changed and a cold war had set in. Walt nagged Josh about chores he hadn't done, and Josh just as often simply stared back defiantly.

When Walt heard Josh practicing his drum set, he sarcastically suggested, "Don't quit your day job. Better yet, you might consider *getting* a job."

Josh replied in turn, "At least I don't spend so much time at work that I let my body turn to Jell-O!"

Things came to a head when Walt unexpectedly got two tickets to a sold-out U.Va. basketball game against archrival Duke. Josh had always loved basketball, and it was one of the few passions that father and son still shared. Walt spent a fair amount to snap the tickets up quickly, but when he eagerly told Josh about them, Josh nonchalantly replied that he'd already made plans for the night of the game, so maybe some other time.

That night as Walt talked to his wife, he was at his wits' end. "He wants to be on his own, fine. Let him. He's got so many sports and activities that he doesn't need to spend time with me anymore. I can take a hint. If he wants to invite me to do something, and *if* it fits my schedule, then I'll consider it. But he's not getting any more invitations from me!" Walt also vowed to give up his (seldom successful) efforts at casual conversation with his son. He was as good as his word, and though Josh would never admit it to his father, he noticed the change and felt more than a little puzzled and rejected by Walt's new approach.

What Walt didn't realize was that Josh had been playing an epic game of tug-of-war with his dad, and Josh thought he'd been holding his own. Now Josh found himself pulling against a rope suddenly gone slack, and he was badly off balance. He'd never given it much thought, but had always assumed that his dad understood that *of course* he still cared. He didn't actually mind (and even kind of liked) doing stuff with his dad every now and then, just not as often as he used to. But if his dad didn't *want* to spend time with him, well, screw that and screw him! Josh went back to his activities and started spending far more time away from home cruising around town with his friends. When they all got arrested drinking at a party a few weeks later, no one was surprised.

That children need strong connections to adults is widely accepted. Adults also need connections to other adults; in fact, those who lack them not only harm their emotional health, we've learned that they actually face greater *physical* health risks than those who smoke cigarettes. In adolescence, however, it's almost as though we believe that this fundamental human need for connection to the adult world takes a moratorium. Teens like Josh pay the price for this belief.

It wasn't until we'd worked together for a while that Walt recalled an experience he'd had with his own father many years earlier. Walt had forgotten he was supposed to meet his dad after school to shop for a new hunting rifle, and he was shocked at his dad's reaction when he didn't show up. Furious, his dad threatened that they might not go hunting anymore. Walt recalled feeling angry, hurt, and confused; he enjoyed hunting with his father, even though he'd been going on fewer trips as he got older.

Luckily for Walt and his father, things were soon resolved when Walt's uncle pulled him aside to talk about what was going on and explained, "Your old man's just hurt and prideful . . . he's always been sensitive, but he wouldn't ever admit it . . . just don't take it too seriously." Walt took his uncle's advice and eased up on his dad a bit, and (somewhat mysteriously to Walt at the time) his dad eased up as well after that conversation and things got back on track.

In recalling this episode, Walt realized that the connection that he'd felt, desired, and valued with his father wasn't one that would have been visible to his father at the time. For Walt, realizing that Josh might feel the same way he once did made the pieces begin to fall into place. We now had a point from which to start.

INDEPENDENCE *WITHIN* RELATIONSHIPS

Other than the misguided notion that teens' immaturity is just hardwired into their brains, the idea that most teens don't want or need strong relationships with adults is perhaps the single most damaging belief we hold about adolescents today. "They don't want to spend time with us." "They aren't interested in adults." "They avoid us like the plague." These notions are almost as common as they are destructive. Like Walt, many people hold the belief that teens are eager to cast off their relationships with adults—a belief that quickly becomes self-fulfilling.

For years researchers made much the same mistake that Walt did. They tacitly accepted the assumption that teens' desire for autonomy and independence rule out a wish to connect well with adults. Parents *could* try to hold onto a connection to their teens, the common wisdom went, but in the end the adolescent autonomy drive was likely to win out and the parent-teen relationship would grow distant. This is precisely what Walt feared was happening with Josh. A plausible enough assumption, to be sure; thankfully, it's one now clearly shown to be wrong.

More recently we have begun to recognize what seems all too obvious in retrospect: A sense of autonomy and strong connections are not at all incompatible. On the contrary, if one stops to think about it, strong adult relationships usually leave both parties feeling both connected and independent. Establishing a sense of independence and self-sufficiency in a relationship can even enhance the sense of connection between two people. In practical terms, this means that the drive for autonomy need not prevent teens from maintaining strong relationships with parents and other adults in their lives. Indeed, our own research findings go much further than that: We find that to do well, teens *must* keep their connections with adults.

We've been observing parents interacting with their teens in our research and practice for more than two decades now, and our findings strongly support this more-positive slant on teen-parent relationships. When we observe teens establishing their autonomy while maintaining a strong connection in discussions with their parents, we find that good outcomes follow in areas ranging from better peer relationships and mental health during adolescence to greater occupational and educational attainment years later in young adulthood. We'll consider just how some families are able to get into such healthy patterns of interaction in just a bit. For now, the point is that when teen-parent connections are lacking, teens consistently fare less well. The overarching principle is simple but critical: *Adolescents want autonomy, but they also want and need strong relationships with adults in their lives.* Walt wasn't just mistaken about what Josh *wanted*, he was mistaken about what Josh *needed*, in spite of his son's apparent disinterest. Walt would not have to give up his relationship with Josh, and indeed *should* not, lest he unwittingly banish his son to a troubled life isolated in the teenage bubble with his friends.

So why is this so hard for Walt and parents like him to recognize and accept?

Well, there's a twist, and it's one that tripped researchers up for years and almost tripped Walt up. The twist is that the adolescent struggle to establish independence in the world takes so much effort, it doesn't always leave teens with a lot of emotional energy left over for maintaining relationships with adults. Making teens' task still more challenging, relationships with parents are often a bit threatening to teens, given their temptation to fall back into the comfortable dependence of childhood—dependence that they are desperately, if ambivalently, trying to shake off. Most teens very much value their relationships with their parents, but also need to show that they can make it on their own. Beyond this, they are also working to manage ever-deepening relationships with peers. None of these goals are fundamentally incompatible; it's just hard for a teenager to pursue them all simultaneously. So in healthy families, teens will often implicitly trust that their relationships with their parents are strong enough to withstand some inattention while they turn to these other tasks.

As Josh put it during one of our individual sessions, "I know my dad is great and really cares about me, and he can be really fun sometimes, but I just wish I could get him to understand that when I want to be with my friends, it's not because I don't like him, but I'm *fifteen* and that's what I'm supposed to be doing!" Not all that deep down, Josh knew that he very much cared about his relationship with his dad, just as Walt had cared about his relationship with his own father. But given the hectic demands of adolescence, Josh didn't have a lot of time and energy left to devote to making sure this relationship was well-tended. He was letting his dad take care of that, or so he thought.

The upshot of all of this for parents is straightforward: *Adults are the relationship maintainers with teens.* This maxim doesn't just reflect a burden, though; it also suggests an opportunity that is too often missed. Most teens, if left completely to their own devices or if asked to carry their full weight in relationships with adults, will flounder. But if we can buttress those relationships with some well-placed scaffolding, we'll often be shocked at how much our teens respond to the chance to engage with us.

EAGER VICTIMS AND AN UNEXPECTED REFERRAL

Now, it's true that as adults (whether parents, therapists, teachers, or neighbors) we often feel we're trapping teens into interacting with us. They protest as if we're victimizing them when we subject them to family dinners, chores, time together, repeated invitations to joint activities, and the like. We don't get all that many positive strokes back from them in these encounters, and that *is* hard and uncomfortable for most parents. What so often gets missed, though, is that while they won't always acknowledge it, our teens are often happy to be included. Indeed, deep down they're even eager for connection with adults and adulthood, as the adolescent bubble gets boring after awhile. But (and this is a huge but) they will rarely show it directly.

I first learned this lesson from a young teenage girl with whom I worked during my clinical internship. Tamara was sullen, badly overweight, and struggling to recover from years spent as a football tossed back and forth between her parents as they continued their marital fights long after a messy divorce. She was brought unwillingly into therapy by her mother, who knew she needed help. I met with Tamara over an eight-month period and did my best to connect with her, though largely, it seemed, for naught. I encouraged her, tried to draw her out, praised her whenever I could find the opportunity, and listened attentively, but her responses were always the same: flat, bored, and guarded. Yes, she would talk to me (she wasn't engaged in a battle as Silent Samantha had been), but I just got the sense that I was boring her and that she couldn't wait for our sessions to end. I knew that without forming a decent relationship with Tamara, I was unlikely to be of any help, yet clearly I was failing miserably on this score with this needy young person.

Or so I thought.

A good while after I'd begun seeing Tamara, I was assigned to see another teen, Christine, whose mother, I learned, had specifically requested me when she called the mental health center for an appointment. Apparently, Christine's mother had often suggested she might benefit from talking to someone, but Christine always resisted, until one day she came home and told her mother she could set up an appointment *if* she set it up with me. She'd heard from her friend Tamara that I was a great counselor!

It was a lesson I never forgot, but one I've nonetheless had to relearn a number of times: Even when things are going well in a relationship with an adolescent, it isn't their goal to show us that in any discernible way. Over time I've gotten better at detecting the clues: *less* resistance about returning for future appointments. Arriving on time. Volunteering at least a little information. The small but genuine smile in the waiting room. But these clues that a teen values an adult relationship are subtle and easily missed if we're not looking for them.

The clues are even more easily missed by parents in the midst of the conflict and contention of parent-teen relationships. Two parents with whom I recently worked, Penny and Paul Turner, described how they realized they'd been missing these clues with their daughter Sasha. Paul recalled turning to her one Saturday after yet another particularly trying and contentious week of angry arguments, and saying, "Sasha, we really need to see if we can get things back on track to a point where we actually get along with each other."

Sasha's quick and sincere reply: "What do you mean? We get along fine." And she meant it.

I worked hard with the Turners to help them accept that they would have to look for and be satisfied with the somewhat erratic signs of connection that Sasha did give them. Penny got good at noticing (and pointing out to Paul) when Sasha chose to share with them her thoughts about her friends or teachers. Paul helped Penny see the connection that was so clearly present when Sasha eagerly called them to the computer to see a humorous snippet on YouTube. The Turners continued to be frazzled by their conflicts with Sasha, but they felt much less discouraged once they saw things from her vantage point: Of course she loved them, of course she was glad they were her parents, and of course she wanted to share things in her life with them. It just wasn't something she thought she had to go out of her way to advertise.

The Turners' experience leads directly to our second relationship principle for moving teens into adulthood: *Teens want adult relationships far more than they show it.*

Indeed, teens very much need such relationships, for the task of taking on the challenges of the adult world is difficult, uncertain, and at times lonely. One of the most important kinds of scaffolding we can provide our teens as they take on adult challenges is emotional: providing warmth and love for teens engaging in an adult world that can be cold and unforgiving at times. Conveying to them our positive expectations for them ("Yes, of course you can do it.") even as they grapple with occasional failures. For a big part of what it takes to make it as an adult is emotional in nature. Learning to persist in the face of setbacks. Being brave enough to seek out new challenges. And while others can teach our teens many of the practical skills needed to function in adulthood, parents are uniquely situated to provide the emotional support. Teens will often be too proud or too afraid of looking dependent to ask for it directly, but they need it all the same, and if we can provide even some of this support, we gain allies for life.

And so we return to Walt, who was so frustrated by Josh's rejection of ninety percent of his entreaties to spend time together. The somewhat unsatisfying answer we had for Walt? Ten percent ain't bad! A teen who truly doesn't want to spend time with his or her parents has no trouble rejecting a hundred percent of the offers made. (We know, we've worked with such teens.) Josh didn't mind spending time with his parents when it wasn't inconvenient, when he wasn't mad at them, and when the activity seemed truly enjoyable. In fact, deep down he counted on a certain amount of that family time and the emotional recharge it provided him. The biggest danger that Josh and Walt's relationship faced was that Walt wouldn't recognize just how significant the relationship was to Josh, and would then withdraw or act in ways that would begin to undermine it.

PARENTS OF CHILDREN, PARENTS OF ADULTS

Letting Walt know that Josh did care about their relationship was helpful, but it still left Walt feeling unsettled. What about all the great times he and Josh used to have together, times when Josh clearly worshipped him? Were these just gone forever? Telling Walt that "ten percent ain't bad" seems like small comfort in this instance, and there is without doubt a good deal of loss and wistfulness that comes with the territory of parenting adolescents as they grow. The childlike hugs and snuggles, the chance for parents to be heroes as they swoop in to solve their child's problems almost by magic, all of these are part of the joy of raising younger children, and watching these days pass is difficult. It has been for us, for our friends, for our clients, and for almost everyone we know. But it isn't our teens' fault that they're growing!

More important, if we accept that such changes are an inevitable part of parenting (not to mention of life), then something else opens up to us. We often can only glimpse it during the midteen years, but we're on the verge of gaining a new, even richer set of relationships with our children as *adults*. Relationships in which we can someday share our thoughts more freely and be understood more fully. Relationships in which we'll be surprised by the depth of the thought and feeling our offspring can share with us. We'll now be able to laugh at some of the same jokes, learn from each other's tastes, and give *and* receive some emotional support in tough times. We'll be gaining relationships in which we can be gradually freed of much of the caretaker role (and perhaps even someday find ourselves being taken care of by our offspring). We'll also be gaining relationships in which our teens love us not just because they need us, but simply because of who we are in their lives. In short, we get relationships that can be among the deepest and richest of our adult lives.

A rare and fine prize indeed, though one that's hard to see from deep in the trenches of adolescence. We can get all of this, but there is a cost and some emotional work involved. The cost is obvious—we lose our little children—but this is going to happen regardless. The work is that during the adolescent transition period, our teens need us to serve as the bridge builders who maintain and buttress our relationships with them even when they are otherwise occupied. This means accepting their need for more space, even if parents end up feeling left in the lurch. We've found it particularly important for parents to build and buttress their own independent social support networks during this time. It's the best safeguard against relying too much on their teens for closeness and good times, and against resentment when their teens can't meet parental needs. All of this is immensely challenging, as in some ways adolescence requires as much emotional work and growth on the part of parents as it does of teens. But for parents willing to make this difficult transition, the return is teens' implicit gratitude and deep sense of trust in relationships that can last a lifetime.

So, while we can't help but notice that the glass is ninety percent empty in terms of how often teens turn down our offers to spend time together (the bridge builder role can indeed be thankless at times), we also need to remind ourselves that the remaining ten percent is potentially pure gold! Time that our teens willingly spend with us. Time that provides the fertile beginnings of a future adult-adult relationship. Time that is so precious, we shouldn't ever minimize its value and meaning.

THE ADULTHOOD PRINCIPLE IN RELATIONSHIPS

Neighbors, Bosses, and Teens

Once we accept the idea that teens actually do want adult relationships, the question becomes: How do we establish these relationships with such ambivalent and mercurial partners? Our overarching refrain of putting the adulthood back into adolescence, and into our interactions with our teens, provides the guidance we need. In the last chapter, we began outlining ways to handle disagreements with teens by moving toward more adultlike ways of interacting with them. As we extend this principle to other aspects of our relationships, we find that one of the best antidotes to teens' fears that relationships with their parents will keep them childlike and dependent is also to make those relationships more adultlike. Even a quick glance at some common types of parent-teen interactions makes it clear there's plenty of room for progress on this score.

Let's start by looking at the ways Walt learned to negotiate with Josh around chores. I asked Walt to imagine he had a next-door neighbor who stopped by regularly, but who often began the conversation by complaining that Walt rarely made the reciprocal effort to walk over and visit on his turf. And then the neighbor would point to the pile of branches that Walt had never quite gotten around to moving from the border between their two yards. "When you gonna get that pile out of there? It looks like a damn snake's nest!" And so it would continue. When Walt was packing the car for a vacation, the neighbor would stop by and remark sarcastically, "Oh, you've got time to go relax somewhere, but not to make your yard look decent!"

The question: How good a relationship would Walt have with this neighbor?

This isn't entirely fair, as Walt noted. Unlike the neighbor, he was *supposed* to be in a position of authority over Josh.

Then what if we weren't talking about Walt's neighbor, but his boss? Imagine if Walt had a boss whose expectations seemed quite high regarding tasks that Walt hadn't yet fully mastered. And what if, in that boss's view, Walt could do little right? Imagine further that while the boss used to be a nice guy, now he was mainly sarcastic and critical . . . possibly because Walt hadn't joined him at a few of the company's social events. Let's say, for the sake of argument, that the boss was even *right* about most of the criticisms. Would that boss's angry and critical approach bring out Walt's best work? Of course not, most people would acknowledge. So why would Josh find it any easier to deal with such a "boss" than an adult would?

Here's where the goal of making our interactions with our teens more adultlike comes into play. *Adults should use the same conventions of respect and politeness when talking with teens that we use when talking to other adults.* Put this way, the principle seems obvious, but based on our experience with thousands of parents over the years, we've found it can be surprisingly hard to implement. Partly we're just so used to treating our young people as other than adults that we don't make the switch easily. And as parents, our offspring bring up such strong emotions in us that we can find it hard to stay rational and polite when we fear our child is wasting her opportunities or damaging his future.

Let's start with an easy example: criticism. Yes, adults sometimes need to criticize one another, but boy oh boy, do they offer such criticism differently to one another than they do when speaking to teenagers. In most workplaces, for example, disagreements do not begin with sarcasm, derogation, or condescension. "I don't suppose you'd be willing to deign to dine with us tonight?" "I can't believe that you thought this drivel would pass for an essay!" "Not that you've ever done this before, but try to pick your sister up on time today." Or, "You may be too spoiled to understand this, but some people work for their money!" Far-fetched? Not for most parents at least some of the time.

The neighbor who makes snippy remarks about one's yard is nothing if not unneighborly. The boss who berates his or her employees while correcting them becomes the butt of watercooler jokes. The colleague who has nothing but criticisms and "suggestions" about how we ought to do things differently gets frequent eye rolls. As adults, we've learned to minimize our contacts with all of these people as much as we possibly can. Why wouldn't we? Who would want to spend any more time than they had to with people who were constantly trying to expound, often in rude ways, on what we should be doing differently? Which, of course, is exactly how our teens often perceive us. Not that teens don't have many other reasons to want to be on their own, and not that adults don't sometimes avoid interacting even with bosses who are respectful and constructive. (Though bosses, like parents, are far less likely to be avoided if they treat their employees like adults.) In short, part of the reason adolescents avoid adults is that adults can be awfully unpleasant for teens to be around *even when there's no need for them to be that way.*

As we seek to create more adultlike relationships with our teens, what if we simply gave adolescents the same courtesies we give other adults when we need to offer criticism? For example, we could preface our criticisms with statements that put them in a more positive overall context. To an employee, we wouldn't hesitate to say, "I know you really want this project to succeed, but I think what you're doing so far isn't working well and we should talk about it." We provide the positive preface so the employee knows we recognize their effort. Why not do the same with our teens? "I know you really do care about school and have been motivated at times these past few weeks, but I think what you're doing isn't going to get you where you want to go." That sure seems easier to hear than, "Your work at this firm just isn't very good this week," or "Your report card stinks." We know and tend to follow these conversational rules implicitly when we're passing on criticism to adults. We just need to take this implicit adulthood perspective and apply it to our conversations with our teens.

Time Without Criticism

Beyond *how* we criticize our teens is the equally important issue of *how much* we criticize them. Even when delivered constructively, a steady diet of criticism inevitably leads to a queasy feeling in one's stomach whenever the critic approaches. In adulthood, relationships grow and thrive primarily based on common interests and pleasant interactions. Criticism has its place, but it will rarely be in a starring role for long if a relationship is to thrive. *No one* wants to be in a relationship in which criticism of their behavior, however well-intended or on target, is the primary topic of the conversation. Adolescents are no different from adults in this respect, yet as parents, we sometimes seem to take on the fantasy that our teens are eager receptacles just waiting to be shaped by our sage advice. We offer lectures endlessly, seeking to pass on our knowledge and guidance. Yet we fail to recognize the fundamental truth captured in the simple equation:

Lectures given ≠ Lectures received!

That is, the number of lectures given by parents often bears little relation to what teens actually hear and take in. In fact, when teens are bombarded with lectures over time, they get more and more adept at quickly tuning parents out whenever they even sense a lecture coming on. We've found that reducing the number of criticisms and lectures offered doesn't necessarily reduce how much teens learn from us—quite the opposite is often the case—but it does reduce teens' desire to run whenever we enter the room.

Here's a novel way to put this into practice. Consciously work to spend some time each week with your teen that is *entirely* free of parental guidance or criticism or advice. The time doesn't have to involve anything fancy or special; it can be any one-on-one time together that allows for communication, even the drive to soccer, as long as neither party is plugged into headphones. Walking the dog together, eating a meal, watching an episode of the teen's favorite series—that kind of thing. But with no corrective comments whatsoever. No advice about their driving, no comments about their manners, no wisdom about friendships, no corrections of their behavior, even when their behavior is undesirable. Short of imminent danger ("You're about to drive the wrong way on the interstate!"), we counsel parents to let all opportunities for criticism pass when it's Time Without Criticism time. Instead, use the time to just listen to and interact lightly with your teen.

This, of course, is precisely what we tend to do when we're with adult friends. And without critical comments, it's amazing how much teens are willing to talk and how much more at ease they become. It may be surprisingly hard at first to carry off, but the magic of it is that parents find themselves enjoying and looking forward to those times with their teen—respites from the monitoring and correcting work of parenthood, when they can be talking more as adult-to-adult. Putting down that monitoring role frees you to enjoy your teen's humor, current passion, or perspective on the world. Not to worry, whatever opportunities for criticism you've let pass will almost certainly arise again (and if they don't, our point is even more well-taken). Understand, we're not at all trying to discourage parents from giving their teens feedback, even critical feedback, and we'll say more about the right way to do this in the next chapter. For now, what's important is to be mindful of how, how often, and when we criticize our teens.

Of course, there are a number of other things that adults don't do when relating to one another, or at least *shouldn't* do if they want to maintain a civil relationship! Adults don't talk about other adults in their presence as though they aren't there. Adults don't launch into important conversations without asking if it's a good time to talk. Adults don't continue talking even after another adult has said they don't want to talk anymore about a topic. And adults don't tell other adults that "someday they'll understand." Parents may take these behaviors for granted, but each of them slowly but steadily pushes teens further away from adultlike relationships within their families. The more we think about the ways that parent-teen relationships differ from adult-adult relationships, the more we think it's a testament to teens' desires for connection that they keep coming back and seeking relationships with adults at all! Fortunately, these problematic relationship behaviors can be changed for the better, and in our experience, teens tend to be eagerly responsive to these changes.

Unsteady Partners

The problem isn't just with adults' behavior, though. To be fair to adults, even when they're doing everything right, getting along with adolescents isn't exactly a walk in the park. Adolescents, for all their good intentions, are *not* adults in terms of their relationship skills. We see this not only in their reluctance to actively pursue adult relationships, but also in their sometimes gratuitous rudeness. Teens will act disinterested in long-term relationships based on passing annoyances; they'll fail to honor commitments; and they'll utter harsh words with little forethought. These are all behaviors most adults routinely try to avoid in relationships they care about, but the same can't be said of most early adolescents. Even more-compliant teens may be too shy or passive to hold up their end of relationships without help.

To be sure, it will help immensely if we treat our teens more like adults in these relationships. But we're also going to want to recognize and take into account some of the ways in which they are clearly still adolescents.

The first point to recognize, going back to our recurrent theme in this chapter, is that teens' immature relationship behaviors should not be interpreted as indicators of *disinterest* in adult relationships. Granted, if adults rejected ninety percent of our overtures, or answered our friendly questions with one-word responses, we might reasonably conclude that they weren't interested in a relationship. But that's because adults have mastered basic relationship skills in ways that teens often have not—not even with one another, and not even in relationships about which they care deeply. This isn't to say we can't have high expectations of our teens in relationships, but we need to be careful about how we interpret their behaviors when they don't meet those expectations.

To some degree, forming close relationships with teens requires, if not combat pay, at least a bit of extra padding against occasional bumps and bruises. The more closely we interact with our teens, though, the more we find the bumps and bruises diminishing over time. We've all seen adolescents rise to the occasion and behave wonderfully in relationships they care about, whether it's with a cherished grandparent, an admired teacher, or a peer in whom they have a romantic interest. The plus-or-minus-five-years rule applies here in a good way: When we get teens to engage with us in adultlike relationships, they can act, much of the time, far older than their years.

What we're proposing is in some ways a simple fix, but it's not an easy fix. Changing long-standing patterns of interaction is difficult, and it is likely to take teens awhile to even notice the kinds of changes we're suggesting. But in our experience, the effects of these changes accumulate over time. We can speed this process along by avoiding criticisms and sarcasm and by relating to our teens like adults in more-positive ways as well. If we're wondering how to do this, we need simply ask: What do adults do in relationships they want to develop? They look for common interests. They laugh at one another's humor. They sometimes show their own vulnerability. They bring interesting ideas to the table. They also have lives apart from the relationship, and don't hesitate to set boundaries and limits on the relationship. They experience conflict, but manage it without belittling one another. If we approach our teens more as adults than as older children, we also help allay their concern about remaining too dependent on us. Most teens aren't afraid of close relationships with their parents; rather, they're afraid of close relationships in which their parents still treat them as children.

THE PAYOFF

Relationships and Discipline: The 24/7 Problem

The adult relationship approach brings some remarkable payoffs to parents and teens even in the short-term. For example, establishing adult relationships with our teens can help address one of the thorniest problems parents confront: adolescent misbehavior. Shelf-loads of sensible (and some not-so-sensible) books have been published detailing behavioral contracts for teens, consequences for misbehavior, appropriate rule-setting, and the like. Without a positive relationship in place, however, all of the advice around appropriate limit-setting, tough love, and the rest is usually for naught. Adolescents are motivated by the material consequences of their behavior, to be sure, but there's an even more basic principle: *The strongest motivator for teens is a close relationship.* Like many of the principles we're suggesting, this is not so much a point about adolescent motivation as it is about human motivation, as applicable to adults as to adolescents.

To understand why relationships often matter with respect to teens' behavior even more than rules and consequences, consider what we call the "24/7 problem." Most parents are lucky if they can find ten minutes in a day to figure out rules, consequences, and responses to their adolescents' misbehaviors. Josh's parents, for example, barely found time to talk about how to deal with his underage drinking in the first few days after his arrest—because they were so busy contacting a lawyer, trying to find out exactly what had happened, and keeping up with their jobs and the rest of their family. In many families, one or two sustained periods of thought or conversation per week to address teenage misbehaviors have to suffice, and for many parents, new problems and infractions arise more quickly than old ones can be handled.

And then there's the problem of enforcement. Even after deciding to "ground" Josh and assign him extra chores, Josh's parents had to remember to enforce these rules, check to see if he had done his chores each day, and make sure he wasn't on the Internet when he wasn't supposed to be. It's a time-consuming process for often-beleaguered parents. Clinicians and counselors have spent countless hours explaining star charts and consequence contracts to parents, and often found that these fail, not because they can't work in theory, but because in practice they're just too burdensome for most parents to maintain. Parents have remarkably limited time, and most adolescent discipline books simply fail to acknowledge this.

Adolescents don't suffer under the same time constraints as parents, however. In contrast to parents' highly limited time to spend on parenting, a teenager like Josh who wants to do something other than what his parents want is often able to devote something close to twenty-four hours per day, seven days per week to figuring out a way around parental rules. Adolescent creativity in such situations knows few bounds (and puts the lie to claims that teenagers aren't capable of advanced planning and strategizing at a high level). Add motivated peers to the equation, and the imbalance of parent and teen resources grows exponentially.

We've often thought that the combined creativity and "processing power" of a network of peers trying to get a grounded teen out to a party would easily rival the capacity of even the most modern massive supercomputers. Given this matchup, parents rarely stand a chance in head-to-head competition. Unless they change the game.

Child psychologist Bruno Bettelheim pointed out that the term "discipline" derives from the word "disciple." While coercion may work to control behavior if accompanied by draconian consequences and intensive monitoring, it just isn't a practical approach in most families. The alternative approach to shaping teen behavior—modeling, persuasion, and modest natural consequences for behavior—requires a good relationship in order to implement it effectively.

We've seen this unfold in several ways in our own studies. For example, we've looked at the extent to which parents seek to exercise appropriate monitoring and control over their teens' behaviors—a long-recognized marker of good parental discipline. What we've found is that parents who use these approaches tend to have teens who behave better, but *only* if their teens also have close emotional bonds with their parents. Otherwise, the efforts at monitoring and control appear to make little difference.

Our colleagues Hakan Stattin and Margaret Kerr have taken this idea a step further. They've found that while parents' keeping a close eye on their teens' behavior is indeed related to good outcomes, how much parents were actually *able* to monitor their teens' behavior was largely dependent upon their teens' willingness to be monitored! So from two different vantage points we're led back to the same conclusion: Relationships are the building blocks of good discipline for teens.

Now, the idea that good parenting involves both warmth and control is something that has been understood at least since developmental psychologist Diana Baumrind coined the term "authoritative parenting" to describe it several decades ago. But what we're suggesting here is the need to go a step further. We're proposing that, especially with seemingly prickly adolescents, the relationship side of parenting must take *top* billing. When trying to deal with a recalcitrant fourteen-year-old, we're saying that the warm relationship is not the frothy extra, but the meat and potatoes of parenting. We've worked with many strict parents whose teens were running amok, and, in contrast, we've always been surprised to find parents who seemed to have almost no formal limits at all for their teens, but whose teens had absorbed their parents' general values and were doing fine. The relationships made the difference.

Looking for Love in All the Wrong Places

What happens when teens don't have strong connections with adults? Not surprisingly, they look for them elsewhere. One of my former students, Mindy Schmidt Rosenbaum, tested this idea while trying to understand young teens' sexual behavior. Mindy wanted to know which teens would be most vulnerable to becoming sexually active at an early age, as Ellen had been with Jake in the back of the bus during school trips.

Conducting this kind of research with teenagers is not for the faint of heart. Aside from getting teens to cooperate in the research (which we do by paying them and, probably more important, providing great snacks and treats when they come in for interviews), there is the issue of getting honest answers. Toward that end we use a "triangulation" method, in which we combine what teens themselves tell us, what their parents and peers tell us, and what we learn by observing them interacting with their parents and peers in our labs. Each perspective has its limitations, but by combining all of these perspectives, we can often get a fairly good picture of how teens are operating in their worlds.

What Mindy found using this approach was that one of the single best predictors of early adolescent sex was a lack of a close connection between teens and their parents. She looked further and found that teens who had sex at an early age also lacked good relationships with their same-gender friends. Fascinatingly, Mindy was able to observe all this *before* the sexual behavior had even occurred. What she saw happening with these teens is very similar to what we've seen in our own practices. Without good relationships from healthy sources, teens turn again and again to premature sexual relationships that not only carry huge risks, but are ultimately unlikely to provide them with the intimacy and support they crave.

RELATIONSHIPS IN THE ADULT WORLD

Teens in the Village

We'd be foolish to place all of the burden on parents to address teens' needs for adult relationships. In fact, connections with adults outside the family can be among the most inspiring connections teens make in their lives. In my tenth-grade English class, for example, I had a teacher I both loathed and loved. He was insanely demanding—seemingly gleeful as he deprived us of our free time with his frequent, complex assignments. He was not an easy grader, and I didn't get my highest grades in his class. Though I later went on to college and graduate school, his was perhaps the most demanding class I'd ever taken. And yet while my classmates and I certainly grumbled, most of us dug in and worked harder for this teacher than for any other.

Why?

We sensed something particular—and something somewhat uncommon—that motivated his demands. He cared about us. He cared about what we were learning (or not) and where we were headed. He noticed if we slacked off, or even slumped in class. He also treated us more as the adults we were becoming than as the children we had recently been. He asked probing questions on writing assignments that made us think not just about the assignment, but about life—not an easy task for a tenth grader (or a teacher of tenth graders). He challenged our literary theories, such as they were, as though we actually had the ability to think, and he listened when we argued back. He didn't just attend to the smartest or most outgoing students, either, but often was successful at drawing wallflowers into the discussion, subtly giving them a vote of confidence. He often *chose* to eat lunch with his students—teenagers!—where he half-jokingly predicted our future careers. He wasn't always right (he pegged me as a future English·teacher and field hockey coach), but the fact that he envisioned a productive future for each of us helped us imagine ourselves positively in that future adulthood, which otherwise seemed so very far away.

Most of us, if we've been lucky, have had such an adult somewhere in our lives. Often it only takes one of these relationships to make a difference. They bring out our best—far more than we thought we could do, actually—not just because of what they ask, but because of the connection we form. Parents, as we've mentioned, tend to offer teens many more lectures and nuggets of wisdom than they could possibly want. The problem isn't that the advice is bad, or that teens don't need advice. When so much advice comes from one source, though, teens find it hard not to feel too dependent on that source, especially when it's a parent. Most parents know the exasperating experience of listening to their teens come home repeating the advice of some admired adult—advice the teen had previously been ignoring from the parent! These other adults can play a crucial role in teens' development. But does it take the heroic adult selflessly giving endless amounts of time to make this happen? Our interviews with young adults who've made it out of adolescence successfully suggest it doesn't.

Twenty Minutes

I conducted a focus group recently with some of our most successful graduating seniors at the University of Virginia, who presented me with a surprising perspective on what it took to form meaningful relationships with adults outside their families. They were a highly thoughtful, introspective group, all of whom were working on my research project on understanding the transition from adolescence to adulthood, and I've used them on many occasions as a sounding board for the ideas we discuss in this book. The topic I put to them this particular week was: Tell me about a teacher who made an impact on you outside the classroom. I was prepared to hear *Stand and Deliver* type stories about heroic teachers or coaches who'd put in hours and hours after school and on weekends working with these teens. Adults who'd gone way above and beyond the call of duty.

These students had no trouble recalling teachers and other adults who'd made a big impact. I was most struck, however, by just how *little* these adults needed to do to have this impact. Student after student recounted stories in which teachers or coaches had simply pulled them aside after class or practice to talk. Sometimes it was because the student had been visibly upset. Sometimes it was to tell the student they had great potential. Sometimes it was to follow up on a point the student had raised in class. Typically, the conversations lasted twenty minutes or less. Rarely did any students describe conversations lasting more than an hour. And while the relationships were often sustained over time, the sustenance often came from quick questions in the hallway, a knowing smile, or a short note on a graded paper. Yet these adults had all clearly had a huge influence in moving these young people toward more adultlike maturity and relationships. It hadn't taken all that much time. And much like my therapeutic work with Tamara, who seemed so bored in our sessions together, I suspect that many of these adults didn't even know anything special had happened. The point, as it so often turns out when we seek to put the adulthood back into adolescence, is not that we have to take on some tremendous and overwhelmingly burdensome task to get adults interacting with our teens. Even modest involvement can make a huge difference.

Will Work for Contact

The strength of teens' desires to connect with adults outside their family emerges most clearly when teens who've been lacking such connections suddenly get the chance to make them. This was the situation with teens attending Wediko, a summer camp and year-round residence for troubled youth. I worked there for several summers during college, and it was one of the formative experiences of my professional development.

One of the more interesting features of this program is an opportunity it presents to its year-round residents. If they do well enough, they are able to earn the "privilege" of working alongside the adult staff members during the day. We put privilege in quotes because the work that teens then do—ranging from landscaping to kitchen work to routine maintenance—is anything but exciting. Teens do get some pay in addition to this "privilege," but it works out to something like two dollars an hour. Further, the hours can't take away from time spent participating in core aspects of the program and hence must come from teens' recreation time. What is striking, though, is that this work is an almost universally desired "perk" for teens attending the program. They work incredibly hard to control their impulses and keep their behavior in shape, so as not to get "fired" from these jobs. They crave the time spent with staff—being treated as near equals—while other kids their age are left to just "play games." Given half a chance to interact with adults in an adultlike role, even these seriously troubled kids jump at the chance.

If We Invite Them . . .

So how do we make these relationships outside the family happen more often? The task largely involves providing opportunities for such connections to occur and then letting nature take its course. In reality, we don't so much need to create new venues in which teens can connect with adults, as we need to stop excluding teens from the venues that already exist. We can do this in large ways and small, and all can add up to make an impact.

When we visited our friends David and Helen for their annual Passover dinner recently, for example, we noticed how nice it was that the teenagers were seated intermingled with the adults. There was no "children's table." The conversations did take slightly more effort to sustain than when there was an adults' table and a kids' table, or even an adults' end and a kids' end, but the evening went just fine. And with only modest effort on anyone's part, our teens all received a two-hour lesson in how to carry on conversations with adults at a formal dinner.

Our friends Matt and Jenny took a different tack at an adult dinner party. As their sixteen-year-old daughter Kira walked through the dining room toward the end of dinner, they invited her to sit down and have dessert with the six assembled grown-ups. The topic at the moment was politics, and Kira came from a politically aware family and school and had numerous opinions of her own to offer. The give-and-take was thoughtful and even provocative at times. What we've found with our own teenagers in such situations is that we often learn more by listening to them talk with other adults than they would ever volunteer in conversations with us. Rather than being awkward, Kira's thirty minutes with us provided interesting punctuation to an already rich evening of conversation.

In our own home, we've found that while we enjoy, and indeed crave, some "adults-only" time at the end of the day, now and again it makes sense to invite our teens into this time with us. Sitting down to watch a slightly edgy movie on DVD, we've invited one or the other of our teens to join us on a number of occasions. As befits their age and interests, they frequently turn us down (yes, we live by the ninety percent turndown rule in our family as well), but when they have joined us, they seemed to revel in being invited to an "adult" event and then asked to carry on conversation afterward about the sophisticated material they'd seen. The occasional sexual content in these movies isn't something we all rush to talk about afterward, but it's also likely far milder than what they hear about from peers at school, and even this exposure serves to normalize a topic that otherwise gets left to the distortions of the teenage bubble. Of course, sometimes our invitations create complications. We've had to establish "adult" rules for these occasions (for instance, no blurting out speculations about the plot or irrelevant questions in the midst of the action). Perhaps we're just teaching our teens how to watch movies with others, but it seems on a different level that we're also welcoming them into adult territory and helping them learn to handle themselves there.

We also look for opportunities to connect our teens with neighbors and friends. The informal "teen swap" is one such idea. The opportunity arises when a neighbor has a home project requiring substantial help. We ask our own teen to join them in helping out ("Mr. Smith and his son really need help unloading some furniture today, and I thought maybe you could take a bit of time to help him, as I know he'd really appreciate it."). Given that the project also involves another teen, the recruitment process isn't usually all that arduous. Our teens may or may not get paid, and they provide help with a real project. More important, though, they get an opportunity to have an extended interaction with another adult.

The teen swap needn't just involve work projects, though. When we vacation with other families whom we've known for a long time, our teens benefit immensely from the occasional chance to chat one-on-one with our adult friends. They get a different perspective on adulthood, on us, and on life in general. They get treated with respect and interest, and typically rise to the occasion and display some of their most mature behavior. We also enjoy reciprocating with our friends' teens. These interactions take little to set up and typically proceed almost effortlessly for all involved. Unless we're aware of just how valuable they can be, though, we can all too easily let such opportunities pass by unnoticed.

Similarly, our extended families often provide rich sources of intensive and sustained connections for our teens. Teens are often willing and eager to stay for a bit with relatives who live at a distance simply for the new experiences they'll encounter, particularly if they're allowed to go on their own without parents. Teens experience somewhat different rules, values, expectations, and lifestyles—all of which can give them needed exposure to the variety of the adult world. More important, relatives are likely to convey adult values to our teens just in the course of living their own lives and talking with them. These nonparental adults are also less likely to fall prey to the Nurture Paradox, and thus may without any effort at all teach our young people to take more responsibility for themselves in basic ways like getting their own food or handling independence during their visits. All in the simple guise of a family visit.

. . . They Will Come

Our neighbors and good friends Steve and Jenny Lambert recalled an incident when their son Will was fourteen and a high school freshman. At the time, our community was involved in a tense discussion about the causes and appropriate responses to the achievement gap between European American and African American students in our highly diverse school system. A set of community meetings was planned to get citizen input on possible responses, and the Lamberts penned the Saturday morning meeting onto their calendar. When the morning came around, they almost offhandedly had the idea of asking Will if he'd like to attend.

Now Will, like most teens, tended to crave his weekend sleep catch-up time. Worse yet, the Lamberts hadn't thought to mention the meeting to him the night before. At nine-thirty they described poking their head into his room, and as he sat groggily in bed, his mother briefly outlined what the meeting was about and said maybe it would be interesting, or maybe having a real student's input might even be valuable. The only catch was that the meeting started at ten. Will said he'd think about it, but as his parents went downstairs to their kitchen, they heard him turning on the shower.

Somewhat to his parents' surprise, fifteen minutes later Will was in the kitchen, wolfing down some breakfast and ready to head out the door. The meeting mainly involved adults arguing with one another, but when the assembled crowd was divided into small groups to gather community input, Will joined his group and put in his own views when asked. He was one of only a few students there and the adults listened to him attentively. In the end he learned something about how *his* school was run, and got a sense that he actually could have input into the adult world, imperfect as it might be. And he found all of this worthwhile enough to violate his cardinal rule of Saturday mornings: sleeping as late as possible, unless explosions or threat of tornadoes rocked his house. Seeing Will's readiness to jump out of bed on a Saturday morning, the Lamberts felt a bit sheepish, realizing they'd almost neglected to ask him if he even wanted to be included in the meeting in the first place.

Organized youth activities like sports, if we tweak them just a bit, offer another great opportunity for teens to connect with adults. Most such activities have ratios of fifteen or so teens to one adult, a structure that seems to preclude meaningful teen-adult connections. But we've found that these activities can be transformed from peer experiences where pressure and hazing threaten to get out of hand into powerful adult socializing experiences. The trick? Well, it may mean little more than doing what Charlie Gordon, a local basketball coach, did, which was to require a different *individual* teen each week to come early to practice and stay a bit late to help set up and put away equipment with him. Charlie's players got both one-on-one time with this thoughtful adult and a sense of responsibility for the team that stuck with them—and it didn't hurt that they became a cohesive and successful bunch on the courts that year!

Along similar lines, helping a teacher organize class materials during lunch can be a high point of the day for some kids. A place where they can feel both needed and, more important, get a bit of one-on-one attention from adults who play a significant role in their lives. Well-organized religious communities often offer lots of opportunities for young people to connect meaningfully with adults, and indeed such contact is believed to be one of the things that explains why teen religiosity has been linked to lower levels of delinquent activity. All of these connections not only serve as a socializing influence and a powerful counterweight to the forces of Madison Avenue, but also are important sources of future connections with the adult world.

The Foreigner in Our Basement

One of the easiest ways we've found to keep the opportunities for adult-like interactions with our teens from slipping by unnoticed is to constantly ask ourselves what if, instead of having a teenager living in a room in our basement, we were hosting an adult from a foreign country? Of course we'd invite them to at least chat with guests at a party we were hosting. Of course we would invite them to join us watching movies on occasion. Of course we'd ask them to help out. Of course we'd welcome their coming along with us to community events.

When we tell new acquaintances that we work with teenagers for a living, the response is often something like, "Wow! Well, more power to you. I'd never want to do it!" But our experience has been that this reaction comes about largely because most adults have encountered teens primarily in large groups (in shopping malls, on the streets, etc.), or when trying to tell them what to do (as parents, teachers, or neighbors with complaints). Outside the peer group bubble and beyond the autonomy struggles, we find that teens are typically good and interesting company. And relationships with teenagers don't necessarily take great effort to establish once we recognize just how important these relationships are to teens. Like Dorothy's ruby slippers in *The Wizard of Oz*, the secret of connecting our teens to the adult world has been with us all along. This secret, to mix our movie metaphors, is quite simply: *If we invite them, they will come* (at least on occasion). The relationships we then establish can help smooth the way as we seek to push, prod, and inspire our teens to take the hard steps needed to grow into handling adult levels of responsibility.

Staples of the Adulthood Diet:
Challenge and Feedback

> # TEENAGERS!
> Tired of being harassed by
> your stupid parents?
>
> ## ACT NOW!
> Move out, get a job, pay
> your own bills.
>
> ## MOVE FAST . . .
> while you still know everything!
>
> —*JOHN HINDE*

We first saw this "ad" printed on a poster in a trinkets store during a family vacation, and even our two teenagers appreciated the humor in it. We all agreed it was a cheap shot at teenagers, but we also recognized that the poster was picking up on a fundamental truth: Teenagers' dissatisfaction with their lives is indeed connected to their lack of exposure to the realities of adult living. The challenge of being on your own, and the no-nonsense feedback the world gives—though presented in the poster more as a threat than a reward—ultimately provide something that most adults see as a positive force in their lives. For all of the stresses that come with adulthood, almost no adult ever wishes they were still a teenager. But as our teens were quick to point out, "It's not like parents would really want or even let their kids move out early anyway." True enough. So aside from the flip suggestion of this poster, just how do we best nurture our teens' developing adult capacities while they're still adolescents?

Thus far we've been focusing on ways of bringing teens into the adult world, whether by exposing them to adult work or to meaningful interactions with adults. In this chapter we're going to come at the problem from the other direction and look at some simple but effective ways of changing the nature of the everyday *adolescent* world. We'll focus on two staples all too often lacking in adolescents' daily diets: challenge and feedback. By increasing the presence of difficult challenges and realistic feedback, even within their adolescent worlds, we can turn the Nurture Paradox on its head and begin raising our teens in a way that gets them ready to take on adult responsibilities (while leaving them less dissatisfied in the process). My experience with teens arriving at Wediko—the residential program for troubled youth we discussed in the last chapter—provides a great example of what we're talking about.

FRESH AIR AND HILLS TO CLIMB

I suspect it was the change in the air they noticed first. Though the bus ride had carried them only a few hours from the shimmering asphalt and housing projects of Boston, the air in the woods of southwestern New Hampshire is chillier and fresher, and, even in the midst of summer, carries subtle hints of winters past and future. The young people who stepped off the bus into the crisp sunlight that morning had arrived at Wediko because the world had treated them poorly, and they'd reciprocated. They had been delinquents and runaways, truants and dropouts, and upon their arrival most were suspicious, frightened (though most of them would never admit it), and very much out of their element. For most of these teens, these eight weeks at the Wediko summer program were a last resort, one final effort by social services or their parents before the system gave up on them. While most were aware that their options were dwindling, they arrived at Wediko with a meager enthusiasm fueled by a lifelong history of failure.

Given this, it might seem odd that the first thing the youth were asked to do when they got off the bus was to climb a mountain. Granted, it was a smallish mountain, in the foothills of New Hampshire, but a long and strenuous hike through the woods nonetheless, particularly for an urban group for whom exercise had not previously been a high priority.

With tons of encouragement from a young, idealistic staff—drawn from colleges all across the country—they *all* made it. Not without a struggle. There was, for example, the teen who took off into the dense woods, only to realize that he had no idea which way to head through the underbrush. A couple of kids sat down repeatedly, protesting that they could go no farther. But with dogged persistence and skillful humor, the counselors coaxed every last straggler to the scenic top, where they were greeted by cheers, Gatorade, and coupons to that night's movie. Even the most sullen, hardened teens usually cracked a smile, surprised that they had made it and shocked that they were— kind of—having fun. And it started a change.

With many other challenges to follow, for at least a brief period that summer these listless, unruly teens became more energized, optimistic, and focused. They experienced a sense of accomplishment. By themselves, these eight weeks wouldn't be nearly enough, of course, but this dawning sense that maybe they wouldn't *always* fail when faced with difficult challenges sets the tone for an intensive, award-winning program that has been changing kids' lives since well before I first encountered it that faraway summer in 1980.

So why did that hike work? Why was it such a powerful experience? Because it was carefully designed to be highly challenging, yet ultimately achievable, for each of these failure-prone kids. With the counselors' intense support (i.e., scaffolding!), the youth were able to succeed at something they could feel proud to accomplish.

Young people crave and respond to a challenge. Yes, even the lazy, baby boomer–raised, overly gratified children of the twenty-first century. Not only do they crave a challenge, they require it. Like the puppies they are at heart, teens will thrash about, seemingly chasing their own tails, when they have too few challenges in their lives. Given adequate challenge, though, they focus and thrive.

While some effects of challenge are large and enduring, as at Wediko, others are simply calming and settling in the moment, though no less valuable. A few years ago, for example, two dads in our neighborhood went on a hike up Old Rag Mountain in central Virginia with their two teens, Kelsey and Ethan, both age thirteen. The outing was originally planned just for several men, but when some of them couldn't make it, the remaining two fathers thought, "Why not bring our kids along with us?" Before the morning had ended, they would question that decision.

The hour-long ride to the hike was winding and tedious, but the kids were just waking up. When they arrived, Kelsey and Ethan bickered with each other in a low-key but annoying way for the first forty-five minutes of the hike, pausing only long enough to complain about their physical conditions. "I'm tired." "Do we have anything good to drink?" "My boots hurt."

The two dads eyed each other and when they got a break alone, questioned out loud whether they'd made a mistake inviting the kids. Why, they both wondered, couldn't these perfectly healthy kids enjoy a walk in the mountains? "Overtired" was the best explanation they could come up with (they'd risen early for the drive), but not one that boded well for the rest of the day, as they were only forty-five minutes into a ten-mile round-trip that would get increasingly strenuous.

About an hour into the hike, the long, gradual incline of the mountain transitions abruptly into a sharp upward climb. At this point the trail becomes demanding enough that guidebooks describe it as "just short of technical rock climbing," with large boulders to scramble over, narrow ten-foot-deep crevices to shimmy through, and very steep, uneven paths. As the dads started to huff and puff, they noticed something else besides their own breathing. Silence. The complaining had stopped. Kelsey and Ethan were working hard. All four hikers became engaged in the challenge of the mountain. As they labored together up the rocky trail, the teens not only stopped bickering, but joked and actively encouraged each other . . . all the while staying well ahead of their dads. When Kelsey and Ethan reached the top, they were elated. All vestiges of fatigue and irritability had disappeared. What had transformed their attitudes? We argue that they had simply needed a sufficient challenge against which to throw their adolescent-brain-and-body-driven energy.

A MOVING PLATFORM

Lack of challenge is often adolescents' worst enemy and can make them as neurotic as any caged and coddled zoo animal. Repeatedly, we've found that our own teens are far more likely to have trouble in situations when too *little* is required of them. But there's good news embedded in this observation: While teens' anxieties often grow unchecked within the adolescent bubble, remarkably enough, these anxieties often quickly melt away when teens are asked to stretch themselves. Again and again we've found that it's not extended therapy, nor self-help books, nor antidepressant medication that's required to jump-start a listless teen, but simply a chance to sink her teeth into something that tests her abilities. Diving into something hard feels good, *if* you get the chance to actually do it.

A neighbor brought this to mind when she told us about her own son's experience. At sixteen, Chris was an exceptionally strong student and a dedicated basketball player on a local recreational team as well as his school's squad. But he was also a bit of a neurotic mess. Not in any terrible way, but in the everyday way that often drives parents crazy and leaves them (with some justification) wondering just how their children will fare in the larger world. "Fragile" was the word his mother used. Chris didn't like change, she explained. He resisted having to do new things and shied away from anything that might disturb the status quo or possibly create conflict with others.

Chris was lucky enough to attend a high school that had an active relationship with the local community college. Accomplished high school students were allowed to take one or two community college classes. He had a long, abiding interest in all things mechanical—he'd always liked building things—though he hadn't been able to do much with this interest thus far. Through the community college program, though, Chris got hooked in with a group of engineering students who had taken on the task of designing and building an elaborate, moving platform for an upcoming city festival. While intimidated by the new campus and older students, Chris was fascinated enough to throw himself into the work, and even contributed a few helpful tweaks of his own.

All was going well until the schedule came out. The city festival, where the moving platform was to be showcased, was scheduled on the same weekend as Chris's recreational team's basketball tournament. The tournament was two hours away, so there was no way he could be at both events. Chris's mom described her and her husband's collective intake of breath when he told them about this conflict, as it was the kind of problem that had often sent him to his room in tears in the past.

His reply this time: "Look, these people are counting on me to help them make this platform work. We're each running one of the parts. There's no way I can not be there."

"What about the tournament?" his dad asked cautiously. "Are you okay about not being there?"

"I wish it wasn't the same weekend . . . but you gotta do what you gotta do. It's just a game, after all!"

His parents were floored. It's just a game, after all? This was a team about which Chris had agonized repeatedly over the past year. Would he start? Was the coach mad at him? Did he blow a key play? They had tried to tell Chris that this was just a recreational league—intended to be low-key—and that it was indeed just a game, over and over, but to no avail.

What was different this time? Well, something valued by the adult world was at stake. For Chris, the only way to realize that the game wasn't the end of the world was to have something real, something that mattered to someone other than a bunch of teenagers, to provide some perspective.

Now, there are many kids like Chris out there, and most will eventually get the message that many of the things they stress about aren't that big a deal in the grand scheme of things. What Chris got was an experience that brought home the message a few years earlier than many teens get it. And, according to his parents, it was a message that stuck well past the city festival (the platform worked magnificently!), and left both Chris and them with less angst going forward. Adult challenges bring stresses of their own, of course, but they also bring the satisfaction of seeing the work and sweat and worry pay off in something real. And the practice of coping with adult challenges also brings a sense of confidence, mastery, and perspective that helps make the more trivial stresses in life a bit easier to manage.

SIMPLE MASTERY

These lessons apply across all levels of education and income, and even across all ages. I found myself walking through a large local big-box store recently, trying to find some small storage bins. I wandered a bit, having no idea what section of the store they would be in. Finally, getting frustrated and finding myself deep within the children's clothing section, I spotted an employee and asked her if she might know where the bins could be found.

"What kind of bin are you looking for? The really large kind, or the kind like you might put food in?"

The smaller kind, I told her, and without hesitating, she said, "We keep those over near the sporting goods section now. We used to have them near the pantry items but we moved them. Let me show you where they are. They can be hard to spot."

As she walked me there, I realized just how grateful I was for her precise knowledge and desire to be helpful. When we got to the bins, I thanked her and asked about one other item I needed in an entirely different part of the store, and she answered with equal assurance and precision and a bit of pride as well. She'd *mastered* this place. And she could rightfully take pride in her mastery and in just how helpful she could be. Her job was one that some people wouldn't want, but it was clear that she'd gained a sense of purpose and competence from it that many teens (not to mention some adults) could desperately use.

Forty years ago at Harvard, psychologist Sheldon White began doing experiments on human motivation. At a time when all of the major research on motivation focused on external rewards as the drivers of behavior, White took a different tack. He examined the extent to which individuals might be motivated by the simple pleasure that comes from mastering difficult tasks. His work, which later led to his theory of "mastery motivation," opened up an entirely new approach to understanding human motivation. The sense of mastery is a powerful reinforcer; often, it seems, more powerful than simple physical rewards. The engaged, helpful worker at my local department store already seemed to get this. The kids at Wediko got a glimpse of it. Most of us know it from at least moments on our jobs and in our lives.

Again and again, however, we pass up opportunities to allow our teens the experience of mastery, usually in the mistaken notion that we are nurturing them and showing them love by doing things *for* them. How do we identify these opportunities in their everyday lives? We've developed a simple rule in our household. Whenever one of us is about to do *anything* for our two teenagers (or our preteen), a little warning bell goes off in our heads and prompts us to ask ourselves: Why don't they know how to do that yet? How can I best teach them? Is this a good opportunity? Now, of course, we hit the same mental roadblocks as every other parent. Worry that the teen won't do it right. Worry that he or she will balk at being asked to learn. And most powerful of all— the sense that we can just get it done faster on our own. When we fall into those traps, we try to remind ourselves, and each other, of what's at stake.

Once parents start to take this approach, a world of possibilities opens up. Activities and challenges come to mind that are totally within teens' capacities, though they night seem totally over their heads at first glance. Individually, the activities are small, even trivial. Over time, however, these experiences can add up to a substantial arsenal of mastered challenges, and, equally important, they provide teens with the confidence that they can learn to handle the basic tasks of adulthood.

Let's take the example of a teen making his or her own doctors' appointments. The first time a parent suggests this, the reaction is often something like, "Huh? I don't have any idea how to do that. Why can't you do that?" Without some guidance and scaffolding, the task would indeed be difficult for most teens. And the first time through, it feels awkward to most. But with a little help—how to find the phone number, how to think through in advance what times would and would not be good for an appointment, what to ask on the phone—and a bit of emotional encouragement ("Come on, sure, you can do it."), the task can be managed with ease, if not grace. And in the process we'll have taught our teen how to look up numbers in the business section of the phone book, how to think about schedules ahead of time, and how to interact with unfamiliar adults over the phone. By taking small steps like these, the seemingly innate sense of helplessness that teens often feel when confronted with the adult world begins to melt away just a bit.

While it takes us longer to guide the teen the first time than to just do it ourselves, that balance pretty quickly shifts and the time invested pays off. Take buying family groceries. In our case it took setting up a credit card for our son to use at the grocery store, clarifying with him what store to go to, trusting him to drive there and handle the credit card, and discussing how to compare prices and make good choices. We also sent him out only for a manageable number of items that he has the experience to choose. Sure, this attempt to have our son master a small, everyday adult task has come with trial and error (and a few items we don't usually buy!), but also with much success. It also comes with the sheer parental joy at being freed from the cry of, "Why are we always out of the good kind of cereal?" We now have the ready answer: "You're free to go get some!"

Prior to their teens learning to drive, our friends the Lamberts found that simply teaching their offspring that they could and should walk places was an awakening for all concerned. The trip home from high school, for example, was about two miles along winding residential streets. Both of their kids had the same reaction when the option of walking first came up (after they'd missed a bus or wanted to stay at some activity on an afternoon when no one could easily come get them), and the reaction was not positive.

"Walk! I can't walk home from school! That would take forever!" the Lamberts' son, Will, practically shouted into his cell phone the first time the issue came up.

But as Jenny Lambert patiently explained that the walk would take thirty to forty minutes, and that given a little thought, he actually did know the route, Will's outrage softened (or perhaps he just changed negotiating tactics).

"But why can't you pick me up?"

To which they replied, "Well, we *can* pick you up, but not for about an hour. You could probably wait in the school library."

"Oh . . . Okay . . . I'll just walk."

The Lamberts were surprised at how easily this went after the initial outburst, but their biggest surprise came when they all got home.

Steve Lambert somewhat hesitantly asked his son how the walk had been. Will barely looked up from his math book. "Oh, fine," he said. Then he added, "And did you know there's a huge tree that's leaning on some power lines and has Rugby Road closed off to cars on the way home? But it wasn't any problem to just walk around it." Will went back to his math while Steve and Jenny stood there for a moment, wondering just why they'd thought this was such a big thing to ask of their son.

As Will, and then his younger sister, Leila, began to walk home occasionally and then to other destinations when a ride wasn't available, the Lamberts found that their teens relished their newly gained flexibility to move about town without needing to depend on parental schedules. If anything, the Lamberts found they had to limit Will's and Leila's walking at times ("No, you can't just walk home tonight from your friend's house because it will be after ten and it's a four-mile walk!"). The fuel savings have been modest but noticeable. The time saved driving has been a great bonus. Their teens' sense of greater comfort moving in and about the world has been . . . priceless.

The simple but profound lesson we derive from these experiences: *Teens thrive on challenge and need as much of it as we can provide.* This isn't just a matter of not babying our teens (though that certainly is an issue); rather, it's a matter of recognizing the incredible value in actively seeking out challenging, growth-producing experiences for them within their everyday lives. The benefits come not only in teens learning essential adult tasks, but also in having a sense of the world as an engaging place and themselves as competent actors within it.

We also find that as teens develop their adult skills, it becomes easier for us to view and treat them as young adults. The relationship principles we outlined in the last chapter dovetail almost perfectly with what we gain from pushing them to master the tasks of adulthood. Good relationships make it easier for us to challenge and support them, and the mastery and maturity they gain from meeting these challenges makes it easier for us to get into the habit of relating to them as young adults, not just as big kids.

HOW MANY TEENS DOES IT TAKE TO CHANGE A LIGHTBULB?

Perhaps our biggest obstacle in applying these principles lies not so much in finding tasks we can teach our teens, but rather in rethinking our own misguided nurture assumptions. These assumptions die hard. A close friend of ours, for example, described working at his home computer one night when he was interrupted by his seventeen-year-old daughter, who reported that two lightbulbs in her bathroom were out and needed changing. He started to get up, but then, partly because he didn't want to be distracted, and partly because he knew his daughter should be able to handle it, told her where the lightbulbs were and returned to the document on his computer, feeling pretty good. But it wasn't so easy.

> DAUGHTER: But one of them is up in the shower where there's something screwed on top of it, and the other bulb is broken. I don't know how to change either of those.
> FATHER [caving in immediately]: Okay, okay. I'll be up to fix them in a few minutes.

Luckily, his wife was sitting across the room.

> MOTHER: Honey, don't you think you should teach *her* to fix them?
> FATHER: Yeah, good point. [To daughter]: Let's go, and I'll show you how to change them.
> DAUGHTER: I don't need you to *show* me. I could probably figure it out on my own. Can't you just change them?
> FATHER [finally up to speed]: Well, if you can figure it out, great, why don't you just go do it?

DAUGHTER [annoyed but resigned]: Never mind. I didn't know it was such a big deal.

And still the father describes feeling a bit bad. He would have *liked* making sure his daughter's bathroom lighting was taken care of (the nurture instinct is a powerful one), and he felt a bit uneasy that he refused a request that would have been so simple to fulfill. After all, this was his daughter's last year at home before college; why shouldn't he take care of her in this small way? The question contains its own answer. The reason he shouldn't "take care of her" in this way is that doing so deprives her of learning, with his guidance, how to do something herself that soon there will be no one else to do.

We could go on and on listing examples of ways we must choose between feeling like we are nurturing our kids versus challenging them and teaching them to manage well for themselves. Changing printer cartridges. Jump-starting a car. Writing a letter to the editor. Cooking a favorite dessert. Finding the best price online for a planned purchase. Our teens have immense capabilities and badly need to learn to use them. We're doing them no favors by keeping them in a state of child-like dependence. On the contrary, our positive expectations of our teens ("Of course you can handle that!") are one of the best things we have to offer them as they make the uncertain journey into the adult world. More than anything else, though, if we stop getting in the way, by pre-empting their efforts to care of themselves, we'll find that they're more than able to step into the breach. (By the way, the daughter did eventually figure out how to change the lightbulbs herself, albeit a few days later.)

LOSING YEARS FROM ADULTHOOD

We can also see the importance of challenge and responsibility in young people's lives in instances where that challenge is suddenly removed. What comes to mind is an unsettling homecoming phenomenon that we've found most young adults readily acknowledge and most older adults can well remember. It occurs almost universally when young adults who are used to living on their own return home to visit their parents. This phenomenon springs partly from the effects of the parental nurture instinct going a bit wild upon these return visits, as well as from young adults sinking back into dependent roles.

We call it the "lost years of adulthood" effect. It's a simple rule, actually: For every day young adults spend living back under their parents' roof, they lose two years of their adult maturity. Short visits lead them to act more like late adolescents. After three days back at home, a twenty-three-year-old begins acting more like she's seventeen. Longer visits can bring her right back to childish needs, whininess, and demands. It's not that the parents of the world are so toxic, but that an environment that expects little to nothing of young adults ("Let me get that for you.") ultimately saps their sense of maturity and efficacy. The surefire antidote for young adults, of course, is a return to their own independent living; for adolescents, we're going to need to make a conscious effort to bring about a similar cure.

THE FEEDBACK PRINCIPLE

As valuable as challenge is to our teens' daily diets, its effects are greatly multiplied when we pair it with that other critical nutrient for adolescent development: feedback. Although it isn't widely recognized, feedback is arguably among the most powerful of human stimulants. It often comes fast and furious in the adult world—enough so that we take it for granted—but teens get strikingly little good-quality feedback in their lives. When they do, the results are often little short of amazing, and we rarely realize just how much power is out there waiting to be harnessed via the feedback principle. To convey a sense of this power, we offer parents a simple riddle.

Imagine you are given the task of motivating a group of teenagers to track and respond to a set of symbols on a computer screen. The teens will be told that the information is completely meaningless in terms of anything happening in the rest of their lives. They'll be instructed that to succeed they will have to pay strict attention to what occurs on the screen, and there will be a penalty if their minds wander even a bit. Now, let's make the task a bit harder. Your job is to recruit teenagers to work on this project for days on end, for hours a day—in their free time and for no pay. Sound impossible? In fact, it's all too easy, as video-game makers around the world have learned. The key: feedback.

Teens will spend hundreds of hours on remarkably meaningless video tasks, in large part because these tasks provide accurate, instantaneous feedback about their performance on a millisecond by millisecond basis. Contrast this with a typical high school history course, where students get personalized feedback that may or may not reflect their actual level of effort at most about once every two weeks. As adults, we know the power of immediate feedback in our own lives. We put off the long-term project (whether saving for college, doing our taxes, or painting the house) to engage in the task that delivers immediate feedback (try not picking your child up from school when she expects it). One of the reasons that exposure to adult activities can be so powerful a motivating force is the feedback it provides—think of the precise, immediate feedback my brother Pete received while folding shirts at the Manchester Men's Shop. Absent such feedback from the adult world, teens will seek out and respond to feedback wherever they can get it. From this perspective, it isn't surprising that many teens get far more worked up deciding what they will wear to school—a decision about which they'll get instantaneous feedback from peers—than about their work at school once they get there.

Occasionally, school does give teens the feedback they need, and those occasions provide the exceptions that prove the rule about the role of feedback in adolescents' lives. For example, a colleague recently described her daughter Jamie's academic awakening. After being a so-so student for years, Jamie's work habits improved a bit in eleventh grade. The change wasn't dramatic; her parents noticed it, but for Jamie it registered as little more than that she liked her teachers a bit better and her parents were nagging her about homework a bit less. Then two things happened. First, Jamie got her end-of-year report card and realized her grades had actually gone up nicely in response to her increased effort. Coincidentally, her report card was followed the next day by her receipt of her SAT scores, which were quite a bit higher than Jamie or her parents had expected. Suddenly, Jamie was truly psyched. She began seriously thinking about college and dove eagerly into her summer reading list, even though the summer was scarcely three weeks old! These two bits of feedback, in rapid succession, had left her feeling as though school could be a real source of success in her life.

Jamie's story is heartening, but it also highlights the overall problem for other students: Our schools are set up so that many students are unlikely to ever have a chance to excel at anything. A's are a fine motivator for top students, but what about the kids who struggle to get B's or even C's? Where can they draw reinforcement? The short answer is that in a system where the chief feedback is in the form of grades, there's little to motivate the bottom half of the class. And we find that these kids get so little positive reinforcement, they frequently don't bother to stick it out through high school. A basic principle—*Teens thrive on feedback that is accurate and immediate*—operates powerfully across all the settings in which teens live.

A SPORTING CHANCE

Unlike school, the athletic courts and fields have a draw that is profound for many teenagers. This can partly be attributed to the sheer joy of physical activity, especially for kids who are required to otherwise sit passively for much of their day. But how much physical joy does the football lineman get from running laps and hitting a blocking sled in practice? Athletic participation also motivates because it offers something more for young people: a chance for mastery shaped by real feedback about how one is doing—feedback that comes fast and furious and with virtually no parental filtering. In basketball, a missed shot is a missed shot, and as a result a made shot feels all that much better. Practice leads to improvement that can readily be seen. Games have winners and losers, and the "thrill of victory and agony of defeat" are well-known to athletes at all levels. In short, sport is the closest many adolescents come to the emotional highs and lows of real participation in the adult world. Objective, rapid-fire feedback is a large part of the reason, even if it is ultimately all "just a game."

In some communities, of course, sporting events aren't just games; they are a community enterprise. In such towns, teens aren't simply playing a game on a team, they are representing their high school and their town. Although these communities occasionally go over the top in their sports passion, it is clear that the players feel they're doing something real. They are acting not only as athletes, but also as performing artists—trying to win, yes, but also providing real pleasure to an entire community that provides intense, instantaneous feedback during and after games. What is most notable among athletes in these communities is the extent to which adolescent negativity, apathy, and lack of motivation appear to vanish from the scene. In their place we see teens who are hyperenthusiastic and motivated, to the point where they're willing to sacrifice their bodies— not always in ways we would want—to achieve the ultimate goal: doing something viewed as meaningful and valuable by those in the adult world.

LEARNING FROM LOCKED DOORS

Many parents readily sign on in theory to the importance of giving their teens feedback, but then feel stymied about how to provide it in a way that gets through. Teens often seem inured, indeed remarkably deaf, to parental feedback. We've watched as the critical ratio of "lectures given" to "lectures received" in many families grows increasingly bleak; frustrated parents provide lecture after lecture as adolescents master blank stares behind which they tune out everything their parents struggle to convey. Most often we've found that the reason is that parents are offering feedback in ways that violate the fundamental principle of getting the adulthood back into adolescence. Adults typically don't learn from lectures and nagging; neither do teens.

Here's a simple principle for making feedback work with teens: Teens learn from feedback in direct proportion to how well that feedback dispassionately mirrors the larger adult world. Conversely, teens are most likely to fight or ignore feedback if it appears to be primarily oriented toward getting them to do what parents want. Sound confusing? It's not actually. The answer is all in the delivery, and the point is surprisingly easy to put into practice once understood.

We've worked with many obstinate, strong-willed, and argumentative teens. Teens whose parents said they *always* had to get their way.

Teens who *never* listened. But no matter how strong-willed these teens may have been, they have all shown a remarkable ability to accept and adapt to feedback *when it appeared as an inevitable part of the larger "real" world.* No adolescent argues that a staircase shouldn't exist in their path or believes that whining will open a locked door if they arrive at a store on a Sunday when it's closed. A staircase isn't subject to the whims of parents. A locked door doesn't respond to teenage rants. It's just the real world giving feedback. Even a referee who makes a questionable call in a high school soccer game generally gets only a grumble. The most stubborn teens are nonetheless primed to respond to and learn from such objective feedback; we just need to take advantage of this priming.

What this means for parents is simple. The goal is to create a home environment that does nothing more or less than *dispassionately* mirror the inevitable rewards and consequences of the larger world. Not doing laundry means not having clean clothes to wear. Not helping with dinner dishes means no special treats for the next week (in the kitchen of the adult world, food comes to those who work for it). We find that figuring out how environments can provide such natural feedback requires a little thought and ingenuity, but ultimately this is the easy part; the hard part is then to simply let these environments do their work. No lectures. No nagging. Just natural feedback, perhaps punctuated every so often with the mildest of suggestions that the system is designed to help teens someday thrive as adults.

The appropriate response when teens fail to meet the challenges before them and are about to suffer the consequences? Parents can and should *relax*. The natural feedback from failure will be one of the best teachers their teens ever have. And what better time to learn from small failures and setbacks than adolescence? Let's take a look at how this works in practice.

MEGAN LEARNS TO COOK

With the guidance we gave her parents, Megan—our teen from Chapter 3 who was paralyzed by anxiety at the thought of leaving her comfy, well-tended home to head off to college—began to get the challenge and feedback she needed. The point we worked to get across to Megan's parents was that their daughter's anxiety would lessen as she learned some of the skills and responsibilities she would need to make it on her own in the adult world. After a bit of thought, they decided a good place to start was by asking Megan to learn to cook dinner one night a week. But how to make that happen? Megan was busy, and her parents already had to prod her just to pick up after herself. So, at our suggestion, they tried applying the feedback principle. They explained to Megan that as an adult, how well she ate would depend on whether she was willing to get good food for herself. Their job was to help her get ready to act as an adult by making life at home mirror the way the adult world worked. So on Sunday nights, they wanted her to cook dinner.

"What if I'm too busy?" Megan asked.

Her parents explained that Megan could swap nights if she did so in advance, but being busy without having planned for it just wouldn't work now, anymore than it would work as an adult. They also explained that of course she could choose *not* to cook on Sundays, but naturally, then, she wouldn't have as good food to eat. She could have yogurt and fruit—things that were always in the fridge—but that would be it. Her parents would manage to get a real dinner together for the rest of the family. Megan listened, then promptly forgot all about this conversation by the next Sunday. Her parents hung in there, though, and Megan ate several apples that first Sunday night, though she made a point of saying it was no big deal. The second week she remembered at the last minute, but said, "Hey, I'll just get food from McDonald's!" Her parents said fine, provided she walked there herself to get it and paid for it out of her allowance. By the third week Megan showed up in time to work with her mother to learn to put together a meal. It wasn't all that hard; Megan found she liked what she'd cooked, and she seemed pleased with herself that she had pulled it off. Now that she was climbing aboard, her parents pointed out that *she* could choose the menu for the following Sunday and they would even get the ingredients. After all, taking charge like an adult has its perks. With a few fits and starts, Megan fell into the groove and realized she even liked cooking (good food provides great feedback). By the time she headed off to college, she had already checked to find that her dorm had a kitchen that students were welcome to use on occasion.

It's key to remember here that feedback won't work if it's meant to be punitive or vindictive. Instead, it needs to communicate that you are on your teens' side in helping them learn to meet the challenges of the adult world. To the extent that teens see feedback as reflecting their parents' efforts to control them, they have tremendous motivation and energy for battle. To the extent that they see feedback as relatively impersonal and objective—more like the locked door than the ranting parent—they are much more likely to respond calmly and pragmatically. Teens won't always do what parents want in these cases, but they will *always* be learning from their actions, which ultimately is the most important goal. The principle we draw from this is simple: *The best feedback comes not from parents but from the real world.*

REMOVING THE MIDDLEMAN

One of the easiest ways parents can depersonalize feedback is to remove themselves as intermediaries or filters between their teens and real-world feedback. For example, an all-too-familiar scenario for teens who underperform academically is the angry confrontation that follows when parents return from teacher-parent conferences. Teens hear their parents rail against their lack of effort, inconsistent performance on homework, and sloppy attitude toward their assignments. But having parents play the middleman in conveying this feedback has a number of negative effects: It dilutes the feedback, clouds it with the fog of conflicts from the parent-teen relationship, and makes the parents play the role of the heavy.

The alternative approach that we've found useful, and which follows both the adulthood principle and the real-world feedback principle, is having teens accompany parents to the parent-teacher conference. This approach has as many advantages as the regular parent-teacher conference has disadvantages. It eliminates all of the he-said-she-said arguments about what the teacher really meant or what the student's counterarguments might be, thus making the feedback more clear and immediate. It takes the parent out of the middleman role, making the feedback more objective.

This approach also has several additional advantages that reflect the value of entering the adult world directly, rather than through a parental proxy. As students learn exactly what's expected of them from their teachers, with nothing lost in the translation, they are put in the position of conferring with adults about their role and taking direct responsibility for it. They are in the classroom with these teachers every day, of course, but for many underperforming students, a meeting during a parent-teacher conference may be one of the few times they get one-on-one time with a teacher to review their progress. We've found these meetings often have the benefit of establishing a stronger relationship between student and teacher than can be formed in the daily whirl of the typical 25-to-one student-teacher-ratio classroom. (We also find that teachers generally appreciate this chance to communicate more directly and forcefully with their students so long as they are given a heads-up that the teenagers will be joining the meeting.) The operative principle here is that the parents are making sure their teens get as much feedback about their actions as possible, but directly from the larger world, rather than through the parental filter.

A family with whom we worked recently experienced a situation with their daughter, Nell, in which getting unfiltered feedback made a big difference. Nell had signed up to go on a weekend youth group trip to a camp about five hours from home. Two days before the trip she decided that she was tired, was going to have a hard time staying caught up in school, and would miss a Friday night party if she went on the trip. Nell's parents saw her predicament but were reluctant to have her back out at that late date, in part because they knew she tended to back out of things that were inconvenient. But rather than explaining to her (yet again) why it was important to keep commitments, they told her that if she negotiated it directly with Karen, the trip director and also a neighbor, she could handle the situation however she wanted.

Karen ended up letting Nell back out, but she did what many adults would hesitate to do—she gave Nell some very clear feedback. Karen let Nell know quite directly that the trip had been arranged for several weeks, there were a limited number of spaces, it cost money, that she herself had put a lot of effort into it, and at least one other student had been counting on Nell to go to make it more fun. In short, Nell got out of the trip, but ended up feeling rather guilty, as well she should, for letting others down. She now knew the costs of her actions, and the conversation with Karen, whom Nell liked, was uncomfortable. Contrast this with what would likely have happened if her parents had simply canceled the trip for her and all Nell experienced was another parental "nag" about how she should plan ahead better and follow through on her commitments.

WHEN EXPERIENCE HURTS AND TEACHES

Nell's experience brings us to a point that's intimately tied both to the feedback principle and to the Nurture Paradox: the growth-producing role of *negative* feedback. Adolescents can learn from what others tell them and they can learn from books and movies, but the most powerful learning comes from direct experience, and sometimes that experience hurts.

Psychologist Albert Bandura has spent a lifetime understanding how individuals learn an endless variety of new skills, and he's found that when comparing books, discussions, lectures, observation of others, and hands-on experience, experience wins every time. We can complain about teens not learning things simply by being told them, but adults appear to be little different in this regard.

My own father, for example, tried for years to quit smoking cigarettes after learning they were bad for him. But somehow the message of just how bad they were never sank in quite enough to overcome the urge for another smoke. But then, in a two-month period, his brother was diagnosed with and quickly succumbed to lung cancer. My father came home from his brother's funeral, threw away every cigarette in the house, and never seriously considered smoking again for the rest of his life. "I guess it just made it real to me," he once recounted sadly when I asked him about it. I've recalled my dad's experience whenever I've thought about the difference between what teens learn by hearing someone tell them something versus what they learn by actually experiencing it for themselves.

What, then, should we do when teens screw up in all the minor ways that adolescents often manage to screw up? We've consistently found that the ideal approach, the point on the compass toward which parents can always confidently point, is to treat those screwups as closely as possible to the way the larger world would treat them if an adult had screwed up in the same way.

For example, Sarah, a sixteen-year-old teen we worked with locally, consistently had trouble learning to get up in the morning. Over and over again she overslept for school. For years her parents had served as her alarm clock, dealt with her grouchy complaints, and driven her to school (even though they were often scurrying about themselves and certainly had better things to do with their time), berating her all the while for her laziness as she groggily stared out the window. Finally, after a bit of prompting from me, they tried a different plan. They told this good, if somewhat lazy, student that the next time she missed the bus they were going to stop "babying" her and just let her handle it on her own, like an adult would have to handle it.

"What do you mean?" she asked a bit suspiciously. "How am I supposed to get to school?"

"Well, if I needed to catch a bus because I didn't have a ride, and I missed it, I guess I would either walk or call a cab," her mom replied. The walk was about two miles and should take about thirty-five minutes, they told her. Or, a cab ride would probably cost fifteen dollars, given how far they lived from the school. They wanted Sarah to know her options, they said, but this only made her a bit more edgy. She quickly ended the conversation.

Nonetheless, a few mornings later the inevitable occurred and Sarah missed her bus.

"But I only missed it by a tiny bit . . . I could see it at the end of the street when I got to the corner! I think it even came early."

"Bummer," Sarah's mom said, and—this is important—she was able to mean it.

"But I've got a biology test today."

"Well, isn't biology just before lunch? If you start walking, you'll make it fairly easily."

Sarah was outraged, and slammed the door on her way out. Later that day she said the walk had taken closer to forty-five minutes and then she had to get a late pass and now she had to stay after school one day because she was late with no excuse.

"Can we help you figure out a way to have your alarm work better?" Sarah's dad asked. Sarah was in no mood for help, but overslept only once more in the next few weeks (and on that day was able to call a friend as soon as she awoke to get a ride).

She ended up oversleeping on occasion after that, but generally got up in time to get rides from friends. She also figured out that putting her clock/radio on the radio setting worked better than her alarm, especially if she turned the volume up all the way.

Part of the reason this approach worked is that Sarah's parents were able to put it into practice without seeming angry or punitive. *Dispassionately* mirroring the adult world is critical to having feedback work. "Letting teens suffer the consequences of their actions" can only work if it's not just a prettied-up way of saying, "I'm glad to see them get what's coming to them." One challenge for parents is to make the consequences of screwups objective enough that the parents can then be free to be on teens' side in lamenting those consequences and in strategizing (if asked) about ways of not screwing up in the future. The second challenge—and often the larger one, in our experience—is for parents to reliably follow through with these consequences. It's almost impossible to convince a teen that consequences are truly objective if parents help their teens circumvent them when they're in a good mood. Harmless as such "exceptions" may seem at the time, they make crystal clear to teens that consequences are far more likely to be imposed when parents are in a bad mood or annoyed with their teens, and hence depend on parents' mood as much as on their own behavior.

Yes, it makes parents tense (and we've held many parents' hands through this process) to watch their kids fail and feel the effects of that failure, particularly when they could relatively easily mitigate those effects. But over the years, we've learned that the real tension and fear should come not when teens fail, but when parents constantly change the rules of the game to help their teens avoid failing at all costs. How sad and ironic we find it to watch parents who would prefer to assure their children's happiness as teenagers, rather than let them use occasional failures to learn to manage their lives well as adults.

THE REAL RULES

Most parents would naturally like to save their teens some of this pain by simply telling them what the rules of the world are and how they work. Even if humans learned well this way, though, most teens have an instinctive and well-founded distrust about whether what they're told reflects how the world actually works. Perhaps surprisingly, the rules that adults *say* apply to a teen's world are often not the real ones. Let's look at a few examples.

"Don't be late." "Don't break the law." "Never cut corners." All of these rules seem simple and clear enough . . . until we try to apply them in practice. Don't be late applies well to high school classrooms, for example, but not so well to casual social events. Over the years, we've hosted undergraduate get-togethers in our home many times. Like most people, we try to prepare ahead, but nonetheless often find ourselves scrambling at the end. Many a grown-up dinner party we've hosted finds us scrambling to pull things together just a few minutes after the appointed hour . . . though by the time guests actually do show up, we're usually where we need to be. But we've found that it's different with undergraduates. The "don't be late" rule gets taken literally by at least a few, so that for the first few years, we were consistently nonplussed when small groups of undergrads would arrive ten to fifteen minutes *early* for our parties. They'd been told and "knew" not to be late!

We've seen teens stumble in the opposite direction as well. Professors running large lectures typically start two or three minutes after the appointed hour in order not to be disrupted by the late rush of students into the class. This works fine for class, but in our holiday travels, we've more than once seen a distraught college student standing in tears outside a closed gate at the airport, having arrived "just a minute" late for their flight, only to find the "don't be late" rule meant something quite different at the airport than at college!

The same principles apply to all sorts of supposedly clear-cut rules. "Don't break the law" is a strong, clear, and simple rule when it comes to bank robberies or muggings or even shoplifting. But the teen who never drives even a mile over the speed limit often finds drivers behind her honking and getting frustrated. The upshot of all this is that most teens have learned to take adults' stated rules with a grain of salt. Words mean little. Seeing, or better yet, acting, in the larger world and learning from its feedback is far more informative and trustworthy as a way to find out what the real rules are.

LOSS AND WISDOM

Inevitably, exposing our teens to real-world situations and challenges that stretch their capacities will also mean exposing them at times to truly significant failures and loss. We've somehow taken on the misconception that such failure is like a pathogen to be avoided at all costs. But this attitude harkens back to the Nurture Paradox, and even to the false belief that protecting our infants from all germs and allergens is the best way to raise them. Although overwhelming experiences of failure are indeed likely to be detrimental, failure and loss in moderate doses can serve not only as a profoundly powerful teacher and motivator, but also as an inoculant against the effects of future life stress.

Indeed, failure and the sense of loss that accompanies it are arguably among the greatest ultimate sources of wisdom about life. The much bemoaned adolescent sense of invulnerability, for example, may only ultimately give way—much like my father's cigarette habit—when people are confronted with the larger truth about life's limits. This confrontation can be brutally painful, as my father's experience made clear, but it is also a source of deep learning. It is striking, for example, how often individuals who have learned that they have long-term, terminal illnesses state that they see their illness as a blessing, in teaching them, as former Senator Paul Tsongas once put it in a valedictory address, that "life is finite, and living it well requires setting priorities." That's a lesson we probably can't teach our teens with lectures and discussions no matter how hard we try.

FORTUITOUS FAILURES

As I was working on this book, I had several meetings with the talented team of young graduate and undergraduate research assistants who do much of the day-to-day interviewing and data crunching that moves our research forward. Wanting to pick their brains, I asked them directly what experiences they felt had most helped them "grow up" or feel like they could handle the adult world. Their anecdotes and thoughts were so similar and so unexpected that they changed the way I thought about the role of failure in teens' lives, including my own teens.

As we went around the room describing the experiences that most helped these young people feel like adults, what they described over and over without prompting were instances of failure and setback. One student described overdrawing her checking account and being told by her parents she'd have to fix it herself. After an initial bout of panic, she ended up going around to all the various merchants where she'd written checks (U.Va. makes it easy for students to cash local checks) and straightening this out. She took out a loan from an emergency fund the university offers for these kinds of situations. And at the end of it all, she realized that she *could* handle these kinds of screwups herself. That it wasn't the end of the world. And that she was acting as an independent adult and solving her own problems. It was a good feeling.

Another student described having to deal with getting his car fixed after it broke down. He called his dad, but the response was, "Well, we're four hundred miles away, so you're just going to have to get it fixed yourself." Again, many small hurdles were surmounted. This student talked to friends until he got a recommendation for a good place to take the car. He found a towing company in the yellow pages. He arranged transportation to pick the car up at the shop. But after it was all done, he knew he could handle challenges like this. He discovered it wasn't even as hard as he thought it would be! It was more of an inconvenience.

Other examples spilled out. Missed appointments. Minor accidents. Lost cell phones. Ironically, what all of these seemingly negative experiences taught these young people was not just that problems in life occurred, especially following acts of carelessness, but that they could be managed and that *they* were relatively capable of managing them! Prior to experiencing these "failures," these highly talented young people described themselves as wandering around with an uneasy sense of vulnerability in the larger world and a nagging sense of continuing dependence upon their parents' almost magical abilities to swoop in and get them out of jams when necessary.

We fear our teens will struggle with these failures, but forget that young people, especially teenagers, are used to falling on their faces and learning from the experience. They fail numerous times each week. They look foolish in front of their peers. They fail as they try to learn new sports. They get tests back with disappointing grades. And they face losses, small and large. Cell phones and jackets, to be sure; but they also get their hearts broken as they fall head over heels in love, only to find their affections not returned. We move past all of this as adults and forget much of it, or block it out.

We then overestimate how much our teens suffer from failure and setback because we look at their failures through our eyes and not theirs. Worse yet, we try to protect them from precisely the experiences that will teach them the most. It can be excruciating to watch our teens fail, or even just to struggle on their own with tasks that we know we could make easier. Indeed, in our experience, it is almost impossible for parents to stop overnurturing their teens in such situations unless the parents are simultaneously developing their *own* independent lives and preparing for life after parenthood. Only then, when parents are busy enough to occasionally turn off the anxious spotlight they cast upon their teens' every sign of progress or failure, are teens likely to get the independence they need while learning from the occasional failure.

We fret about our teens' potential failures, but one of the traits we know that young people possess in abundance is resilience. As adults, falling on our faces, or losing something we want, is often a wrenching, painful, even traumatic experience. That can certainly be true for teens in extreme cases, but we've been struck by how differently they process the more minor setbacks in life than adults do. Teens' brain wiring no doubt comes into play here in a helpful way, as we discussed in Chapter 2. "They focus on the positive more than the negative," is how Aristotle summarized it. While it's true that sometimes failure brings little aside from pain, much of the time—especially when failure comes as part of learning to make it in the adult world—it provides the crucial feedback that our teens need to grow.

A colleague once remarked to me that there is nothing more motivating than feeling as if you are completely responsible for your life. We can't make our teens *completely* responsible for themselves within their adolescent worlds (in spite of what the poster in the trinkets shop suggested), but if we allow ourselves to move in that direction, we take a large step toward helping our teens make the transition from adolescence to adulthood.

Ending High School as We Know It

Schools, unless discipline were doubly strong,
Detain their adolescent charge too long.

—WILLIAM COWPER, 1785

Adolescents spend one-quarter of their waking hours in school, mostly in large classroom groups led by single teachers, yet we would be hard-pressed to find adolescents or adults who think the time is being particularly well spent. While a college education has become almost a required ticket for entry into a good job, many people don't realize that most of our teens actually drop out of the system well short of this basic goal. For every 100 students entering ninth grade each year, only 68 will graduate four years later with a regular diploma. That's startling and depressing to most people, but the numbers get even worse from there. Of that group, only 40 will go directly to college, and only 27 will still be in college the next year. Ultimately, only *18* of these initial 100 students will finish with an associate's degree within three years or a bachelor's degree within six. If we accept that at least a two-year college degree is going to be important to thriving in the workplace of the twenty-first century, then our current system is an abject failure for more then 80 percent of the teens moving through it!

Now, for some teens, family backgrounds and parental expectations will provide a significant push toward a college degree. Even in these cases, though, many find it hard not to get lost, sidetracked, or just demoralized along the way. Although we've worked with a fair number of teens locked in battle with their parents about school, it's the experiences of kids like Ray, who never wanted to battle anyone, that we've found the most disconcerting and, ultimately, the most informative.

RAY'S LESSON

Ray was a delight to most adults who met him. Slender-framed, pale-complexioned, and a bit shy beneath his shaggy blond hair, he almost always wore a warm, open smile. Even as an early teen Ray would cheerily carry his end of a conversation with most of the adults in his life. At home, he'd had his outbursts, but they were few and far between. Ray wasn't a star student, but had always worked hard and done well in school.

Until ninth grade. At first Ray's parents attributed the slippage in his grades to the tougher workload. But as Ray's friends seemed to adjust, he kept slipping, until this formerly B+ student was coasting along with just barely passing grades. In the midst of it all, Ray's disposition never changed. After each report card, he sheepishly acknowledged that he needed to work harder, and many long talks with his parents ended with his sincere promise to do just that. Each time, his parents let themselves feel some hope that the "old Ray" was back . . . until his next set of grades came in. Ray always said he "didn't know what had happened" and he guessed he hadn't worked hard enough. His teachers said it seemed as if he'd just stopped caring.

In some sense he had. For many kids, the pressures of the Endless Adolescence gradually sap motivation to keep on "preparing for the future." For Ray, these pressures also built gradually, but he could later recall the specific day and time when his motivation snapped. He had been asking his dad, a pediatrician, questions about college. Would he get into a good one? How did you pick a college? What was it like? He had long heard that starting in ninth grade, his report card mattered for college, and he was nervously gearing himself up for the long push to get into a good school.

Perhaps sensing his son's tension, Ray's dad tried to put things into perspective, "You know, Ray, a good college is important and all, but it's only just the start. Once you get to college, you need to get good grades there too. And for me, how I did after that in medical school was also really important. So it's not just all about college."

His dad's remark went off like a flashbulb in Ray's head, but not in the way his dad had intended. Ray suddenly realized that high school wasn't his one big chance to become well-situated for adulthood. He didn't have four years left, but *fourteen*! At least if he wanted a career like his dad's. Though Ray didn't let on, the thoughts in his head now came rapid-fire. How much was it going to matter when he was in his twenties if he learned about Charlemagne's reign tonight? If he pushed himself to get into a good college, wasn't that just going to make him have to work harder once he got there? Wasn't he getting old enough to start worrying about what *he* wanted, and not just what other people wanted him to do?

Ray never said a word of this to his dad, and so his father was left thinking he'd made his intended point that not everything in life rested on success in high school. Ray still wanted to work and do well, but found he just couldn't motivate himself like he used to. It was only many months later that the meaning of this conversation became clear to all involved. The problem, of course, was that Ray's dad couldn't take back what he said, because all of it was true. Ray's epiphany was more sudden than most, but the dawning, often implicit sense that the path out of adolescence leads through a seemingly endless array of irrelevant hoops takes its toll on most teens' academic motivation.

COLLEGE AS THE NEW HIGH SCHOOL

Even for the most motivated students, the sense of just jumping through hoops abounds. Almost all of the teens we've described in this book felt it to at least some degree. For the academic elite, the current college admissions frenzy epitomizes this problem, and the frenzy has become wild. Consultants multiply. Books on gaining admission proliferate. And top high school students compete with one another to pile on as many extracurricular activities as possible (in leadership positions, of course), not because they are intrinsically attracted to these activities, but because they want to win favor from college admissions officers. Alas, given current demographics, the ultimate Ivy League prizes in college admissions are open to only a tiny percentage of the three million or so students who finish high school each year.

But the real irony is that the top prizes don't even mean what we once thought, and the Endless Adolescence helps explain why. Research has now shown, for example, that after college, the graduates of elite Ivy League–type schools don't appear to fare any better than similarly qualified students who graduate from good state institutions. The top schools can select stronger students on average, who then do better later in life, but when we look at equally strong students who gained admission to top schools but chose instead to attend less-prestigious schools, the school prestige effect largely disappears. Whether we look at future income or at entry into prestigious graduate programs, the strong student from the weaker school does just about as well as a similar student from the most prestigious school.

Why don't strong schools have more of an impact on future outcomes? One of the explanations that seems most plausible is that as adolescence has lengthened, college has increasingly become the new high school. Consider how we used to think about the role of high school in one's future life. For most young people, going to a great versus a good high school, while advantageous, wouldn't be expected to make a major difference later. While stronger high schools clearly provide advantages, it is what a student does within those schools and after leaving them that really counts. For at least a generation we've recognized that high school, at least for the upwardly mobile, was just a way station on the road to something else.

Increasingly, the same has become true of college. As the period of education has become extended for the highest achievers, coming from a strong college is useful mainly to the extent it helps gain entry into a good graduate or professional program, or a good entry-level job in business. But such entry is typically open to students from all sorts of colleges, provided they've done well while they were there. Where one went to graduate school will matter far more for the most accomplished than where one went to college. And mostly it's what a young person does after finishing his or her education that makes the difference in a career. And that's often years later, as even Ray realized.

This message should be reassuring to parents and high school students facing the college admissions frenzy. But it also carries within it an important cautionary note: Bending over backward to get one's child into a good college will not matter nearly as much as preparing them to function independently and to thrive once they are there. Certainly the college admissions process is important enough and new enough to the teens who are stressed by it that some parental hand-holding is warranted. But ultimately this process provides just one more opportunity to let our teens learn about challenge and feedback and the effects of their own actions.

We've known many adults who say they "blew it" in high school and went to a lower-tier college as a result, but learned from there and went on to thrive after that. When we see U.S. presidential candidates describing cocaine use during their teenage years or ranking near the bottom of a college class, it becomes clear that *entry* into college is but a tiny step and not a surefire marker of future success (or future mediocrity). Rather, learning to live and act in a mature fashion as an adult will matter for our teens long after the college admissions frenzy ends. The simple message for parents from this: *Relax* a bit about the college admissions process, and *refocus* your efforts on your teen learning to take responsibility for his or her own education, and not just relying on parents to help, prod, and steer them toward getting into the best possible school.

But that's about the college years. If college has indeed become the new high school, what does this say about what's going on in high school and its relevance to teens' future lives? The problems, as we'll see, pop up consistently across the board, from the most remedial to the most advanced classes and students.

$6X^2 - 2X - 20$

If we take a look at what's going on inside high school classrooms, the reactions of teens like Ray come to seem quite understandable. Recently I was watching a videotape of a teacher trying to explain to his remedial algebra class how to factor quadratic equations like the one above. Many of these kids were taking the class a second time, having failed it previously, but needing it to graduate. I was working with colleagues to think about how this teacher could best motivate his clearly disengaged students when the teacher's real problem hit me.

$6x^2 - 2x - 20$?

This problem didn't have any current meaning or relevance to his students. And for at least ninety-five percent of them, it *never* would. They would never use this material, would never again care about it once they left this class, and in all likelihood would promptly forget it. They might as well have been told that learning ancient Sanskrit was a key to their graduating from high school. We'd wager that most of you reading this book will struggle to factor this equation within the minute or so these students are given on a typical test, and that this "deficiency" doesn't cost you anything in your daily lives. Indeed, even living in a college town, we know few adults who actually factor quadratic equations as part of their work. Yet we make quadratic equations a hurdle for all teens to move successfully into adulthood. The kids in this class may not have been the most academically gifted, but they were smart enough to know they were being asked to jump through hoops that weren't preparing them for anything.

The problem of the irrelevance of what's being taught in school isn't limited to those who struggle academically, as Ray realized. Much of what schools try to teach has only very minimal apparent importance to teens' future lives, other than as hurdles that (for reasons teens find hard to fathom) they need to overcome to someday get good jobs. Yet we ask them to learn this seemingly obscure material in incredible detail. Important generals in the War of 1812. The precise role of ADP in the energy chain of cells. Synthetic division. Whatever the value of a broad education and cultural capital—and learning for learning's sake—it's clear that if most adults not only don't routinely use this information but don't even *recall* it, then teens are right to at least question its relevance to their lives.

It is unclear whether school has ever been particularly engaging for students (witness the quote at the outset of this chapter from the year 1785). What is different now, though, is not only that school goes on longer than it used to, but that the cost of doing poorly, of *not* going on in school, has gone up dramatically over time. Those who drop out of the educational process early, and thus try to escape the Endless Adolescence, often find themselves foreclosed from the kinds of jobs that provide real entrée into adulthood.

YOU CAN LEAD A KID TO TEACHERS

None of this is at all to deny the value of a generalist education, especially in a fast-changing, information-driven society. Even knowledge that isn't directly useful often trains the brain in other ways, not to mention carrying a certain aesthetic and cultural value of its own to many people, *if* they put in the effort to master it. But knowledge can't be force-fed. And while exposure to the higher learning of a culture seems an unarguable good, much of the exposure schools provide occurs only on paper and in theory, not in reality.

Given how many students drop out, and how many others hang in there with decreasing enthusiasm over time just to obtain a diploma, we need to recognize that lofty cultural goals for a generalist education aren't going to be realized with just stricter standards or more tests. I've even had a number of talented U.Va. students describe their high school years as a waste. As one put it, "I didn't learn anything in my classes. I just crammed the night before a test, took the test, then forgot it all by the next day."

In some ways it seems like the ultimate *adult* intellectual laziness to design a secondary school curriculum based only on a hypothetical vision of the knowledge one should ultimately acquire across a lifetime, without considering what adolescents are most and least primed to absorb during this phase of their lives. Teens have incredible capacities to learn complex material *that they care about*, whether it's mastering online games, athletic trivia, or even music or politics, but they need to be engaged in order to put these capacities to use. We can argue over the relative merits of core curricula, cultural capital, or high-stakes testing, but if we have no way to engage and motivate teens in that learning, then these arguments are for naught. As Ray's story shows all too well, you can lead a kid to teachers, but you can't make him think. What you can do, though, is alienate him from the educational process.

CHANGING THE CLASSROOM AS WE KNOW IT

If we've made the case that substantial changes are worth considering in our flawed educational system, then the principles outlined in this book can help us start to change the way education unfolds for adolescents, both in small ways and in large, from changing high school classrooms to changing the way parents interact with their teens around school.

Working together with my partner, Bob Pianta, dean of the Curry School of Education at the University of Virginia, we've begun a $1.25-million project funded by the William T. Grant Foundation that tests some of the ideas we've been putting forth. The project, ongoing in ninety classrooms spread across half a dozen different school districts serving a wide range of students, is designed to change the secondary school classroom in order to improve students' engagement, motivation, and ultimately their academic performance. The program builds on a high-tech, collaborative approach for working with teachers called "My

Teaching Partner," which Bob and his colleagues previously developed for the elementary grades.

Our goal was to use this collaborative approach to put into practice what we've been learning about the unique needs of adolescents in the classroom. We took the principles we've outlined thus far—about teens' need for connection, exposure to challenge and feedback, and a sense of how their efforts are linked to what goes on in the adult world—and applied them in settings where we could carefully measure the results. As such, this project provides a great acid test of the principles we've been discussing, and does so in one of the most stressful and important environments in teens' lives.

FEEDBACK FROM REAL EYES

We've already described some of the ways in which the high school classroom offers only delayed and poor-quality feedback to students. Part of our effort in My Teaching Partner goes into increasing the quality of the daily feedback teachers give students in the classroom. One of the joys of this project, in which we observe videotapes of all manner of teachers repeatedly over the course of a school year, is that it lets us learn from some of the most effective teachers we observe—teachers who have intuitively learned to implement the principles we describe. They've provided some great approaches for offering feedback to spark immediate interest on the part of students.

For example, one of the high school teachers with whom we work described a simple intervention she made with one of her writing classes to remarkable effect. As the end of the school year approached and the students' final writing project loomed, this teacher dropped a small bombshell into her class. She was going to exchange favors with a friend who was a professional writer: While the teacher did some editing work for the writer, the writer was going to read and evaluate each of the students' final papers as he would a written project that came across his desk. The students were instantly intrigued, curious, and more than a bit intimidated by this upcoming brush with the adult world. Was their work good enough? Would this person judge them harshly? Some of the best students hoped that their work just might stand up well under real-world scrutiny. This led to several intense class discussions about just what kind of writing actually did fare well in the adult world. The essays, when they came in at the end of the year, were the best this teacher had ever seen. A number of parents remarked on how motivated their students were by the assignment. The students, having gotten a chance at real feedback about how their work might fare in the world of adulthood, had responded accordingly.

English teachers across the country are gradually catching on to a similar though less dramatic approach to motivating students' writing: the peer-supervision group. The idea is simple: All student writing is passed around within a small group of peers who comment on each draft's strengths and weaknesses. It's a small change, and one that partly saves teachers some of the tedium of commenting on obvious errors. But done well, it has a much more profound effect on motivation, since students are now writing for an *audience.* Of course, in order for this approach to work, teachers must instill in the teens the recognition that they can contribute, in adultlike fashion, to advancing one another's writing skills. This approach doesn't just help the student whose writing is being critiqued, it helps the peer critics as well, who come to see themselves as contributors, and to think about writing in a different way.

Parents, too, can play a role by looking for opportunities for their teens to get feedback for their work from outside the school building. Writing contests, letters to the editors of local papers, volunteer work that uses developing skills, and even showing good work to relatives can all make at least a bit of an impact.

ADULTS ON BOTH SIDES OF THE DESK

We've also worked with and learned from teachers who are gifted at forming connections with their students. Not with one-of-a-kind heroics, but with simple courtesies and interest. For example, one teacher begins class each year by having students pair off to talk for a bit, then asks each student to introduce the other to the class, providing at least

206 · Escaping the Endless Adolescence

five relevant facts about the other student. This is a fairly typical group-building exercise, but what this teacher does that makes it different is that she furiously takes notes as the kids are being introduced. She then learns a bit about every student, commits it to memory, and uses it routinely to connect with students in the weeks that follow.

We've seen this same teacher handle students not being prepared in early classes by confronting them with direct, forceful, and immediate feedback. "You *will* do the reading each night in this class. It's the only way we can work together. It has to happen." And while either the attention to personal details or the forceful and confrontational feedback alone might do little, the combination consistently gets results in an approach that we're now teaching to other teachers. In some ways this teacher has replicated the Manchester Men's Shop approach we described in Chapter 5 of making clear she cares about her students while demanding nothing less than their best efforts. Students, sensing an adult who cares and notices, tend to respond.

We also find that teachers form their best connections with students when they are focused upon drawing out the student's inner adult. In conveying this to teachers, we ask them to recall their best and worst teachers from their own adolescence. We then ask them about the characteristics of these teachers, and find some remarkable consistency in the answers. Almost universally, the best teachers are remembered as treating their students as a bit older than they actually were. It's the teacher in ninth grade who says, "Ladies and gentlemen" to start the class (and means it) and who tells students they'll be given assignments that require them to work at a higher level than they've ever done before (and also means it). Conversely, some of the least-effective teachers do just the opposite. "Boys and girls," I can still recall one high school teacher beginning a class of mine that she never successfully managed to control.

Teens have an innate radar for adults who are working to pull them toward greater maturity. It's partly the language the adults use and how they frame their actions, but those are just the outward signs. The best teachers already see the inner adult in teens. They don't see themselves so much trying to lead kids into adulthood, as simply trying to help already fledgling adults make their way in the world as effectively as possible. And year after year these teachers bring out the very best in their students.

A BIAS FOR ACTION

Some of the simplest interventions we introduce into classrooms come from recognizing that adolescents' bodies simply aren't designed for sitting endlessly, engaging in no activity more strenuous than taking notes. Like drivers of high-performance cars stuck in city traffic, most teens feel a strong urge to step on the gas occasionally. The best teachers take advantage of this energy. They have kids move their desks around, gather into groups, display projects, and build things. As we've worked with new teachers around these principles, though, we've had to reassure them that this wouldn't just become a drain on productive classroom time. Quite the opposite, we've found that a bit of structured movement throughout almost every class significantly increases the degree to which students remain engaged for the entire period. Yes, kids can be forced to sit passively through forty-seven-minute lecture after forty-seven-minute lecture. But sitting passively isn't the same thing as learning. If we go beyond simply leading kids into classrooms to sit passively, their natural desire to learn occasionally gets the chance to take over.

Although parents are unlikely to change the nature of what takes place within high school classrooms (other than by giving teachers a copy of this book!), they can at least work to see that teens' bias for action gets addressed outside of school. All too often the inertia and passivity of the school day carry over at home as teens plop themselves in front of the TV, Internet, or Xbox. "Getting them moving" isn't just a figurative prescription, but a literal one. This prescription was second nature to parents just a few generations back, but seems to have been lost of late. Almost any activity can help break the stupor, but the more enjoyable and engaging, the better. The list of options is by and large obvious, ranging from team sports to active work to just shooting a basketball. Teens are built for physical activity, and with enough of it, will function better in all areas of life. Schools may ignore this, but that only increases the urgency for parents to make the push. In our experience, students who have a real chance to expend their energies in at least some venue in their lives—whether connected with school or not—are far more able to tolerate the enforced passivity that much of the school day brings.

IN SEARCH OF RELEVANCE

And then finally we get to our toughest challenge, given the current structure of our educational system: How do we make what happens in the classroom seem relevant to teens' lives? The question itself illustrates the problem: What does it say about the material we're teaching our teens that making this material *seem* relevant becomes such a challenging task?

In the second half of this chapter we'll get to some more extreme solutions that go directly to the heart of the problem. But even within our current system, it turns out that teens are willing to work hard to absorb material with only tangential relevance to their lives *if* we can at least make a nod in the direction of their interests and inclinations. Relevance doesn't mean that what is taught in school must be something teens can turn around and use the following weekend; they simply crave some sense that the knowledge they're trying to absorb can be connected in *some* meaningful way to their current or future lives.

One U. S. history teacher, for example, faced with the challenge of engaging her students in learning about the post–World War I period (not the most intrinsically fascinating time for most students), approached it as follows:

"Okay, so imagine you've had a big end-of-year standardized test and you've been slogging through studying for it for weeks and then you take it, and it's incredibly long and hard and painful. How do you feel at the end of it?"

"Exhausted. Shot. Worn-out," the chorus replies.

"That's the United States after it made it through World War One," the teacher notes. She then goes on, "Okay, so what do you want to do?"

"Party!" says one student, and others quickly join in the cry.

"Okay, so you enter the Roaring Twenties and it's party time. Then you party and party and party all night. Then what happens?"

"You crash!" they said, as if the answer had been planted. And so these students now had a way of understanding and remembering the period leading up to the Great Depression. They were introduced to the intriguing notion that maybe adults at times acted in the same irresponsible ways that they did. Even if it was just an analogy, the students could now make the connection between what they were learning and real experiences in their own lives. The course came alive.

We've seen another world history teacher require her students to watch the news or read about current events every single day as part of the class homework. Her explanation? "The *only* reason to learn anything about world history is because it helps us understand what's going on today."

I still clearly recall my first-year college faculty advisor telling me that if I was going to take French in college, I should only do so if I could do it with the expectation that I was going to go to France and *use* what I was learning at some point. I'd never even considered going to France before that conversation, but realized the idea had some appeal; I decided I would in fact plan to go to France someday. This simple change in my thinking increased my motivation significantly as I worked through the tedium of drills and vocabulary over the following year.

Mathematics is one of the trickier subjects to tackle if our goal is to have students understand the relevance of what they're being asked to learn. Unfortunately, many of the well-intentioned efforts that have been made to make such material relevant to students can only be described as rather lame. For example, for decades math teachers have been explaining the applied principles of geometry by telling students to imagine that they were putting a ladder against a wall at a sixty-degree angle, and asking how long the ladder would have to be to reach up twenty feet. To which most students reply (either directly, or under their breath), "I don't care about ladders against a wall, and if I ever do, I'll just lean it up and see if it's long enough!"

In contrast, we've seen teachers bring architects and engineers into their classrooms at various points—not to describe, for instance, exactly how they employ sines and cosines in their work, but to show pictures of what one can do if one knows how to employ them. Elegant suspension bridges, clever electronic gadgets, beautiful buildings. These can grab kids' imaginations. They are real, and obviously useful in the adult world. Teens are indeed capable of making some inferential leaps in finding the relevance of what they're doing if we at least make an effort to assist them.

GETTING THEIR EYES ON THE PRIZE

What some of the best teachers in America do, parents can also do. Parents can and should be looking constantly for ways to show their teens the relevance of what they are learning. Finding and bringing home a foreign-language newspaper. Engaging teens in conversations with other adults whose careers require knowledge learned in high school. Even for teens like Ray, there are ways to get across the idea that working hard now will have payoffs that come sooner than a decade in the future. Making the idea of attending college more real and less abstract is one place to start.

Recently, for example, we were traveling near a college that seemed like a great potential institution for one of our children to attend someday, and even though college was still a ways off (our oldest two were in the eighth and tenth grades at the time) we stopped by for a visit. The college was beautiful, but it was our kids' reaction that we most appreciated. They thought the school seemed really cool, and now had something concrete and positive that they *wanted* to work for. While most teens at least suspect that the goal of "getting into a good college" is a reasonable one, when it's put only in that abstract way, it provides pretty thin gruel for motivation at ten o'clock on a Tuesday night, sitting in front of a long list of geometry problems. Making the goal more vivid and three-dimensional, even in a small way, provided our children with a motivational boost at least in the short-term, though they were years away from college. Even if our adolescents are stuck in a world that is largely frustrating, showing them concretely where that world is leading at least gives them something to hang on to.

The other principles we've outlined thus far in this book also can go a ways toward helping teens see the relevance of their education. For instance, taking on tasks at a volunteer level—as Tonya did in the child-care center as part of her work in the Teen Outreach program—can help teens see the educational requirements needed to take these tasks on at a higher level of adult employment. Helping teens form close enough relationships with adults so conversations can occasionally take place about real jobs those adults hold can also be a great help. As adults, this is a two-way street. We need to not only look for other adults who can educate our teens, but to seek ways we can engage teens from other families in conversations and relationships that begin to transmit such knowledge. Ultimately, contact with the world of adult work—where education actually gets used—is the best way to show teens the relevance of this education.

Similarly, at the other end of adolescence, a graduate student of mine described a small epiphany she had her junior year in college when she worked abroad as an exchange student. By her own description, much of her first two years of college were spent goofing off, but then in her junior year in Costa Rica, she found people asking her to perform research and writing tasks that she felt ill-equipped to handle. "But you've been to college for two years. We assumed you could handle this," her supervisor gently scolded. And then it suddenly hit her, that "I'd better be learning something in my time at college because when I get out, people are going to assume I can handle all sorts of tasks and I need to be ready."

For all of their complaining, our teens are often remarkably good sports about diving into the material we put before them. And while it is worth recognizing that the examples above barely make a dent in the larger relevance problem, for many teens even a small dent makes a difference. Even within the framework of the current high school system, we're finding that putting together these various pieces—connection, relevance, feedback, and action—has a real impact. Our intervention experiment and study are still ongoing, but in our early results, we're already seeing significant, measurable improvements in students' motivation, engagement, and sense of academic efficacy in the classrooms of teachers who participate in the program.

BEYOND HIGH SCHOOL

While working to help teachers in high school classrooms may be the most practical, immediate approach to helping today's students (and practical, immediate help is certainly desperately needed), the effort brings with it an inherent frustration. We can work hard to enhance the sense of feedback, connection, challenge, and relevance students experience within classrooms, but feedback is still mainly about grades of questionable long-term import, connections are limited by student-teacher ratios, challenges are inevitably partly manufactured, and relevance comes from analogies, occasional guest lectures, and visions of even more education in the future. How do we tackle this larger problem?

There are some radical options we think should be considered. We raise these not because we are naive enough to think these options would be easy to implement on a large scale—or wouldn't bring new problems of their own—but to make clear that there is a universe of possibilities available for restructuring and enhancing adolescents' lives, and it may be that only by considering the extremes will we gain a sense of just how vast the opportunity (and the need) for change truly is.

THE AMISH LESSON

I was in my first year at Yale Law School when I first came across the idea that we might be able to structure education for teens differently than we currently do. I was taking the required Constitutional Law class and found my interest piqued while reading a famous Supreme Court decision, *Wisconsin v. Yoder*, involving the rights of the Amish people. I am one-fourth Amish myself, and Yoder is actually the surname of my Amish relatives, which made the case that much more interesting and relevant to me. The case was about religious freedom, education, and parental rights, but what particularly caught my attention was the specific Amish approach to education upon which the case turned.

The Amish educate their children intensively, and, by most people's standards, quite well, up through eighth grade. Most would argue that they continue to do so quite well afterward, but *not* through traditional schooling. At the age when most teens in the United States are entering high school, the typical Amish teen spends most of his or her days not in school, but working with other adults in the community. The Amish reasoning is that they want their teenagers—in the years when their values are crystallizing—to be socialized not by other teens running in packs, but by adults.

Do these teens miss out on some things educationally? Undoubtedly—that was, after all, the reason for the Supreme Court battle (although given how badly our educational system fails so many teens, the loss of a few years of traditional high school may not be as great a loss as it seems). But there also seems to be little question that Amish teens also gain something in maturity and socialization through this system. We think the Amish have something to teach the rest of us. Not that we should necessarily replicate their approach, but that it is possible to approach schooling for adolescents in ways radically different from our current approach, and still end up with reasonable outcomes. The Supreme Court ultimately ruled in favor of the Amish, in part concluding that they educated their teens as well as a few more years of mandatory high school would have. Perhaps, however, we can have it both ways—educating our children for the technology of the twenty-first century while also spurring their movement into adulthood. Let's take a look at just how we might do that.

AN EARLY LAUNCH

What if high school weren't just about putting in "seat time" until one had put in enough years to graduate, but about crossing milestones *in terms of what's learned*, and then moving on to something else as soon as those milestones were crossed? A group sponsored by the National Center on Education and the Economy has proposed just that. At first glance this principle seems benign and sensible enough, and not that different from current practices. But imagine the practical application of such an idea: If high school was about accomplishing specific goals and moving on, rather than putting in time, then once the goals were reached, there should be no need to remain in high school. Might motivation be different if students were actually trying to achieve a goal so they could move on, rather than put in a fixed number of years in place? The commission's suggestion for implementing this principle: a set of comprehensive "gateway" exams. We might call them "Get Out of High School" tickets. The key: Learn enough to pass these exams and you can immediately move on beyond the constraining world of bathroom passes, befuddled substitutes, overcrowded hallways, bored teachers, and loudspeaker announcements.

What do you move on to do in this scenario? It depends. In the commission's vision, academically motivated students could get a head start on traditional postsecondary education. Yes, we would need to enhance and modify our postsecondary system to accommodate them. Community colleges, for example, might get a jolt of energy from an influx of advanced young students looking to use these colleges as a springboard toward eventually pursuing advanced degrees.

Less academically inclined students could move into strong vocational/technical programs. Not just in traditional areas such as auto mechanics and bricklaying, but in high-tech areas such as software engineering, Web design, and the like—vocations that are in demand in the modern workplace yet receive minimal attention within our current educational system.

But the biggest change would be in what happens during the time teens are in high school. They would no longer be simply earning "six letters on a sheet of paper" (as Perry described it in Chapter 1). Instead, they would be working to get out and move on with their lives. The students who hated high school the most would have the greatest incentive to work to get out quickly. Students who did not pass exams on a given try would be able to retake them frequently, and would know exactly what they needed to learn in order to pass in the future.

And those students who did get out early would face entry into adultlike choices: selecting curricula to pursue, managing greater independence, choosing courses based on their relevance to their future adult lives. Yes, there would be limits. The value of a solid grounding in the basics and in cultural literacy would remain, but the options open would be much more like what we provide to college students than the typical high school curriculum.

The commission estimates that, with other changes to our educational system at earlier points in students' careers, three percent of ninth graders, sixty-five percent of tenth graders, and ninety percent of eleventh graders might someday meet these standards and be able to leave high school early. Even if these numbers are overly optimistic, it seems likely that we could bring about a significant change in education for large numbers of teenagers with an approach such as this. This idea seems radical, and no doubt would bring on other difficulties and challenges—whether in deciding just what level and type of testing would be required to leave high school, or in providing scaffolding for youths not ready to make the leap to even a modified college environment at sixteen. But when we compare these problems to the "leaky pipeline" of our current educational system, which tries to keep all students in high school for four years regardless of how much (or little) they may be learning, there's less to lose than we might think.

This is all more than just an interesting intellectual exercise. One bit of evidence that it might be a viable real-world solution is the endorsement of the idea by the highly respected members of the commission, including Joel Klein, former chancellor of the New York City public schools, and former U.S. senator Bill Brock. But the more serious evidence that we haven't lost our bearings in pushing this idea comes from the fact that a variant of it is *already* being pursued successfully in several fascinating programs around the country.

BARD COLLEGE

Bard College at Simon's Rock has been a unique institution in American higher education since its founding as Simon's Rock College by Elizabeth Blodgett Hall in 1964. One of its most unique features is that it admits students to its college curriculum as early as the completion of tenth grade. These highly motivated students are then able to take a regular college curriculum in the following two years, and by the time they would have completed high school, typically have an associate's degree and two years of credits toward a regular four-year college degree. They can then either continue at Simon's Rock for their full four-year degree or transfer to another more traditional four-year college.

Students leaving home and asked to begin acting like college students as early as eleventh grade?! This surprises and alarms some parents. A little reflection, however, reveals that Simon's Rock "freshmen" aren't quite as young as they first seem.

Over the years, many school systems have changed birth date requirements so that students begin kindergarten (and hence all subsequent grades) at ages that are three to four months older now than they were just a generation ago. Further, parents now routinely hold their children back from school entry if they're on the margins of these age cutoffs or if they seem at all immature, which again delays entry into all subsequent grades. The result is that students at Simon's Rock are in fact only starting college something closer to a year and a half earlier in terms of chronological age than students used to. We then add to this the fact that students today almost all began their formal education with a year of kindergarten (which has become the norm only within the past generation), and we realize that those finishing tenth grade now have eleven years of schoolwork, not ten, under their belts. In addition, means of communication with parents (and thus the ability to get support from parents at a distance) have all improved dramatically.

Put all these factors together, and, arguably, Bard College isn't so much moving kids off to precocious independence and challenge compared to prior generations as it's swimming upstream to give kids *at least as much* independence and challenge as previous generations experienced at similar points in their development. More persuasive than all of these arguments, though, is the history of the college, which shows just how viable this system can be.

Recently, for example, Bard opened a Manhattan campus, the Bard High School Early College. It comes without the residential features of a traditional four-year college, but with the same goal of giving students two years of college credit by the time they complete high school. Though the program began only in June 2001, it has been a stunning success thus far. In the most recent year for which statistics were available, 4,000 students applied for 148 spaces in the school! This means that a high school that ends high school as we know it and successfully helps kids move more quickly through adolescence is so attractive, it can be more selective than Harvard and Yale!

So there's good evidence that letting our more-qualified teens skip much of the mind-numbing high school experience and move more quickly into adulthood is not just a pipe dream. But the Endless Adolescence is a disaster for teens at both ends of the socioeconomic spectrum. What about the teens who are at great risk to not even escape from high school in twelve years with a degree? If the ideas we've put forth in this book are correct, shouldn't they be at least as likely to benefit from changes in the educational system designed to move them toward adult-level academic competence more quickly?

A COLLEGE DROPOUT PREVENTING HIGH SCHOOL DROPOUTS

Perhaps addressing the needs of youth most at risk of dropping out requires the perspective and wisdom of someone who so understood adolescent impatience with school that he himself dropped out of college to become self-employed. Enter Bill Gates. Or more precisely, the Bill and Melinda Gates Foundation. In 2002 the Gates family, through their foundation, launched a program called the Early College High School Initiative. Unlike Bard College, and other similar programs like it that have been developed around the country, the Early College High School Initiative is targeted directly at those young people most likely to struggle to complete high school. Based on the most recent available data for the program from the 2006-2007 school year, most of the students being served were poor (sixty percent qualified for a free or reduced-cost student lunch program that targets low-income students), were disproportionately members of minority groups, and had unimpressive records of academic achievement when they began the program. Overall, they were about as far from a highly selected, Ivy League–bound group of teens as one could get.

Even still, and remarkably, the goals for these at-risk students were much the same as those for Bard College students: to make it to the end of their high school years with two years' worth of college credits. At each program site, a high school is teamed with a college to serve this difficult population. The program explicitly utilizes many of the adulthood-focused principles we've discussed in this chapter and in this book, including: building strong relationships with adults; directly establishing for students the relevance of what they are learning; and setting rigorous standards with constant feedback and high expectations for adult-level work. The program provides a great deal of support and scaffolding for students, but it also challenges them. Students are typically integrated into regular college courses with other high school graduates. In some instances they have struggled; in many, though, college professors have found themselves unable to distinguish these students from traditional college students. In a few instances these students are "blowing some pants off," as one college professor put it.

These schools, now serving more than 20,000 students in twenty-four states, have strikingly high attendance rates. More important, as the first cohort of students graduated, eighty percent moved on to four-year colleges, and eighty-five percent had between thirty and sixty college credits upon graduation. The program appears to cost somewhat more per enrolled pupil, but significantly less per *graduating* pupil! And this is without even factoring in any of the savings in college costs.

Attendance rates of eighty percent at four-year colleges for students who would typically find it difficult to graduate from high school? The incredible magnitude of these results is strikingly reminiscent of the Teen Outreach program findings we considered in Chapter 5. What both programs share is that they achieve results that seem truly remarkable from approaches that focus on moving teens toward contact with adults and adulthood more quickly. From this perspective, these results are not necessarily so surprising.

These findings could be taken as an indictment of our current educational system, but more relevant for our purposes, they illustrate the power that can be harnessed by making even modest changes to the environments that have supported the Endless Adolescence. Obviously, there are many formidable hurdles to overcome to implement programs such as these more widely. Not all students live near colleges. High schools currently also serve as athletic, social, and extracurricular hubs, and the need for these functions would not disappear. Colleges would undoubtedly find it hard to ramp up to handle an influx of sixteen- and seventeen-year-olds. The more-incremental approaches we're currently pursuing in our classroom-based research may serve as a way to bridge some of this gap. But even more-radical programs, like those we've been describing, can serve to orient not only our educational efforts, but also our thinking about adolescent development more generally. For interventions such as these provide powerful clues as to just how much potential is currently lying fallow in the fields of the Endless Adolescence.

Water for the Thirsty

In this book we've argued that adolescence can and must be restructured in fundamental ways and that this call for change is neither a naive wish nor just another ivory tower theory. Far from it. It's a powerful idea that's already being proven on the ground, from volunteer programs to redesigned high schools, and from years of work with our patients to countless experiences with friends, neighbors, and even the teenagers in our own family. Formal programs such as Teen Outreach and the Early College High School Initiative provide glimpses of just how dramatically we can change teens' lives, but the approach we outline doesn't require formal programs. The changes that are needed can begin in almost every interaction we have with teens, and they can begin today.

We've outlined some of the many routes by which we can bring adolescents into adulthood more successfully. We see these primarily as jumping-off points, though, which we hope can inspire others to discover and create additional routes by which to move our youth toward maturity. The essential ideas we've outlined are not complex, but they are also not obvious, and we've found it helpful in explaining them to parents to boil them down into the following five simple principles to guide our efforts:

1. *Include them.* If we want our teens to gain a sense of what the adult world requires and rewards, we need to give them the chance to participate in it, whether through volunteer activities or the right kind of paid employment. As might also be true with our metaphorical foreign visitor living in our home, if we want to make our teens at home in adult society, we need to give them not just a place at the table at dinner, but a task in the kitchen where they can help out and truly become a part of the adult world.

2. *Go with the flow* by building on the strong current of healthy, adulthood-seeking motives in teens' behavior. The view of teens as irrational, hormone-crazed creatures not only flies in the face of much of what we're learning about adolescent development, it actually undermines this development. In recognizing teens' autonomy strivings as a positive force in moving them into adulthood, rather than a threat to be countered, we become their allies in helping them grow up. They'll need some support—or scaffolding—to make the leap into adulthood, but we consistently find teens more than eager to make that leap.

3. *Connect, connect, connect.* Teens may not appear to want adult connections, but they desperately need them, provided the connections don't just move them back into a childlike role. It takes emotional resilience for parents and other adults to keep offering adult connection in the face of apparent rebuff and disinterest, but the reward, if we can be patient, is well worth it as we slowly build mature adult relationships that can last and grow over a lifetime— and help our youth grow up in the process.

4. *Ramp up the challenge.* Adolescence is potential energy waiting to be engaged. We need to move beyond the Nurture Paradox and the idea that doing things for our teens or giving them more gadgets, activities, or lessons has much to do with helping them grow up. Rather, what they need and want is challenge: tasks just beyond their current level of competence and comfort that leave them feeling more adultlike after they've been mastered. Fortunately, the challenges are all around. What's on your to-do list that your teen could do for him- or herself? Move it from your column to his or hers.

5. *Give it to them straight.* Teens thrive on feedback from the adult world. Engaging in the adult world in real ways—from the rigors of adult work to the rewards of adult relationships—can easily provide this feedback as long as we don't step in to shield teens from unpleasant aspects of the feedback they might receive. Failure, setback, and loss—these aren't just unavoidable problems our teens will have to face, but teachers from which our teens can learn much.

Together, these principles and the routes they suggest can not only move teens more quickly toward adult responsibilities, but also provide them with the fundamental nutrients—the adult connections and the adult rewards of autonomy, competence, and mastery—that have been missing from their diets for too long.

ADEQUATE NUTRITION

In our experience, some teens' diets are deficient in just a few of these nutrients, but for others—like Perry, the young anorexic boy we described at the outset of this book—almost all are lacking. Helping young people like Perry often means addressing several deficiencies at once. But his story provides a nice illustration of how even a few modest strategic changes—working in tandem with a teen's innate desire to move toward greater maturity—can often be enough to help even very troubled young teens begin to spring back to life.

Though it took much persuading and reassuring, Perry's parents eventually allowed him the freedom to ride his bike to the local tennis courts to hit a ball against a wall for practice each summer morning. This small step led to a fortuitous cascade of events after Perry one day encountered a neighbor there teaching nine- and ten-year-olds in a summer tennis program. The neighbor saw him hitting the ball alone and asked if he might like to volley with some of the kids. Perry said sure, and was paired with a quiet, talented young boy who berated himself harshly after every missed shot. Perry had no trouble empathizing and being supportive, and turned out to be a great and encouraging "coach" that morning.

He made sure to return at the same time the next day, and was asked to help out again, and then the day after, and the day after that, and ended up serving as an informal junior coach in the program. The kids loved Perry and even argued over who would get to hit with him (though he was also asked a few times why he was so skinny). His long summer mornings of monotonous boredom at home had now been replaced with a new refrain. "I'm running late, gotta go!" he'd yell to his parents just after breakfast each morning as he hopped on his bike to head to the courts. Perry's sense of urgency didn't so much reflect the heavy pressure he'd always known, however, but rather a new and unfamiliar feeling: eagerness.

Perry's dad also got him a "job" volunteering a few hours a week that summer with a political science professor at the local community college. Much of the work was clerical, but Perry sensed that it was important, and often reminded his parents, "Professor Steuben once testified before Congress, you know." Eventually the professor asked him to skim newspaper articles for relevant information and outline what he found, and Perry eagerly dove in. When he returned to school that fall, he still found math and science a stressful chore, but could now see the relevance in his journalism and government courses—and never failed to point out instances where the course content in some way overlapped with "the project Professor Steuben and I worked on together this summer." Perry was adding pride to his emotional lexicon.

In spite of these encouraging events, his progress was not without its fits and starts. His parents were struggling not only against his entrenched eating habits, but also against their own impulses, and even more important, against a society that reinforced many of the impulses that maintain our teens as overgrown children. Over time, however, Perry's parents got on board, treating him as the young man he was becoming, not the child he had been. As he took on more adultlike tasks both in and outside of his home, his mood continued to improve, and as it did, his weight gradually increased. Perry was going to make it. His problems did not totally vanish, of course, and he came in for occasional booster shots of therapy when home from college over the next few years, but he was now getting enough of the nutrients he needed—figuratively and literally—to resume his growth toward adulthood.

As the human life span has lengthened and our society has advanced, it is perhaps not surprising that the fundamental nutrients—the challenge, feedback, connection, and eagerness—that were lacking in Perry's life have also been gradually stripped from the diets of many of our teens. History is replete with such trade-offs following societal change and progress. As sailors first learned to cross oceans, for example, scurvy became a worrisome and mysteriously common illness. The nutrients that sailors had taken in effortlessly on land (in this case vitamin C) had slipped out of their diets unnoticed. Similarly, as we learned to take full advantage of the automobile, exercise that was previously built into our daily lives fell by the wayside and heart disease loomed large. And as technology let us live off processed foods, fiber tended to disappear from our diets and cancer rates shot up.

In all of these cases, though, the solutions have not required going back to the primitive ways of the prior era. In fact, the answers have often been deceptively simple, *once we understood the problem.* Scurvy could be avoided simply by by adding citrus fruits to shipboard diets. Thirty minutes a day of exercise would largely pay back to our bodies what we'd lost by relying upon the automobile. Fiber became a fairly easy addition to diets, once we recognized its importance.

So too with adolescence. Over and over again we've found that as we add missing nutrients back into teens' diets one by one, they spring almost magically back to life with the energy and enthusiasm they seemed to have lost somewhere back in the childhood years.

UNLEARNING HELPLESSNESS

Many years ago psychologist Martin Seligman began studying animals exposed to punishing environments with no chance of escape. The animals were placed in situations in which they saw no feedback or success no matter what they tried; they had no way to escape the stresses before them. These animals, Seligman found, developed a strong and fixed response that looked like depression and could at times even be fatal, a state he termed "learned helplessness." Even when opportunities to act did present themselves to these poor creatures, they often just waited anxiously. They became passive and barely took care of themselves. Without intervention they quickly progressed from being in a helpless situation to becoming helpless organisms.

As our societal changes have shielded teens from most venues where their actions might matter to themselves or to others, it's little surprise that we've come to see human behavior patterns that resemble those that Seligman observed in animals. Fortunately, Seligman's was not the last word on the story. Not long after he conducted his research, Ellen Langer at Harvard and Judith Rodin at Yale—both aware of Seligman's work—experimented with a simple intervention in a nursing home for the elderly. Langer and Rodin gave some of the residents—who in many ways appeared as helpless and passive as Seligman's animals—the chance to exert modest control and have a modest impact upon their environments: to again begin acting like adults and not just as extremely old children. The residents were given simple activities—like arranging their rooms and caring for plants—and were allowed a choice of which nursing home activities to attend. The emphasis was on the residents being responsible for guiding their own lives in the home. The remarkable result from this simple intervention: Residents given even this modicum of increased control and input into their lives were only half as likely to *die* over the course of the study as their less-fortunate peers. The efficacy, input, and impact of Langer and Rodin's experiment had literally saved lives.

For adolescents, the good and somewhat surprising news is that *none* of the problems we've been discussing appears to come prebaked into their brains or into their hormones. And there is every reason to believe that teens can gain as much from our modest, well-directed interventions to address their learned helplessness as Langer and Rodin's nursing home residents. What we've found most striking about the approach we've described is just how *responsive* teens are to it. Perry's growth is the rule, not the exception. As we view the modern adolescent environment, it's not a matter of asking whether the glass is half-full or half-empty. Rather, like water to the person dying of thirst in the desert, it's simply the case that even a little goes a long way. In part, this is a testament to natural human resilience. But the responsiveness of our teens to the right kind of interventions doesn't just tell us how resilient they are, it also tells us just how thirsty they've been for the chance to enter the adult world in a meaningful way.

PLATFORM 9¾

Once we're attuned to it, we can see this thirst all around us. The power of the Harry Potter series, for example, derives at least in part from J. K. Rowling's success in creating a world in which teenagers get the chance to play an active, indeed central, role in the adult world which they magically enter via Platform 9¾ of a London train station. Part of the appeal of the series lies in its description of young people discovering adult powers they didn't know they had, which lets them influence the adult world in ways no one thought they could. Indeed, a little reflection reveals that this theme of youth's deep thirst for adulthood has been a growing part of successful young adult fiction for at least a generation. From the Hardy Boys to Nancy Drew, young people have been feeling the same pull and thrill at the fantasy of being given the chance to perform as adults in the adult world. This vision needn't be a fantasy.

CHANGING ADOLESCENTS, CHANGING OURSELVES

There's one final benefit to the changes we've been suggesting, and it's one we've left largely implicit thus far. Perry's story hints at it. For if we look at Perry's environment, we see that a few other things of note changed in the world Perry inhabited that summer a few years back. The neighbor who was running the tennis program found it useful to have an extra person help tend to the young kids on the courts. The political science professor enjoyed chatting with Perry and having some of the more mundane parts of his work taken off his hands. Perry, like most of our teens, had something real to offer.

Over the years, we've found that parents often start out worrying that they're simply too busy and overtaxed to implement the suggestions we offer. In the end, of course, it's far more taxing to live with a bunch of perpetual children in one's midst (cloaked as teenagers) than to live with budding adults. Once parents realize this, their energy for making the changes we suggest typically skyrockets—and, of course, they then find that the changes make their lives as parents *easier*, not to mention far more gratifying. But while the practical contributions teens can make to our households and our communities are not to be underestimated, we've found over and over again that when we engage them in the adult world, what teens have to offer actually goes far beyond such practical help. Adolescence is a challenging age, but the challenges have at times been of immense benefit—not just to teens, but to the larger society.

While modern society struggles to shape and socialize its future generations, it's important to remember that the role of young people since at least the dawn of recorded history has been to look afresh at the mores of the larger society. And that fresh look can at times bring real benefits. The challenges presented by engaged, contributing, and questioning adolescents are at times uncomfortable and even irritating, but irritants don't just annoy, they can also prompt an organism, or a society, to grow stronger.

Whatever you may have thought about the war in Vietnam, there is little question that the movement that brought our country home from Southeast Asia derived its greatest energy from mid- to late-adolescents. Some of the most heated (and no doubt productive) debates of this era occurred not on the floor of the Senate, but within millions of homes across America, as teens and parents discussed and disagreed. Teens were forced to grow in maturity and sophistication to put forth their arguments effectively. Equally important, their parents almost inevitably also found themselves extending and broadening their own perspectives as they listened to their teens' views of the world. These adolescents were engaged in changing society in part because they were forced to contribute to it in a large way (and for some, the largest possible way) via military conscription. Much of what those in the "youth movement" back then supported and indeed pushed upon their parents' generation—from civil rights to attention to the environment—turned out to represent real advances. Engaged youths not only learned from their parents, they also taught their parents . . . just as those parents had themselves done with *their* parents a generation earlier, and so forth back into time immemorial.

But for any of this to happen, youths must actually *be* engaged with the larger society. "Society gets the teenagers it deserves," author J. B. Priestley has observed. Throughout this book, we've made the point that strong and vital connections between teens and the adult world determine not simply how teens act, but who they become. At least as important, these connections also go a long way toward determining who *we* will become and what we will learn from future generations as we all march forward together.

ACKNOWLEDGMENTS

This book would not have come into being without the support, wisdom, and guidance of many people, all of whom we're delighted to have the chance to acknowledge.

Our agent, Susan Arellano, graced us with her enthusiasm and patience, which were matched only by her perspicacity and skill in helping us distill and frame the nuggets of insight that form the core of this book. Without her efforts, this book might never have come to pass.

We'd also like to thank our editor at Random House, Marnie Cochran, for her steady support, gentle suggestions, and attentive guidance. And our copy editor, Peter Weissman, for his thoughtful efforts to beat our prose into reasonable shape.

We're also indebted to the graduate students, postdocs, and research associates—Kathleen McElhaney, Nell Manning, Judith Wasserman, Sharon Deal, Amanda Hare, Claire Stephenson, Erin Miga, Dave Szwedo, Emily Marston, Joanna Chango, Megan Schad, Jen Heliste, Meredyth Evans, Katie Higgins, and Amanda Letard—who read and commented on early drafts of this book and added to it with their own experiences and ideas.

The institutions that have funded our research over the years have played a critical role as they have literally paid for many of the insights in the book. Support in particular has come from the National Institute of Mental Health, the National Institute of Child Health and Human Development (Grant #'s R01-MH44934, R01-MH58066, and R01-HD058305), the Spencer Foundation, and the William T. Grant Foundation. At the latter, Bob Granger and Ed Seidman have been sources not only of financial support, but also of considerable intellectual support and stimulation.

We'd also like to thank some of those who've provided mentoring and inspiration to us over the years. Joe would particularly like to thank: Seymour Sarason, for his wisdom and gentle, persistent inquisitiveness; Larry Aber, for his friendship, warmth, support, and thoughtful career input on numerous occasions; Bonnie Leadbeater, who put up with the end of my own adolescence in helping me collect my dissertation data and provided very helpful comments on early drafts; And Bill Kahn, for everything from helping us think through challenges with our own adolescents, to serving as a sounding board for our ideas as they developed to providing critical reactions to our evolving prose to providing consistently unbounded friendship and support.

Claudia would like to thank: Harry Parad and the late Hugh Leichtman of Wediko Children's Services, a brilliant training ground for budding therapists as well as a haven for children who others have written off as doomed to failure; David Waters for providing invaluable clinical mentoring and sharing his unique gift of finding the best in people; and several colleagues who have provided clinical wisdom and personal support: Deborah Cohn, Karen Loftus, Ted Siedlecki, Carol Manning, Steven V. Heim, Deborah Strzepek, and Susan Kaufman. Finally, Dick Reppucci has been an enormous source of support to both of us over many years and several careers.

Friends and neighbors who have shared their stories and let us bounce our endless ideas off them and their experiences are also owed our enduring gratitude. Janet and Jeff Legro, Cori Field, Charlotte Crystal, Dave Mattern, Saphira Baker, Tal Brewer, Matt Jones, Karen Shapero-Jones, Helen Rosenthal, Carmen Marino, Dawn Johnsen, John Hamilton, Howard Shapiro, Shirley Brandman, and her own thoughtful late-adolescent, Zach, all provided key pieces of help, insight, and support along the way. Bob Emery also provided helpful input about the writing and publishing process early on as we were developing our ideas.

We particularly want to acknowledge the many teenagers and their families with whom we have been privileged to work in many different ways over the years. Though we've rearranged their stories into composites to preserve their anonymity, it is their spirit of hope, optimism, and energy that was our touchstone as we wrote this book and to which we have tried to do justice.

Finally, we want to thank and acknowledge our families. Claudia's brother Pete Worrell contributed directly and indirectly to the book by sharing his experiences and injecting his enthusiasm. Kareen Worrell and Judy Thornton also read drafts and provided valuable comments and encouragement. Kathryn Newton was an early inspiration as an example of an adolescent who discovered quickly how to contribute to the adult world. Bob and Loraine Worrell understood the idea behind this book before either of us were even born and passed it on to Claudia implicitly. And last, but not least, we want to thank our children. They've put up with hearing our ideas bounced back and forth at the dinner table. They've challenged us continually to explain how our lofty-sounding notions really worked in their lives. And they've inspired us to develop and try out these ideas repeatedly. To respect their privacy, their names are attached to none of the stories in this book, but their spirit lives throughout it.

NOTES

Point of View

As we noted in the introduction, although we wrote this book together, we've used the first-person singular throughout as the simplest and least distracting way to present our thoughts and recount our experiences. The clinical cases we present are all composites, and thus attributable to both of our experiences. Beyond that, the personal anecdotes can be attributed to Joe, with the exception of the following:

> Chapter 4: Although "Barrett" is a composite, he primarily reflects work Claudia has done in her role at the U.Va. Medical Center as director of Behavioral Medicine in the Department of Family Medicine.
>
> Chapter 7: Claudia is describing her experiences with her tenth-grade high school teacher.
>
> Chapter 8: Claudia is recounting her experience at Wediko in this chapter.
>
> Chapter 9: Claudia is describing her law school experience and Amish background.

Citations and Relevant Notes

Chapter 1

8 *On the contrary* . . . Kett, J. F. *Rites of Passage: Adolescence in America, 1790 to the Present.* New York: Basic Books, 1977.

8 *For example, the average college student* . . . Twenge, J. M., "The age of anxiety?: Birth cohort change in anxiety and neuroticism, 1952–1993," *Age, 79*(6), 2000, 1007–21.

13 *Recent analyses make clear* . . . Yelowitz, A., "Young adults leaving the nest: The role of cost-of-living," in S. Danziger and C. Rouse (eds.), *The Price of*

Independence: The Economics of Early Adulthood. New York: Russell Sage Foundation, 2007.

13 *But many find themselves . . .* Robbins, A., and Wilner, A. *Quarterlife Crisis: The Unique Challenges of Life in Your Twenties.* New York: Jeremy P. Tarcher/Putnam, 2001.

16 *"My parents and I talked" . . .* Hofer, B. K., et al., "The 'Electronic Tether': Communication and Parental Monitoring During the College Years," in M. K. Nelson and A. I. Garvey (eds.), *Who's Watching? Practices of Surveillance among Contemporary Families.* Vanderbilt, Tennessee: Vanderbilt University Press, 2009.

16 *Indeed, Hofer and her colleague . . .* Kennedy, E. K., and Hofer, B. K., "The Electronic Tether: The Influence of Frequent Parental Contact on the Development of Autonomy and Self-Regulation in Emerging Adulthood," paper presented at the Biennial Meeting of the Society for Research on Child Development, Boston, Massachusetts, 2007.

19 *We see the problems in . . .* Luthar, S. S., "The culture of affluence: Psychological costs of material wealth," *Child Development, 74*(6), 2003, 1581–93.

Chapter 2

23 *Stated in everyday terms . . .* Salthouse, T. A., "The processing-speed theory of adult age differences in cognition," *Psychological Review, 103*(3), 1996, 403–28.

27 *Rather, this passage . . .* Patty, W. L., and Johnson, L. S. *Personality and Adjustment.* New York: McGraw-Hill, 1953.

28 *They look at the good side . . .* (~350 B.C.E.). *Rhetoric, Book II,* Chapter 12. W. R. Roberts, trans.

28 *Some would trace it to 1904 . . .* Hall, G. S. *Adolescence: Its Psychology and its Relations to Physiology, Anthropology, Sociology, Sex, Crime, Religion, and Education.* New York: Appleton, 1904.

29 *With its vivid prose . . .* Ross, D. G. *Stanley Hall: The Psychologist as Prophet.* Chicago: University of Chicago Press, 1972.

29 *For example, most adults . . .* Dahl, R. E., and Hariri, A. R., "Lessons from G. Stanley Hall: Connecting New Research in Biological Sciences to the Study of Adolescent Development," *Journal of Research on Adolescence, 15*(4), 2005, 367–82.

31 *And yet as I recently sat . . .* Giedd, J. N., "The Teen Brain: Insights from Neuroimaging," paper presented at the Biennial Meeting of the Society for Research on Adolescence, 2008.

31 *That's precisely the dilemma* . . . Schlegel, A., and Barry, H. *Adolescence: An Anthropological Inquiry.* New York: Free Press, 1991.

32 *Historian Joe Kett* . . . Kett, J. F. *Rites of Passage,* op cit.

32 *Susan Hull has written* . . . Hull, S. R. *Boy Soldiers of the Confederacy.* New York: Neale Publishing Company, 1905.

33 *This pejorative tendency* . . . Ross, L., "The intuitive psychologist and his shortcomings: Distortions in the attribution process," *Advances in Experimental Social Psychology, 10,* 1977, 173–220.

34 *In fact, had he looked* . . . Kett, J. F., op cit; Hine, T. *The Rise and Fall of the American Teenager.* New York: Bard, 1999.

40 *We've also recently learned* . . . Cauffman, E., et al., "Responding to Reward vs. Punishment: How Adolescents Differ from Adults in Performance on the Iowa Gambling Task," paper presented at the Biennial Meeting of the Society for Research on Adolescence, Chicago, March 2008; van Leijenhorst, L., Crone, E. A., and Bunge, S. A., "Neural correlates of developmental differences in risk estimation and feedback processing," *Neuropsychologia, 44*(11), 2006, 2158–70.

42 *The very timing of* . . . Ellis, B. J. "Timing of Pubertal Maturation in Girls: An Integrated Life History Approach," *Psychological Bulletin, 130,* 2004, 920–58.

44 *It seems far more likely* . . . We would like to acknowledge the broad relevance here of the work of Robert Epstein, whose book *The Case Against Adolescence: Rediscovering the Adult in Every Teen,* (New York: Quill Driver Press, 2007), argues persuasively that teens often have capacities for adultlike tasks that rival the capacities of many adults. For the interested reader, Epstein also focuses upon the problematic nature of modern adolescence and offers somewhat different routes to addressing these problems than we outline in this book.

44 *Experiments have shown* . . . Draganski, B., et al., "Neuroplasticity: Changes in grey matter induced by training," *Nature, 427*(6972), 2004, 311–12.

Chapter 3

48 *The Bubble Boy* . . . For further information, see McVicker, S. (1997). "Bursting the Bubble," *Houston Press News,* April 10. http://www.houston press.com/1997-0410/news/bursting-the-bubble/. Also see, PBS (2006), *The Boy in the Bubble/* PBS American Experience Series. Program website: http://www.pbs.org/wgbh/amex/bubble/.

51 *Psychologist Erik Erikson* . . . Erikson, E. H. *Identity: Youth and Crisis.* New York: W. Norton & Company, 1968.

52 *His principles apply well . . .* Frankl, V. E. *Man's Search for Meaning*. New York: Pocket Books, 1985.

58 *"Without high school . . ."* Hine, T. *The Rise and Fall of the American Teenager*. New York: Bard, 1999.

59 *In contrast, across history . . .* Hine, T., ibid.

59 *In those relatively rare societies . . .* Schlegel, A., and Barry, H. *Adolescence: An Anthropological Inquiry*. New York: Free Press, 1991.

60 *Cultural observer Thomas . . .* Hine, T., op cit.

60 *If we extend Hine's notion . . .* Moffitt, T. E., "Adolescence-limited and life-course-persistent antisocial behavior: A developmental taxonomy," *Psychological Review, 100*(4), 1993, 674–701.

62 *Adolescents today spend . . .* Steinberg, L. *Adolescence* (8th ed.). New York: McGraw Hill, 2008.

63 *Victor was first discovered . . .* Lane, H. *The Wild Boy of Aveyron*. Harvard University Press, 1976.

66 *Similar research by other colleagues . . .* Osgood, D. W., et al., "Six Paths to Adulthood: Fast Starters, Parents without Careers, Educated Partners, Educated Singles, Working Singles, and Slow Starters," in R. A. Settersten, Jr., F. F. Furstenberg, Jr., and R. G. Rumbaut (eds.), *On the Frontier of Adulthood: Theory, Research, and Public Policy*. Chicago: University of Chicago Press, 2005, 320–55.

67 *Large numbers of teens . . .* Patel, D. R., Greydanus, D. E., and Rowlett, J. D., "Romance with the automobile in the 20th century: implications for adolescents in a new millennium," *Adolescent Medicine, 11*(1), 2000, 127–39.

67 *Recent evidence suggests . . .* American Medical Association, "Harmful Consequences of Alcohol Use on the Brains of Children, Adolescents, and College Students," American Medical Association, Washington, D.C., 2006.

67 *Homeowners, consumers, retail shopkeepers . . .* Taylor, N., and Mayhew, P. *Financial and Psychological Costs of Crime for Small Retail Businesses*. Australian Institute of Criminology, 2002.

68 *He pieced together . . .* Dishion, T. J., McCord, J., and Poulin, F., "When interventions harm: Peer groups and problem behavior," *American Psychologist, 54*(9), 1999, 755–64.

Chapter 4

79 *But by 1930 the percentage had increased . . .* Kett, J. F., op cit.; Coleman, J. S. *The Adolescent Society: the Social Life of the Teenager and Its Impact on Education*. New York: Free Press, 1961.

85 *Each year the actual odds* . . . Finkelhor, D., Hammer, H., and Sedlak, A. J., "Nonfamily Abducted Children: National Estimates and Characteristics," *Juvenile Justice Bulletin No. NCJ196467,* Washington, D.C.: Office of Juvenile Justice & Delinquency Prevention, 2002.

87 *They coined the term* . . . Tversky, A., and Kahneman, D., "Availability: A heuristic for judging frequency and probability," *Cognitive Psychology, 5,* 1973, 207–32.

89 *For the one in 3,500 teens* . . . Prevention, C. f. D. C. a. (2006). Web-based Injury Statistics Query and Reporting System (WISQARS) [online] publication. Retrieved [Cited 2006 Dec 1] from National Center for Injury Prevention and Control, Centers for Disease Control and Prevention (producer): www.cdc.gov/ncipc/wisqars.

93 *Worse yet, for every hundred women* . . . Institute of Education Sciences. *Digest of Education Statistics.* Washington, D.C.: U.S. Department of Education, 2007.

Chapter 5

98 *Quite the opposite. Under the most* . . . Allen, J. P., Philliber, S., and Hoggson, N., "School-based prevention of teen-age pregnancy and school dropout: Process evaluation of the national replication of the Teen Outreach Program," *American Journal of Community Psychology, 18*(4), 1990, 505–24; Allen, J. P., et al., "Preventing teen pregnancy and academic failure: Experimental evaluation of a developmentally based approach," *Child Development, 68*(4), 1997, 729–42.

98 *When we published the initial* . . . Matthews, J., "Teenage girls who volunteer are less likely to get pregnant, study finds," *Washington Post,* August 28, 1997.

104 *The term coined* . . . Bachman, J. G., "Premature Affluence: Do High Schools Students Earn Too Much?" *Developmental Psychology, 18,* 1982, 385–95.

106 *Poorer grades and a greater likelihood* . . . *Protecting Youth at Work.* National Research Council, Washington, D.C.: National Academy Press, 1998. Mihalic, S. W., and Elliott, D., "Short- and Long-Term Consequences of Adolescent Work," *Youth & Society, 28*(4), 1997, 464.

Chapter 6

136 *For example, in a long-term study* . . . Allen, J. P., McElhaney, K. B., and Bell, K. L. "Autonomy in Discussions vs. Autonomy in Decision-making as Predictors of Developing Close Friendship Competence," paper presented at

the Biennial Meeting of the Society for Research on Adolescence, Chicago, 2000.

136 *Similarly, our own research* . . . Allen, J. P., et al., "Longitudinal assessment of autonomy and relatedness in adolescent-family interactions as predictors of adolescent ego development and self-esteem," *Child Development,* 65(1), 1994, 179–94; Allen, J. P., et al., "Autonomy and relatedness in family interactions as predictors of expressions of negative adolescent affect," *Journal of Research on Adolescence,* 4(4), 1994, 535–52; Bell, K. L., et al., "Family factors and young adult transitions: Educational attainment and occupational prestige" in J. A. Graber and J. Brooks-Gunn (eds.), *Transitions Through Adolescence: Interpersonal Domains and Context,* (345–66), Mahwah, New Jersey: Lawrence Erlbaum Associates, Inc., 1996.

137 *The concept was first identified* . . . Newman, F., and Holzman, L. *Lev Vygotsky: Revolutionary Scientist.* New York: Routledge, 1993.

Chapter 7

141 *Hardwired to Connect.* We gratefully acknowledge the title for this chapter, which is taken from the intriguing report of the same name put out by the Commission on Children at Risk in 2003 (New York: Institute for American Values).

142 *Adults also need connections* . . . House, J. S., Landis, K. R., and Umberson, D., "Social relationships and health," *Science, 241*(4865), 1988, 540–45.

144 *When we observe teens* . . . Allen, Hauser, Bell, et al. (1994); Allen, Hauser, Eickholt et al. (1994); Bell, Allen, et al. (1996). Allen, J. P., and Hauser, S. T., "Autonomy and relatedness in adolescent-family interactions as predictors of young adults' states of mind regarding attachment," *Development and Psychopathology, 8*(4), 1996, 793–809; Allen, J. P., et al., "Prediction of peer-rated adult hostility from autonomy struggles in adolescent-family interactions," *Development and Psychopathology, 14,* 2002, 123–37; O'Connor, T. G., et al., "Adolescent-parent relationships and leaving home in young adulthood," in J. A. Graber and J. S. Dubas (eds.), *Leaving Home: Understanding the Transition to Adulthood. New Directions for Child Development, no. 71,* 39–52, San Francisco: Jossey-Bass, 1996.

158 *Child psychologist* . . . Bettelheim, B., "Punishment versus discipline," *Atlantic Monthly, 256*(5), 1985, 51–59.

158 *What we've found is that parents* . . . Allen, J. P., et al., "Attachment and adolescent psychosocial functioning," *Child Development, 69*(5), 1998, 1406–19.

158 *Our colleagues Hakan Stattin* . . . Stattin, H., and Kerr, M., "Parental monitoring: A reinterpretation," *Child Development, 71*(4), 2000, 1072–85; Kerr,

M., and Stattin, H., "What parents know, how they know it, and several forms of adolescent adjustment: Further support for a reinterpretation of monitoring," *Developmental Psychology, 36*(3), 2000, 366–80.

159 *What she saw happening* . . . Rosenbaum, M. S., et al., "Looking for love in all the wrong places: The developmental context of adolescents' early initiation into sexual intercourse," manuscript submitted for publication, 2007.

167 *And well-organized religious communities* . . . Harden, K. P., "A behavior genetic study of religiosity and adolescent problem behavior," unpublished doctoral dissertation, Charlottesville: University of Virginia, 2008.

Chapter 8

188 *Psychologist Albert Bandura* . . . Bandura, A., "Self-efficacy: Toward a unifying theory of behavioral change," *Psychological Review, 84*, 1997, 191–215.

192 *It is striking, for example* . . . Tsongas, P. *Heading Home.* New York: Vintage Books, 1985.

Chapter 9

196 *Schools, unless discipline were doubly strong* . . . Cowper, W., (1785), *Tirocin, 219.*

196 *Ultimately, only 18 of these* . . . Estimates of high school dropout rates vary widely and are a source of controversy within the field. Lower estimates can be obtained if one counts adolescents getting graduate equivalency diplomas (GEDs), although labor force studies show these adolescents fare no better than dropouts following high school. Estimates of young people not graduating high school often don't include adolescents incarcerated at an early age and those who are severely handicapped and not in regular schools. On balance we think the figures presented provide a good estimate of the extent and severity of the problem. Hunt, J. B., and Tierney, T. J. *American Higher Education: How Does It Measure Up for the 21st Century?* San Jose, California: National Center for Public Policy and Higher Education, 2006; Heckman, J. J., and LaFontaine, P. A., "The declining American high school graduation rate: Evidence, sources, and consequences," *National Bureau of Economic Research Reporter: Research Summary, 1*, 2008.

199 *Research has now shown* . . . Dale, S. B., and Krueger, A. B., "Estimating the Payoff to Attending a More Selective College: An Application of Selection on Observables and Unobservables," *Quarterly Journal of Economics, 117*(4), 2002, 1491–1527.

202 *Given how many students drop out* . . . Evidence of declining student

enthusiasm and motivation for school during adolescence is extensive. Among the key studies supporting this finding are: Eccles, J. S., and Roeser, R. W., "Schools as developmental contexts," in G. R. Adams and M. D. Berzonsky (eds.), *Blackwell Handbook of Adolescence (Blackwell Handbooks of Developmental Psychology)*, 129–48, Malden, Massachusetts: Blackwell Publishers, 2003; R. W. Roeser (ed.), "Academic and emotional functioning in early adolescence: Longitudinal relations, patterns, and prediction by experience in middle school," *Development and Psychopathology, 10*(2), 1998, 321–52; Marks, H. M., "Student engagement in instructional activity: Patterns in the elementary, middle, and high school years," *American Educational Research Journal, 37*(1), 2000, 153–84; Steinberg, L., Brown, B. B., and Dornbusch, S. M. *Beyond the Classroom: Why School Reform Has Failed and What Parents Need to Do.* New York: Simon and Schuster, 1996.

211 *Our intervention experiment . . .* Those interested in obtaining the latest results from this ongoing project or other information about it can do so by going to www.myteachingpartner.net.

213 *A group sponsored by . . . .* National Center on Education and the Economy, *Tough Choices or Tough Times: The Report of the New Commission on the Skills of the American Workforce.* National Center on Education and the Economy, Washington, D. C., 2007.

216 *Though the program began . . .* Bard High School Early College, overview, 2008, http://www.bard.edu/bhsec/.

216 *This means that a high school . . .* Yale University, for example, reports accepting nine percent of applicants in 2006–2007 and having 21,101 applicants for 1,315 slots, which is slightly less selective than Bard College, "Statistics on Current Freshman Class," http://www.yale.edu/oir/facts06.html#Statistics%20on%20Current%201995%20Freshmen%20Class.

218 *At each program site . . .* Early College High School Initiative: 2003–2005 Evaluation Report. American Institutes for Research and SRI International. Seattle: Bill and Melinda Gates Foundation, 2006.

218 *And this is without even factoring . . .* "Jobs for the Future," *The Early College High School Initiative,* Boston: 2008. http://www.earlycolleges.org/contact.html.

Chapter 10

225 *Without intervention they quickly progressed . . .* Abramson, L. Y., Seligman, M. E. P., and Teasdale, J. D., "Learned helplessness in humans: Critique

and reformulation," *Journal of Abnormal Psychology, 87*(1), 1978, 49–74; Seligman, M. E. P., "Depression and learned helplessness," *The Psychology of Depression: Contemporary Theory and Research*, 1974, 83–113.

225 *The efficacy, input, and impact* . . . Langer, E. J., and Rodin, J., "The effects of choice and enhanced personal responsibility for the aged," *Journal of Personality and Social Psychology, 34*, 1976, 191–98; Rodin, J., and Langer, E., "Long-term effect of a control-relevant intervention," *Journal of Personality and Social Psychology, 35*, 1977, 897–902.

INDEX

ABOUT THE AUTHORS

JOSEPH ALLEN, PH.D., is a professor of psychology and director of clinical training at the University of Virginia, and a licensed clinical psychologist who specializes in working with adolescents. He has served as associate editor of the prestigious journal, *Child Development*, and as chair of the National Institutes of Health review group responsible for funding research on preventing child and adolescent mental health problems. In an ambitious ninety-classroom study funded by the William T. Grant Foundation, he is presently collaborating on a teacher-training project designed to improve students' engagement, motivation, and ultimately their academic performance.

CLAUDIA WORRELL ALLEN, PH.D., J.D., is associate professor and director of behavioral science in the Department of Family Medicine at the University of Virginia, and for fifteen years has been a licensed clinical psychologist with an active private practice for adolescents and their families. She also holds a law degree and served as the editor in chief of the prestigious *Yale Law Journal*.

Married and the parents of three preteen and teenage children, the Allens live in Charlottesville, Virginia.

ABOUT THE TYPE

This book was set in Caslon, a typeface first designed in 1722 by William Caslon. Its widespread use by most English printers in the early eighteenth century soon supplanted the Dutch typefaces that had formerly prevailed. The roman is considered a "workhorse" typeface due to its pleasant, open appearance, while the italic is exceedingly decorative.